TENACITY & I

A Sales & Marketing Titan's Story
of Tribulations, Victories, and Love

By Daniel E. Reed and Lauren M. Oujiri

Especially For Lynette and Mervyn - - Hope you understand me better after reading my stories.

All best allways, allways!

Dan Reed

ISBN-13:
978-1548330149

ISBN-10:
1548330140

Disclaimer from Daniel E. Reed:

This is my story and how I remember it. I tried to the best of my ability to provide factual information, but I don't claim my memory - or me - to be perfect. You might disagree with some of what I have written, facts or opinion, and you're entitled to that, but it's my story, and I'm sticking to it. I hope you wouldn't sue me over something you don't like in it, but if you do, my attorneys are glad to speak with you. I write and share all this in good faith, and hope you enjoy all the tales within. There's lots more I could have written, that some would surely like to sue me over or at least argue about, but I am wiser than that at this point!

Best,
Dan.

Acknowledgements

This book is dedicated to my many friends, some of whom are not mentioned in my stories.

Also, to my families, blood and inherited. I hope some of my logic is especially helpful to my grandchildren, great grandchildren, nieces and nephews, great nieces and great nephews. I mention this purposely to the younger set in hopes some of my life encounters will improve their future choices.

Most of all, I would like to thank Laurie (Lauren) Oujiri (my niece) and Pat Byram. When Laurie came to visit Pat and me months ago, she and I had conversations about many things late into the night. We really got acquainted and she mentioned that all of the experiences I had would make a good book. Her encouragement caused me to spend many hours getting the accumulation of events gathered together for this book. I put my stories to tape, and Laurie edited it into reading format for you. As I thought of more stories as we went along, my partner, Pat, as usual, was there to help in composition and decipher my scribbling, type it and send it to Laurie. Without these two ladies you would not be holding this book and have the opportunity to learn about me. I am deeply grateful to both of them.

It's been a ride to remember.

MOVING AND SCHOOLING

1.

February 16, 1928, I was born and lying in Cook County Hospital in Chicago, Illinois with Lucille Reed, my mother. I find it difficult to even use the word "mother," because I rarely have used it during my life.

I don't recall much of my really early life, but I was told by my Aunt Lucy, my grandmother Elizabeth "Lizzie" Robinette's youngest child (and one of thirteen aunts and uncles; there were fifteen to start), that as a young boy my father, mother, and I visited his mother (Lizzie), in the hills of Southern Ohio, in the very poorest county in the state, Vinton County. Aunt Lucy told me that Grandma Lizzie said, "He is such a cute boy," and Lucille responded, "Would you like to have him?" and my grandma said, "Well, of course! He's such a nice boy!" And my own mother said, "Well, here," and handed me to her on the spot. That began my journey away from knowing much of anything on my mother's side of the family.

At age three, when you first begin to remember things, I recall living in a two-story house, the old house that my grandfather, Moses Heenan Reed, had originally built as a log cabin when he married my grandmother. Years later as the kids kept coming along, he built around the log house and added an upstairs. There were three bedrooms and a living room upstairs, and downstairs there was a master bedroom, and a kitchen in the back. It had no electricity and no running water.

My dad and me

My first memories are of picking eggs out of the chicken house, which was across the little road that ran up the hollow. There was always a white goose that would chase me around and bite me on the legs, and I was always trying to get away from it.

In the summers, my grandma and I worked in the garden together. She always wore an apron all day long, as women did in those days, and she picked all the different fruits and vegetables; I remember there were always a lot of pole beans. She always used that apron as a bowl to carry them. We had a water pump outside between the garden and house, and when I finally was big enough, I'd go out and pump the water, and carry it awkwardly inside.

I remember one time when I was about four years old my Uncle Lindley Reed, my grandma's youngest son, came to visit, and she was complaining about the water tasting funny. He pulled the top off the well and went down into it. It was a hand-dug well with rocks lining it, probably four feet in diameter. He said, "Well, no wonder," pulling a few turtles out of the water. He killed them and later I ate turtle for the first time; I'll have turtle to this day, it's very good. We drank that well water as long as I lived there.

2.

When it was time for me to go to school, it was decided by someone that I should go live with my Aunt Elma Downs, and her daughter, my cousin, Geneva, who lived out on highway U.S. 50 going through southern Ohio, East of Londonderry about five miles. Apparently a big reason for that decision was transportation: There was a bus that would carry me to school.

I began my school days in 1932 in a one-room schoolhouse named Boblitt, grades one through eight, with about fourteen kids total. My teacher was a lady named Thelma Graves; my father had had her as a teacher, too. I was a straight-A student during my first four years of schooling.

I grew up through the depths and the heights of the Depression, and times were tough on all families, but I never remember going hungry, nor going to bed hungry, like so many unfortunate people did. We didn't have a big variety of foods,

7

and we ate a lot of beans, a lot of side pork, and a lot of cornbread. I didn't eat eggs, in fact I never ate eggs until I was nearly twenty because they made me sick, as it seems I was allergic to them. I outgrew that eventually.

At school we would play Annie Over, a game with a hollow rubber ball, about three inches in diameter. There were two teams, one on each side of the school. We'd throw the ball over the roof, and if the other team didn't catch it we got a point, and vice versa. That was some of our entertainment when we went out to the schoolyard.

When I was in the fourth grade, in '36 or '37, for some reason it was decided that I should move to Montana where my dad was working on a new dam, what is now the Fort Peck Dam. He had been sending money to my aunt to pay for my board and keep, as there hadn't been very much money floating around for her then. My dad had done okay, though, as he had worked on the Boulder

Dam in Boulder City. The conditions were simply awful, with temperatures every day exceeding a hundred degrees, with no air conditioning and nothing modern. They lived in pretty sparse conditions. It was hard work, and they worked two twelve-hour shifts, seven days a week. My dad was actually one of the first welders in the U.S., beginning in 1932.

I think it was President Franklin D. Roosevelt who renamed the Boulder Dam to the Hoover Dam, and my dad was just furious over that name change. They had started this dam up in Montana on the Missouri River, called Fort Peck Dam. It was going to be the largest earthen dam in either the world or United States, I'm not sure, and they were going to be working on it for years. There was nothing out there except desert. He had a friend he worked with who visited us in Ohio. His name was James Gunnerware, and he had a nice wife and two kids, Billy and Lorraine. Billy had six fingers on his hands; he had an extra thumb and was kind of club handed. He was a nice kid, though, and my age.

Cole's Studio
GLASGOW, MONTANA

We rode cross-country in a Chevy, a new car, because everybody was making good money by then. We moved to Glasgow, Montana when I was about nine. We moved into a little two-bedroom apartment that was on a street just a block from the school, named for Glasgow, which was grades one through twelve. Up on the hill behind that where there were no trees whatsoever, there was a big "G" made out of rocks painted white. Years later I discovered that most of the towns in Montana had the first letter of the town high on a hill like that.

The Great Northern Railway ran through Glasgow in northeastern Montana, and it paralleled U.S. Highway 2. That Christmas I got the first present I ever remember getting: I got a bike.

My dad had a "live-in" at the time, Midge, and she was good to me. She would wash my neck and ears and everything. Apparently that was important back then, as I remember my grandma always used to say, "Wash your neck and ears now, wash your neck and ears!" I don't remember Midge being around there for very long; I guess she came and went.

In wintertime in Glasgow you could get a lot of snow and a lot of cold weather. I made my first money out shoveling sidewalks for ten cents, and it would take me all day just to make a dime. This is when I started getting my education not only in school, but in a lot of other ways, too.

In 1937 my dad decided I should go back to Ohio and live with his younger brother. Uncle Harold had been a professional boxer, and at one time my dad was his manager. My uncle fought some pretty tough people, and he was a pretty doggone good boxer. He fought some of the big names: Max Schmeling,

11

Max Baer, and Jim Braddock. He never fought Joe Louis, but the guys that he was fighting had fought Joe Louis.

I moved into to a beat up, run down, ramshackle hillside farm in Overton, Ohio, which was in north central Ohio, quite far from where I started. I walked a little over a mile each way down a gravel road to a one-room schoolhouse. I was in sixth grade, and went to school there with my cousin, Doris, who was in first grade.

One of the chores I had to do every morning, because my uncle left for work early, was to go out and feed the horses and one or two cows that he had already milked. One time I was out there with a pitchfork getting hay to bring to the horses, and one horse kicked me and it threw me clear across the barn. I landed in a pile of horse manure. The kick caught me right in the midsection, and it really hurt. I got up and got back up to the house, which was a pretty good walk up the hill, but I couldn't go to school that day, I was just hurting too much, and so I stayed in bed all day. I remember that vividly.

I lived in Overton for a year, then for some reason my dad decided I should come back to Montana. By this time the dam was well underway, and the government had built a town called Fort Peck. Every single thing, every building in the town was government-owned, and they were all built alike, although some of them were a little bit larger than the others. There were four units to each house and eight houses on a block. You could get lost in a New York second there because all the houses looked alike. We lived across the street from a huge reservoir. In the winter that would freeze over and I would go ice skating on it.

My life in Fort Peck was quite interesting. It didn't have a hospital, but it had an infirmary, a school for grades one through twelve, one movie theatre, one grocery store named Buttreys, one gas station, and so on. There was a park with headquarters at Fort Peck, and they kept a lot of fossils and arrowheads and other interesting artifacts there. They built a great big fence around the whole town, and yet coming into town on the road from Glasgow the gates to town were always open. Why they built that fence I don't know!

I will never forget my schooling at Fort Peck because in the seventh grade I got a teacher named Mrs. Germain. Mrs.

Germain and I didn't get along, so she moved me from the middle of the room up to the front row in the front seat next to her desk. Up until that time I had always gotten good grades in school. However, I wrote left handed, and she didn't think that students should write left-handed. Time after time she kept telling me to take my pen and put it in my right hand. If I didn't do it, she'd make me come up front so she could get her yardstick out and I would get hit with the yardstick across my back. Moving me closer made it easier for her to do that. That went on for a year.

There were a lot of king snakes in Montana; some called them bull snakes, some called them king snakes. There were great big, just huge king snakes around in the spring when the weather was getting nice and warming up. They're harmless, and they are long, seven or eight feet. They had their babies in spring, so I caught a young snake out in the schoolyard, and it wrapped right around my arm. All the kids knew it, and they were all around me giggling about it. I carried it into the school because we were on lunch break and Mrs. Germain wasn't in the room. I carefully slid it into the top left-hand drawer of her desk, which I was sitting right in front of.

Mrs. Germain came into the room. We sat there, and every kid in that room knew what was going to happen. So we sat there and sat there and sat there, and everybody was giggling and she didn't know what was going on. She went to the blackboard behind her desk, and while writing, broke the chalk, so she went to the drawer to get another piece. When she pulled that drawer open that snake came crawling right out! It scared her and she wet her pants, and made a huge puddle right there on the floor. She screamed, "Danny, you did that!" and she came over and just beat the daylights out of me with her ruler.

Mrs. Germain took me by the arm and dragged me down the hall to the principal's office. I got expelled from school, which didn't make my father very happy, mostly because he had to take time off from work. He was a foreman and worked twelve hours a day, 7:00 to 7:00; they blew 7:00 o'clock whistles out in the dam, which were heard all over town.

In each of the apartment buildings there was one common shower and bathroom for the men and one for the women in the center of the building, and every apartment was alike: You walked into the kitchen, which was off to the right, and the rest was all open, no partitions, it was all a living room. It wasn't very big, but it wasn't sparse. Off to the left was one bedroom and a closet that didn't go all the way to the top for some reason. All the walls were Celotex, a type of insulation. They weren't painted or wallpapered, that was just the way it was. There were cracks in the walls, and they were filled with bedbugs. I'd wake up in the middle of the night and find them on me, and I'd kill them. I learned quickly not to sleep with my arm next to the wall. Twice a year they would come in and fumigate, so we'd have to leave for a few days.

The entire time I lived in Fort Peck, about three years, I apparently liked tomato soup, so my dad would buy tomato soup by the case and it sat right inside the kitchen door. I had some type of cereal for breakfast because he'd be gone to work already. I'd get on my bike and ride about a mile and a half, all downhill, going to school and then all uphill coming home.

There were bike and walking trails for the kids alongside the road. There were caves down on the right hand side of the coulees, which are small undulations in the ground, not big enough to be a 'hill.' There were a lot of artifacts out there in the high desert, and a tremendous amount of arrowheads just lying around everywhere, and so it was an interesting topography. The town theater had an area in the front where people had brought in dinosaur bones, and they had a big display of them.

When I came home from school, I'd have my tomato soup and a grilled cheese sandwich. My dad gave me thirty-five cents every day to have lunch at the diner close to school. I'd have either an open pork or beef sandwich with gravy on it, and potatoes. That was my diet, and that's what I did. I don't remember eating fruit or candies or vegetables or anything else.

Also when I got home from school, I would turn on the radio and listen to the Lone Ranger and to Jack Armstrong, the All-American Boy. I'd make my supper and then listen to the Lucky Strike Hit Parade, which played the top songs of the week. I'd usually go to bed at 8:00 o'clock, and sometimes I'd stay up until my dad got home. Most of the time I'd get up by myself, go to school by myself, and come home by myself.

At about ten years old, I kept having colds, and Dad took me down to the infirmary. It was just a one room infirmary: When you got past the waiting room there was one hospital "bed" that actually was just a table that you would lie on. The doctor told him that I had to have my tonsils and adenoids removed because they were swollen and inflamed, and they weren't going to get any better. He made an appointment for that, and so I went.

It was summer so I rode my bike to the infirmary, parked it outside, and went in. They gave me ether, did the operation, and when I woke up the doctor said, "Now, who is going to pick you up here? You need to go home and get some ice cream into you." I said, "Well, I rode my bike." He exclaimed, "What?" I said, "I rode my bike down, I'll ride my bike home." He reached in his pocket and gave me a quarter, and said, "I want you to take this quarter and go down to the store. Do not buy chocolate, buy vanilla ice cream, and you take that home and eat it and get to bed." So, I went to the grocery store, got my vanilla ice cream, got on my bike and pumped back uphill for a mile, ate my ice cream, and went to bed.

3.

I read somewhere about a job selling Grit newspapers, a compilation of news from all over which was printed in Williamsport, Pennsylvania. On the front banner, there were two elves holding the banner on the masthead, which said, "Puck, what fools these mortals be." I always found that interesting. It was a weekly publication delivered all over the country. Delivery men would pick the bundles of papers up in Glasgow at the trains, and one would bring them to my house in Fort Peck. They were always a week late due to the trains. Since I had my bike, I decided that was a job I could do.

There were a few people selling Grit newspapers like I was, but I established a route of subscribers. The paper cost a nickel a week. I would go around once a month to collect the money and send it in to Williamsport minus what they owed me. That worked out pretty well and I did that for quite a few months.

I got subscribers at an apartment building, and, boy, it was nice and easy to just to go up there and drop those papers ten feet apart at all those doors. I had a good customer base there. I usually went down on Saturdays to collect the money, and sometimes went on Sundays as there was one guy that was never home. I finally caught him at home, and I said, "Sir, I came to get the money for the Grit Newspaper." He said, "Kid, get out here, I'm not paying you for that rag sheet," and he slammed the door in my face. That really irritated me, and this became my first lesson in vindictiveness.

Soon after that, when he was at work, I left school and I went to the apartment. There was nobody in the whole building because they were all working. I kicked his door in and I trashed his whole apartment. There wasn't anything left that wasn't broken or messed up. I closed the door, and walked out with a smile on my face. Somebody that would screw a kid just ten years old out of money just deserved that. So, that was my justice.

In the downtown area they built two-story apartment houses for single people; if you were married they tried to put you in a house. Housing was limited, and they had hundreds maybe thousands of people working on that dam. Because they couldn't get housing, some workers commuted nineteen miles to Glasgow, and then some of them started building what they called the Tip Up Towns.

The most famous Tip Up Town was Wheeler, Montana, and Life Magazine featured it on its cover in 1936. There were all these "Tip Ups," these little shacks that people built with just two by fours and black tar paper around them. They were livable and a little bit 'upscale' from a tent, but that was about it. There were hundreds and hundreds of people living in Wheeler, and it developed into a little cowboy town.

At that time the cowboys, and a lot of other people, including my dad, wore guns on their hips. My dad didn't wear his at work, but when he went to Wheeler to drink beer, he'd strap his gun into his holster. There were a few saloons in a block long building there. The boardwalk was elevated and the saloons were lined up one after another, and there was one hardware store. And, like every other town like it, there were two or three houses of prostitution that were out in back of the saloons.

Wheeler, the Tip-Up Town, was about two miles from Fort Peck all uphill getting there and, and all downhill coming back.

At the time, if you brought beer bottles into the beer joints and it was a brown bottle, they'd give you a penny, and if it was a green bottle they'd give you two pennies. I was picking up bottles in Fort Peck and I'd put them in my basket, as many as I could carry, and I'd pump my bike all the way up that hill to Wheeler because there was no alcohol, no taverns, nothing like that in Fort Peck. I would park my bike, get up on the boardwalk, take those bottles into the taverns to redeem them, and they'd give me pennies in return. Every Saturday that was the routine for me: I'd spend all week long picking up beer bottles and then on Saturdays I'd take them to Wheeler.

One day I was up in Wheeler and I decided, being nosey, to go around the back of the boardwalk buildings to see if there were any bottles laying out there, and I found a real catch, I found the golden egg. There were bottles piled up out there taller than I was, great big piles. Not one pile, but two or three of them, and I thought, "Good Lord!" I started picking up those bottles, and about that time a young woman comes to the door of this little shack back there and asked, "What are you doing?" and I said, "I'm getting these beer bottles." She said, "You leave those beer bottles alone, they belong to us." I said, "Oh, I didn't know that." She asked, "What's your name?" and I said, "Danny," and she said, "Danny, come in here." So I went in, and there were four or five women having breakfast even though it was maybe close to noon. And, oh my gosh, it's as if they had never seen such a cute little boy, so they all started talking to me and asking me questions, and getting me something to eat and giving me candy, which I never had, and well, I was in hog heaven. These women were all prostitutes, but they liked a little ten-year-old, blond-haired kid. So, I became their favorite.

From then on I would collect my bottles in Fort Peck all week long, go to Wheeler to get all my pennies, and then I would go around to the back of tavern, get my breakfast, and have the ladies make a fuss over me. I'd never had that before, women who hugged and kissed me and treated me like I was a halfway decent kid. That was pretty important to me.

There was a postcard that came out in 1937 that showed a picture of Wheeler in the wintertime with an outhouse. They had communal outhouses to serve four or five families living out there; they just dug a hole and put Tip Ups around it. And, on this postcard it said 'Wheeler Montana 1937, temperature 62 below zero.' And, there was a little verse on the front of the postcard and it went like this:

'You remember when you were a wee, wee tot.
And they took you out of your warm, warm cot,
And they set you on a cold, cold pot,
And told you to wee, wee whether you could or not.'

I always remembered that and I still say it to this day.

We went back and forth once or twice from Montana to Ohio and Cedar Rapids, Iowa in Dad's '37 Chevy. On one of those trips, I was with my mother, her sister, and my cousin; I think his name was Richard, but I'm not sure. The only thing I remember from that family visit was that they put me in bathtub and washed me all over.

Me at Cave of the Winds in Wyoming

On the way back we stopped at Cave of the Winds in Wyoming, a state park, which I've always remembered: the wind just shoots up out of the ground, and it was dangerous, it could lift you right off the ground.

We got back in the car, and while driving to Montana, there was news of the election on the radio. Wendell Willkie was running, I remember that. Something came up in the conversation, I don't recall what it was, but I said, "Oh, doggone you, Dad." And, boy, he hauled off and hit me - with his fist - and that knocked me right up against the door. I never forgot that. I couldn't understand why anybody would get so mad because I said 'doggone you'. That was an expression that the kids used at the time. That was a memorable trip, one of the most memorable trips to Iowa and Ohio and then back to Montana.

After the Fort Peck Dam was built and the lake formed, they tore everything down, removed every last thing, and that was that.

YOUNG ADULTHOOD

4.

When we left Montana, my dad and I moved to Philadelphia. I was going into eighth grade, twelve years old, in 1940 or '41. Now, you talk about a culture shock - that was quite a bit different. Street cars, running water, showers, telephones. Man, what a departure from where I've been up until that point in my life.

He moved me into an apartment in Nicetown, which is in the northern part of Philadelphia, south of Germantown. Nicetown was all Polish. Dad always reminded me when he left for work never to go out of the house, that I wasn't to leave the house

under any conditions, so I didn't; being as young as I was, it was illegal to leave me alone all day.

He finally found a place with a family that had a son living at home that was about a year older than me, and it was in Germantown. It was technically for my dad to stay, too, but he never did. He never ate there, but I did. He went to work in the Navy yards down in south Philly. He rode a streetcar when he came "home" on Saturday evenings.

I shared a room with Matt Shields. His father's name was Matt also, and his mother's name was Mae. They had three children. Catherine was the oldest, Allen was in the middle, and Matt was the youngest.

I went to Gillespie Junior High School, which was quite a walk, but I walked every day, in every kind of weather. I walked with a kid named Reid Watson, whose father was a very prominent attorney in Germantown. He had a couple of sisters that were really good-looking gals, but they were older, going to Swarthmore, which is a very pricey college.

I remember that when I went to his house in the mornings to walk with him to school, one sister had a record that she loved to play, and the music was called "Frenesi." I've always remembered that song from those mornings. Reid and I walked past the home of the Vicks VapoRub company which was next

21

to the home of Burpee Seeds company. I started taking Spanish, and I was a really good Spanish student. To this day I can speak limited fluent Spanish as a result of that junior high school.

We lived at 4900 North Germantown Avenue, which is a historic route from Philadelphia to Scranton. I went to Germantown High School for tenth through twelfth grades, and I just barely turned sixteen when I got out of high school.

High school was a lot of fun for me. There was a gang of eight kids I hung with. There were lots of gangs all over Philadelphia. We didn't get into trouble, we just had fun. The eight of us - "The Glorious Eight" - we had a diversity of ethnic backgrounds, Italian, Irish, English, and so on.

Frank Goffredo was my best buddy going into high school. His folks were from Sicily, and he worked in a shoe repair shop that his dad ran, and which his uncle ran for years after his dad died. I ate my first pizza and rigatoni and so on that his mother would make by hand, before pizzas were even heard of, the big dish type pizza with a lot of meat and fillings in them.

We had fun in high school. Sometimes a bunch of us would hitchhike down to Atlantic City on the Blackhorse Pike to Steel Pier. We Philly kids didn't have any money, so we would go down to the sand underneath the pier. There were big bands like Tommy Dorsey, Glenn Miller, Harry James and a lot of other big names that played there. We would dance down there in the sand, take our shoes off, and because you couldn't exactly dance, so you'd do the Shuffle. That's where the Shuffle started, down there on the sands of Atlantic City. Then we'd hitchhike back.

One time there was advertisement in a newspaper for people to pick carrots in Jersey, so I said to my buddies, "Hey, let's go down there and make some money on a Saturday and pick carrots." They said, "No, you don't want to go so early and pick carrots and work your butt off. No, that's too hard of work." I couldn't get anybody to go with me. But I decided to go make some money.

One Saturday I got on the streetcar early, 5 o'clock in the morning, and rode it all the way down to South Philly, as far as it went to where the carrot buses were there waiting. There were a bunch of us kids, mostly Italian kids or black kids on that bus down into Jersey where there was really good farm land. That's why it's called the Garden State.

On the carrot farms, they'd give you crates, and you got ten cents for every crate of carrots you filled. I was down there on my hands and knees all day long, and didn't leave until about 6 o'clock at night. I think I made $3 and some change picking carrots. I was so tired I could hardly walk. I rode the streetcar all the way back home. The guys then kidded me and chided me about going down there when they told me not to. I never went back. It was awful, hard work, but it created an appreciation in me for the hard labor of the Mexican and other laborers that worked in the fields for years. And, I can understand why a lot of people don't or won't do it.

I never got my high school diploma. I was not a good student. World War II was on and they made exceptions for people who would go to work in war plants, and so I got a job at Leeds & Northrup. It was about five blocks from where I lived, above La

Salle University. I'd get out of school early, at 2:00, and walk; I rarely rode a trolley. The trolleys were fifteen cents a round; you got two tokens for fifteen cents and you got free transfers so you could go anywhere in Philadelphia for eight cents, which we used to do on Sundays.

I worked four hours in that factory from 3:00 until 7:00, and made, for me, good money at the time. So I never did much homework.

I went to a lot of dances. I love dancing, and they had dances all over the city, mostly at the Catholic schools. There were dances different nights of the week, but mostly Fridays, Saturdays, and Sundays. You'd have a different group of kids and different girlfriends at each one. That was a good thing. In

Germantown on Saturday nights up on Green Street they had dances with big bands playing.

As kids we went to Gratz High School, which was next door to Gillespie where I went to junior high, and one time there was a guy in there singing. He was a kid from high school, and his name was Eddie Fisher. Eddie Fisher used to sing, and girls would all swoon and would go crazy. That was before Frank Sinatra really started coming on. About a year or so later, Sinatra got really popular and Eddie Fisher became old hat.

I grew up loving jazz and blues and was always going to hear a lot of music. I've loved it all my life. Big dance era, swing era, and a lot of jitterbugging, and a lot of what they call slow dancing, which is really ballroom dancing, and I was good at it.

I'll never forget one summer when I was a sophomore, I was walking down to Hoover's Bakery on the corner at Germantown Avenue. We lived on Clapier Street, which ran perpendicular to Germantown Avenue. There was a girl up there in the second floor by the post office in an apartment, and she leaned out the window and she said, "Hi, how you doing?" I looked up and here was this really, really cute girl. And I said, "I'm doing great." She said, "My name is Inez. I'm here for the summer with my aunt. What's your name?" I said, "Danny. Danny Reed." She asked, "Where do you live?" I said, "I live up there at the top of the hill." She said, "Well, do you want to come up and visit for a while?" I said, "Sure."

I went in and upstairs to the apartment. She was there alone, and we just did what kids do. We talked about this and that, and the other, and something else. After about the second or third trip of going to see her, she said, "Do you know how to kiss?" And I said, "Yeah." She said, "No, I mean, really kiss." I said, "I'm not sure." She says, "Well, let me teach you." She taught me how to French-kiss. At that time, the vernacular for kissing amongst high school kids was "batting."

Well, I guarantee you, I made a lot of trips upstairs that summer to see Inez. It never went beyond French kissing, but it was just a brazen indoctrination. I call these my "educational years" for lots of different reasons.

One thing about Philadelphia, as I already mentioned, they had gangs. About five blocks north on Germantown Avenue was

Manheim Street, a heavily traveled street, and it dead-ended on Germantown Avenue coming from the west to West Philadelphia. There was a theater there called the Lyric Theatre, and on Saturdays you'd go there and you'd buy two comic books, and then you got to see the movies, all for ten cents. So I took Inez to the movies regularly, and she'd give me her comic books. They tore the covers off of them so they could give them away as used, but that was the kind of promotions we got on those Sunday afternoons. You'd go and see Tom Mix or Buck Rogers in westerns, it was always westerns, The Lone Ranger and all that kind of stuff, and the good guy always won.

But, up there about five blocks north of Manheim Street, was the beginning of an area of a really, really mean gang of kids. They were all older than we were in our group. We never got into fights with them or anything because they were older. There was a guy by name of Hoodie in that group. Some of us were walking up there one time, and he got hold of me and said, "What are you doing up here?" I said, "I'm going up to Chelten Avenue." He said, "Well, if you walk through here, you pay me." I said, "What do you mean, I pay you?" He said, "Did you hear what I said? You pay me. You got a dollar?" I said, "Yeah." He said, "Well, if you're going to walk through here and you want to get through okay, you got to pay me a dollar." So I started paying and got more "education" about the highbinder, a bully.

As time passed, Hoodie went into the Service as The War was still on. When he came home on leave from the Service, he was a drunk. We were up at the YMCA dancing on a Saturday night, and he came in there drunk. Hoodie saw me, came over and said, "I'll meet you at Germantown and Chelten." I said, "For what?" He said, "You're going to get what you should have gotten a long time ago," and then he left. So all the kids that were there with me said, "You don't want to go down there," and I said, "Well, I'm not afraid of him. I'll go down there."

When the dance was over, we went down, and sure enough, there he was with a smaller portion of his gang, because most of them had gone into the Service. As we were going down there to the corner all of a sudden he took off running, and he ran down Germantown Avenue towards where they lived. When we got down there, a kid was lying on the sidewalk. Hoodie had stuck a knife in him, had walked around to his back and just dissected him. I don't know if the kid lived or died, but they got Hoodie, who was a Marine, for attempted murder or murder, whatever the case was, and he went to jail. I never saw Hoodie again, but if I had gone down there, maybe he would have put a knife in me, I don't know. I'll always remember that.

Back to high school, and graduation... Mrs. Shields had always prided herself in taking care of me. She used to give me a quarter a week to take piano lessons. I took piano lessons for about two or three times, and I didn't like it, so I stopped going. I never told her I quit, and I practiced at home with the lessons I learned. I'd take that quarter and I'd take Inez to the movies on Saturday. I'd have broken Mrs. Shields' heart if she'd known that.

In the meantime, Matt Shields had joined the Coast Guard. He was older than me and had left, and so I was living alone on the third floor. There was no air conditioning, and boy, in the summertime it got hot, and I mean it got really hot on those black, tarred roofs. There were two bedrooms on the third floor, and my dad had all his stuff in the front bedroom. The only time I saw him was on a Sunday when he'd come home. I don't know where he stayed when he wasn't there, and don't know what he did.

My dad, Mr. Shields, a fellow named Spike McNeil, and Mr. Shield's son-in-law, Jack Maher, would play pinochle every Sunday afternoon for hours after we had dinner; we called lunch 'dinner' and supper 'supper.'

Usually for Sunday dinner we had leg of lamb with gravy, and boy, it was good. We ate lamb a couple of times during the week, but Sundays we had meatloaf or leg of lamb. Before Matt went into the Service, his mother would give him money and he'd run down to Hoover's Bakery and come back with a mixture of doughnuts, which is what we had for breakfast during school.

While I lived in Philadelphia, I learned to love Scrapple. Most people don't even know what Scrapple is. It's a meat product made from seven different kinds of meat. It's usually served as breakfast with syrup on it. It's different, but if you ever get a chance, give it a try.

One night my dad came into my bedroom, and he was drunk. He said, "Danny, you got to promise me you're never going to drink until you're twenty-one." I said, "Oh." And he said again, "Now, you've got to promise me." He got me to shake his hand and said again, "You got to promise," and I said, "Okay, I promise."

And, I never took a drink of alcohol until I was twenty-one years old. And let me tell you, at age nineteen and twenty, everybody was drinking beer. Not me. I gave my word, I was going to keep it, and I did keep it.

When it came time to graduate, I knew I wasn't going to get my diploma because I had flunked a couple of courses; I had to go to summer school to make up the grades, and then I'd get my diploma later. Rather than break Mrs. Shields' heart, I went in there and got a gown and everything so I'd be in the graduation ceremony.

They had bleachers set up just like those old style churches – if you'd ever been in an old church back East like in Philadelphia, they looked just like our high school auditorium with balconies up on top, and people sitting all around. There were 507 kids in my graduating class, and we were on the bleachers, and, my Lord, it was hot! I remember they put buckets of ice underneath the bleachers while we were standing and sitting there and going through the routine. There was a kid sitting in front of me that everybody picked on, including me. I had a knife in my pocket so I cut his suspenders. When we walked up the aisle, the graduating class, he was walking up there holding his pants up! I'll never forget that.

And so, Mrs. Shields got to see me graduate. My dad wasn't there, but she was, so she got to see me graduate, as I didn't want to disappoint her. I never did get a high school diploma. I always told everybody I graduated from Germantown High School, but I never actually graduated. They put out a yearbook, and I was voted "Mr. Most Pleasing Personality, Danny Reed, graduating class of 1945.

DANNY REED

24 E. Clapier St.

MECHANIC ARTS

Senator E, F; Alternate C, D; Lunch room Committee F; Basketball C, D, E, F.

Danny has a super personality that does things for him. When it comes to laughs or jokes, you can be sure that Danny will contribute his share of the fun. We know you will make out in life, but here are some good wishes to follow you.

Danny Reed

I bought my first car, a 1933 Chevy with the money I made working at Leeds & Northrup while I was a senior in high school. I was really proud of that.

All the way to senior year I had dated one girl. Her name was Ruth Doyle and she lived three streets up from me. Her brother was in the Navy. He came home one time and he grabbed me and said, "If you mess around with my sister, I'm gonna come back here and kill you. Just keep your hands off of her." And that's just the way things were, getting educated on all sorts of things.

One day my dad came home and said, "Well, we're going to move to Ohio." I said, "Ohio?" He said, "Yeah." By that time I was working full-time at Leeds & Northrup, and again I said, "Ohio?" And again, he said, "Yeah. Why don't you sell your car and get us a truck?"

He had a new '41 Chevy, because they didn't make cars during the war, and he sold it, and had me trade my car for a Ford pickup truck. We loaded all of our belongings in it, and that was the end of my time in Philadelphia. I went over and said goodbye to my girlfriend, and never did see her again.

Off we went on the Pennsylvania Turnpike, which was way ahead of its time for high-speed transit, the first in the United

29

States. We went through seven tunnels going through the mountains. I was very impressed.

5.

I was sixteen when we moved to Ohio. We moved back to his old home where as a kid I had lived with my grandma, and the place was about ready to fall down. I had an upstairs bedroom, and he had the adjoining bedroom. We'd converted the bedroom that was downstairs next to the living room into the kitchen because in the area where the kitchen had been the roof had fallen in. There was no electricity, no plumbing, no running water. Now you're talking about another culture shock and more in my education after moving from Montana to Philadelphia, Philadelphia with all the lights and all the glitz, so for me as a kid from high school, moving back to the hills, into the woods, I saw that Ohio wasn't too enchanting.

My dad wanted to start a sawmill but I never understood his reasoning. He had lots of timber there on the land and he thought he was going to make all kinds of money on a sawmill.

In order to get the logs down to the sawmill, he had to have a team of mules. Well, to have mules, you had to have a barn. So, he and I built a barn, a lean-to, one-direction barn with a corrugated steel roof to house the mules that I did the logging with.

The mules had to eat, so then he decided, "I should put in corn." He rented a piece of flat land about three quarters of a mile from our house. I went down there with those damn mules and I plowed the ground with a sixteen-inch single-bottom shovel plow. I seeded the corn. I tilled the ground. I had what they call a "wiggle-assed" cultivator. You'd swing your butt back and forth as you went down the rows so the shovels wouldn't pull up the little two- to three-inch corn plants so that they would be nurtured and grow big and tall.

I did all that work for those mules to get them fed so I could take the mules up on steep, steep hills. And, they weren't just hills, they were just totally woods. There was no open land anywhere. My dad showed me where I should go up there to cut timber with a crosscut saw five feet long. He hired a guy to work with me, Johnny Applegate, who would later become my brother-in-law. My dad paid him $3 a foot for every tree that we fell and trimmed, and they all had to be trimmed. My dad paid me zero.

We would fall the trees, most of which were poplar. We did some pine, but when we did pine, it was just awful. They'd gum up the saws and we had to put kerosene on the saw, as every time you pulled twenty pulls, it'd be all gummed up with rosin. It was hard work, very hard work, and dangerous on the steep hillside. After we cut trees down, we'd trim them, and then we cut them into either eight-, ten-, or six-foot lengths, starting with the base of the tree where the tree was the biggest which was usually ten feet. As you progressed up the tree trunk it would change to eight feet, then six feet. I would take chains up the hills and drag those things down the hillside, trying to stay out of the road of the rolling logs, and not letting the logs run over the mules. It was tedious but I learned a lot. I learned a lot of things not to do, and gained more education about hard physical work.

Once we got them down and made a log pile, my dad set up the sawmill. We'd use cant hooks to move the logs. And he hired a guy that he drank with, a total alcoholic, to work on his sawmill. I did the off-bearing, which means when you cut the board off the log, it goes to the side and you ride over the saw, which is a fifty-six- or a sixty-inch diameter saw. My dad would gum those every morning before we started. That meant that he'd go with the file and he would sharpen every one of those teeth all the way around.

While he was doing that, I was getting logs pulled up by mules to the to the sawmill before we were about to saw during the day. Then I would ride on the tail saw right over that blade. He would look at those logs and he'd turn them this way or that way so he could see how many boards he'd get out of the logs. He was smart that way.

Then I would off-bear those and throw them in a pile called the slab pile. That's when I started chewing tobacco because it was so dusty and my mouth would get dry. In the meantime, I'd started smoking when I was in Philadelphia at age fifteen, and I really started chewing tobacco by the time I was about seventeen years old. I chewed tobacco all the time I was on the sawmill; when I wasn't on the sawmill, I didn't chew, I smoked (and I didn't quit smoking until I was about thirty-two).

With some of those logs, my dad would make cribbing for the railroads. They were cut triangularly and they sat in a corner of a box car and they would keep things in place. He also cut ties for the railroad. They had to be oak and they were heavy, six foot long by six inches square. We would take three or four days to get a truckload. I'd get in the truck and drive those about twenty-five miles to a junction where I had to unload them and stack them neatly by myself. It was not easy work.

The hell of it was, my dad paid the guy who helped cut down the trees, he paid him every day based on how many feet we had fallen. And the old guy who was an alcoholic, he got paid. I never got paid. *Ever.* It was slave labor.

I did that for about a year and a half, and during this time I had met this girl. Her name was Patty Applegate. She was from a dirt-poor family living on a small dirt-poor acreage, about eight miles from where I lived. We started dating when she was a junior in high school.

I saw an ad in the paper at the time the W.P.A. was in existence, which employed mostly unskilled men on public works projects to help them earn money. They were doing all kinds of road and reclamation work and projects, digging ditches, and whatever. Those who worked on the projects, they really didn't do much work, they did a lot of talking, a lot of spitting, and a lot of leaning. I never did work for the W.P.A. because I had all kinds of work to do for my dad.

I saw the W.P.A. ad and this other ad looking for workers in the beet fields in southern Michigan, in the town of Blissfield, for a couple of weeks while the beet season was on, and it said that there was a bus leaving from MacArthur, the county seat. I told my dad that I was going to do this, and he was upset about it, but I went up there to get myself some money.

The bus would take you up there, and well, was there ever a motley crew on that bus, let me tell you. A lot of ex-convicts, a lot of drugs. I had never been around drugs; the whole time I was in high school I never did drugs.

Once you got to Blissfield, you would live in boxcars on the railroad tracks, you'd sleep in bunks, and they would feed you; they had a cook there for breakfast, lunch, and supper. There wasn't much to do except go to bed after supper. We worked ten hours a day. The pay wasn't much but it was a lot better than what I was getting.

In Blissfield, a lot of drinking went on in the evenings, and there was a lot of fighting and card games. One time I saw a guy chase another guy out of a place with a hatchet. He chased the guy and they went around and into the boxcar, and he threw the hatchet, which landed right on the side of that boxcar, and it just quivered there. It didn't hit the guy, but if it had, it would have killed him.

Then another night, we were sound asleep when in comes a whole bunch of Michigan State Patrol Troopers with flashlights. All of a sudden they were there, going through about five or six box cars up and down that old rail line. They put the flashlights under each one of us, one after another, so they could see our face. A woman who was with them would say, "No. No." And it went on like this down the row for a few minutes, and then she said, "There he is!" and they took this guy off the boxcar that had apparently raped this gal that night. And, so, we all went back to bed. That was the process of growing up when you're seventeen years old. That was 1946.

I was on an unloading job in Blissfield where the trucks pulled in and you pulled a lever and they would dump those beets onto a huge conveyor that was recessed below the ground. You had to unhook the trailer, pull the clip pin on the tractor, unload the trailer, let it sit there, and go back and open up the drawers, and they would dump all those beets on the trailer into a conveyor belt that carried them over to the processing plant.

I was out there trying to get the pin of the fifth-wheel on the tractor unhooked from this long trailer, and it was stuck. I told the driver to pull it up a little bit, or back up just a little bit so it would come loose, so he did that, but we just couldn't get it. He said, "Here, I'll get it."

He came out and, like me, he put his back to the tractor and the trailer. He pulled on that pin and when he did, the tractor was sitting just right to where the wheels rolled over his feet, his heels, and just crushed them. He was screaming and they carried him away in an ambulance to a hospital in Tecumseh, Michigan. He wrote me a card eventually, as he had my address because we'd worked together, to tell me that they were hiring at Tecumseh Products, and it would be a good place to work, a really good place to go to work.

I went back home and had money so I could start dating this girlfriend of mine, and we'd go to movies, and do this, that and the other thing, nothing fancy. I went back to work for my dad.

When I turned eighteen, President Truman announced that the country was going to have the last conscription call for the draft; people who turned eighteen would be eligible, and after that it was going to stop. The draft requisition for the county I lived in was five people, so they put ten of us on a bus and we went to Fort Hayes, Columbus all day for a physical.

We took our physicals, and out of the ten, five were classified as "1-A" or eligible for service, and the others were "4-F" or ineligible for whatever reason. We were all just eighteen. They needed three of us, and they decided, in order to be fair, to have a drawing of us five that were 1-A eligible on the county courthouse steps on a Saturday night. They drew three names, and my name was not drawn.

My dad was overjoyed, as were my aunts and uncles. They were glad I didn't have to go off to Japan for occupation, so I guess I was, too. But in retrospect, as time went by, I discovered had I gone to Japan, had my name been drawn, that would have made me eligible for a college education, for G.I. insurance, for V.A. benefits, and a G.I. loan. At that time it was a big deal because you could get a $5,000 loan and buy a house. I should have enlisted. The biggest mistake I ever made was not going to Japan for occupation because it would have made a big difference. But again, as I've said all along, these were the education years.

In the winter of 1945-46, I made the decision to sleep out on the overhead porch on a corn shuck mattress. It had a roof, but the snow blew in, the rain blew in, and my dad thought I was nuts, but I persisted and created my first lesson in perseverance.

I was working on the sawmill again, asking my dad for money every now and then. Every Saturday, he and Lowell, his worker and friend, would go to town and get drunk, and they'd come home with gallon jugs of wine and would spend the week drinking. They went to town one Saturday when it was raining. This thing kept burning in my head about Tecumseh Products in Tecumseh, Michigan.

36

I went upstairs where my dad had an old beat up cardboard suitcase. I got what clothes I had, my boots and various things, and piled all of my belongings into that suitcase. About 4:00 o'clock in the afternoon, I walked up over the hill behind the house, which is the way all my aunts and uncles had walked to their one-room school and to church, I walked up over and down the other side of the hill to highway U.S. 50. It was about three quarters of a mile. It was raining. There was a grove of real dense Scotch pine trees, and when you got underneath those trees, it was dry as could be on the needles. I spent the night sleeping on the needles.

6.

In the morning I got up and I started hitchhiking up U.S 50 towards Chillicothe, and then Highway 23, all the way to Tecumseh, Michigan. I don't recall all the details about hitchhiking, but I do remember one ride in central Ohio in the back of an open pickup truck. It was blowing cold snow all around me the whole time.

I got to Tecumseh and I found my way to the Tecumseh Products Company, a manufacturer of refrigeration products, and they were indeed hiring. I filled out some papers, and was hired on the 30th day of April. The reason I remember that date so distinctly is that Tecumseh Products was a union shop, and the day of hiring was very important for your future years in a union. One of the union rules was that if you wanted jobs that others had because the positions made more money and you liked the jobs better than your own, you could bump anyone in the factory as long as you had one day seniority on them. April 30th was a really big day for me because they hadn't hired many that week, and then May 1st they started hiring a lot of people: That one day of seniority was very important to me in future years, relative to income.

After I got my job, I had to find a place to stay, so I walked downtown, which was only about four blocks. The downtown Tecumseh area was two blocks east and west, and one block north and south either way. That was the whole district. Tecumseh was a town of about 6,000 people, and it was located in Lenawee County, which is the southernmost county in

Michigan, bumped up against Ohio. Adrian was the county seat, and there was Adrian College and a lot of manufacturing such as for car springs for Ford Motor Company.

There was one hotel on one of the four main corners of downtown. It would years later become the Bank of Tecumseh, but at that time it was a rundown hotel. I went in, and there was a man behind the desk wearing a hat, chewing a toothpick, and his name was Maynard Mulvany. I never forgot that. I said, "Sir, I just got a job at Tecumseh Products, and I need a room to stay until I get paid. I don't have hardly any money right now." He said, "Get out of here." I persisted, "Sir, listen I'm as honest the day is long, and I've got a job, and I will get paid in two weeks and I'll pay you."

He said, "Well, all the rooms I've got are more expensive than what you want. But, I'll tell you what I'll do. Come with me." We went up two flights of stairs to the third floor which apparently was hardly ever used. The hotel rooms on that floor were used for storage. He unlocked one door, and there was a old single iron bed with metal springs, but no mattress, no blankets, nothing, and said, "I'll get a mattress pad for you, and a pillow and some sheets, and a blanket." He said, "You better pay me." I said, "I promise I'll pay, as soon as I get my check I'll come and pay you." So, I had myself a room!

Then I was hungry, and I had five dollars and ten cents in my pocket. I'll never forget that. There was a Kroger grocery store at the end of the first block going north downtown. I went in, and I bought a loaf of bread, and a jar of sandwich spread, and I was in business. I started back to hotel and noticed there was a restaurant on the back end of the hotel across from the store. I went in and said, "Ma'am, I wonder if I could borrow a knife from you. I don't have much money. I just got a job down at Tecumseh Products, and I got my sandwich stuff here to make my lunch for tomorrow, and I'm wondering if I could borrow a knife." She said, "Well, sure you can." I said, "I'd like to get some lunch. I don't have much money, but I'll pay you," and she said okay. I got an open beef sandwich, like when I was a kid.

I ate the sandwich, and said, "You know I don't have much money, but if you would do my lunch for me until I get my

38

paycheck, I'll come right in and pay you, because I'm living right here at the hotel."

She said, "I can't believe you're living in that fly trap." I said, "Well, I got a room." She said, "All right, I'll trust you, so I'll do your lunch for you every day, and then, you better pay me when you get paid." I said, "I will Ma'am, and I'm honest." I got my lunches set up for every day, and I had my sandwiches to make for dinner because I worked in the afternoon shift that started at 3:30 and got done at 12:00.

That was my first day in Tecumseh, Michigan.

The second day, I went to work in the factory on the second shift. They gave me a heavy duty job of putting compressors on long racks, hooking them up to tubes, and then they'd blow hot air through them to remove moisture. You closed the doors, then it was a big oven, and they'd blow hot air through there and take all the moisture out of the compressors so that when they put Freon in it wouldn't lock up. With a wrench, I had to hook up all these tubes from the compressor itself.

Each compressor weighed about twenty-five pounds; the heavy ones weighed about forty, but they sat on the floor so you didn't have to swing them up. And there was hot air that ran about eight feet in the oven on both sides. It was only about four feet wide on both sides, and there was just racks and racks and racks of these compressors. By the time you got to the top rack, you would throw on some weight up there, making a swing up to get them hooked up. That was my first job.

I came in the next day, and found out I had screwed it up. I had cross-threaded most of them and destroyed all the threads on the things that they took off later from the compressor. They had them on there so they could remove and reuse them.

There was a big guy, strapping big, and he had been working there for years, and when I came in, he and my foreman were waiting for me, and I really got blasted. I mean to tell you, that man was hot mad, because he had to take downtime and go through and change all of those copper tubes that were screwed onto the compressors. I was scared to death. So my foreman chided me about it, and the other guy chewed me up.

The foreman was a nice fellow, though, and told me to be very, very careful. His name was Homer Cliff, and I've never forgotten that.

Homer ran what they call the White Room, where they assemble the compressors, and they had to wear white masks and white hats. It was just a really clean room, and air-conditioned all the time. They ran two shifts. I discovered that Homer was the foreman for the second shift in the White Room, and they were working overtime every night. They were working three, four, five hours and the most overtime they could allow was four hours.

Everybody in there had been working overtime for so long they didn't want to anymore, so I went over there and got a job on the line that I could handle, and after working my shift until midnight, I got four hours of overtime after that. I went to work at 3:30 in the afternoon and got off at 3:30 in the morning, and I walked home to the hotel, and I did that for weeks and weeks and weeks.

The wages when I started in Tecumseh were $1.10 an hour. When it came time to get my first paycheck, because they paid every other week, I discovered I'd hired in on an off week. So, instead of waiting two weeks, I had to wait three weeks, and after that, it would be every two weeks. I had to go and tell the restaurant owner and the hotel owner about me hiring in at the off time, and thankfully they were okay with it. And when I finally got my check I went right away and paid the hotel owner, and I went and paid the restaurant owner, and then I got a place with room and board somewhere in town.

My clothes were getting dirty by this time, so I would turn my t-shirts inside out because they were getting all black, and I got chided about that by some guys that were older than me.

During my shift, all I would have for lunch was my sandwich. It was really hot in there, and I became weaker from not eating right and working so much. One night I passed out, fainted right there on the floor at work. A Clark truck was coming down through there and the driver saw me, stopped the truck, got me revived, and I sat up and there were people all around me. I was okay pretty quickly, and I got up and went back to work.

But that is just the beginning of the story.

40

Tecumseh Products Company manufactured refrigeration products for various refrigerator manufacturers like Kelvinator and Westinghouse and all those, and they had two plants. In Plant 1 they put all the components together. There was what they call the Gray Iron, which was dirty, dirty, dirty. They take the castings from the foundry, and they drill on those, and it was all piecework, and people just worked their butts off.

Then, as you're going down through the factory you would come to the White Room, and my ovens were right there on the other side. Then, you got on a ramp and you got on to the assembly lines. That was down where they assembled all of what were called the high side units. And in the other plant, Plant 2, they would take those units and transport them over on big trucks. They had ovens over there also. Everything was for Admiral refrigerators, Westinghouse, Sears, and so on. We'd run fifty for Admiral and thirty for Sears, but it didn't really make a difference as they were all the same.

Tecumseh Products had about 3500 employees, and they drew farmers in from all around southern Michigan. They were all union, the U.E.W., Union of Electrical Workers, and everything was piecework and timed. The big factories in Detroit, Ford, Chrysler, GM, they were timed at fifty-five minutes: You worked fifty-five-minute increments of an hour. So, it was a time rate of fifty-five per hour. Well, at Tecumseh Products it was fifty-six and two-tenth seconds per hour. I'll never forget that. This caused a lot of hypertension and heart problems with the employees due to the stress; you just worked like the devil.

The assembly line would start up either the overhead conveyors or the belts on the conveyors on the flat, and those things ran until it was break time. They had what they called a relief man that would come around, and everybody got a relief time or break, not to exceed ten minutes. The relief man made good money. He had to know how to run every job, he had to know every one of those facets on the lines.

That was the way it was set up. It was a closed shop union. You had to belong and you had to pay dues, there was no other option. The union had a steward for every forty people. If there was any disagreement between the company and the employee, the union steward would give out a complaint and then take it to

41

the union board, and the union board, along with the steward if it merited it, would go into the company's general manager. His name was M.W. Wilson, "Red" Wilson. He had very short hair, was a short stocky guy who had played football with the Detroit Lions, and he was a one-man warhead.

A couple of years later, after I put my time in there, I was elected as the union steward because I used to argue for the guys because of what they thought the company was doing wrong, and I argued pretty strongly about it.

Every time a case came up, I went to the union board. I presented my case and if they thought it had some merit then we would have a hearing. I would have to come in mornings and sit with the union board. There were five on the board and we had two or three cases per month. I was the union steward for two years, reelected once, and that was interesting and taught me a whole lot.

In 1948 I made enough money to buy a car from one of the guys that worked on the line. He had a '37 Pontiac Coupe in excellent condition. He had taken very good care of it. I couldn't go to the bank and borrow money, because I didn't have any credit, so I talked him into carrying me with the credit on it, and I paid him for the car plus interest.

When I got that paid for, I traded it for a '41 Ford with two doors. The model normally didn't have heaters in it at the time, and this one had a gas heater siting on the floor that they'd plugged into the manifold. Well, I thought, now I was downtown!

7.

I could now go back to southern Ohio to see my girlfriend, Patty Applegate, who lived down there in the hills. Every now and then during that first year I'd been writing letters to her. I don't recall going to see my dad, because we had a falling out and he hadn't heard from me nor I from him, because he didn't know how to get a hold of me and that's what I wanted.

I went back and forth down there, and I did stop to see my Aunt Elma and my cousin Geneva. I'd always gotten along well with them. However, I was smoking then, and they just hated it.

They wouldn't let me smoke in the house and chastised me for my smoking, which I deserved.

I maintained a long distance relationship with Patty, and kept working, and eventually we decided to get married. In the meantime I had gotten her father and her brother a job at Tecumseh Products. They were both hard workers, working on the dirtiest, hardest, toughest jobs in the plant.

John Applegate and his wife Mary bought a Quonset hut and set it up on rented property next to the railroad tracks about twelve miles out in the country, and that's where Patty was living. They had a table in it and some chairs, a bed and a cot, and not much else.

When we decided to get married, John tried to be benevolent. He said, "Well, we don't have much to offer you, but you can have all these chairs that we've got. We'll give you that," which I thought was gracious of him, because he didn't have anything to begin with. But, I had discovered a house trailer park. It was close to the factory, about five blocks east of the factory and other railroad tracks. I went over there and met the owner, Roscoe Ferris, and his wife, Mae, and I rented a nineteen-foot long, seven-foot wide house trailer that was up on blocks.

Patty and I got married on July 31, 1948. She was Catholic so I had to go and take instructions from the Catholic priest about what I would do and what I wouldn't do. The priest asked, "Well, who are you going to have for best man?" I didn't know anybody up there except those working in the factory, so I said, "well, I don't know. I don't–" and he said, "I'll get a best man for you."

He got a fellow by the name of Gene Drouillard who was a very strong Catholic. He had a younger brother, Bernie, and years later they both wound up working for me on the production line.

We went to the only Catholic Church in town and walked up the steps. There was the priest, and me and Patty, and my best man, and so we were married.

I had made arrangements for a seven-day honeymoon for us to drive to Detroit and then get on the Detroit-Cleveland Cruise Lines, and go on a cruise that went from Detroit all the way up to

Lake Huron, Lake Superior, Upper Michigan, and back down Lake Michigan to Chicago, and then back to Detroit.

In the afternoon we got on board the ship, and since we were newlyweds, of course we were doing the natural thing to do, when suddenly sirens went off and the loudspeakers came on saying we had to do a lifesaving drill! We heard directions to get life vests on and all that jazz. We looked at each other, laughed, and we went right back to doing what we were doing, and didn't go to the drill. If the ship had sunk I guess we would have gone down with it!

So, that was our honeymoon, and then we got back and went to work. Patty had previously applied for work at Tecumseh Products, and was waiting for two weeks to get the job, so when we got back, she immediately went to work, and we were both working at the Products. She went to work at 8:00, and got off at 5:00. I went in at 3:30 and was off at 12:00, except for working overtime wherever I could find it.

Patty and I moved into the little trailer park. Everybody who lived there went to a common shower and latrine, one for the men, one for the women, and that's where you'd take care of your necessities. I would always shower when I got off work because I was just stinking from that shop; I'd shower every night before I got in bed. Patty would have been home since about 5:30, and I wouldn't get home till 3:30 or 4 o'clock in the morning. We didn't see too much of each other right away, and that was my beginning of married life.

In April of 1949, we were blessed with a daughter who we named after Patty's sister, Celine. At that time fathers weren't permitted in the delivery room, so Patty went to the hospital to have the baby and I went to work. When I got off work, I went over and saw our daughter for the first time. She cried a lot! And the doctor, Dr. Dustin, I'll never forget him, incidentally, billed $35 for the birth, and the hospital bill was $40. Of course we didn't have any insurance of any kind, but that's what the prices were then.

Because Celine cried a lot, the doctor determined she had a collapsed lung, and told us she was going to need to lie in crib to sleep. We had a little area there in the trailer where we could set one between two closets, and so I told him, yes, we would do that. He said, "Well, set it up, and just let her cry." She cried constantly for a couple months, and then the lung healed and she stopped crying.

In that little, narrow, nineteen foot by seven-foot trailer, the kitchen was in the front, and when you walked in, right across from the door, there were two benches with a table in between. You walked further down and there was a bathroom, which we never used. We stored stuff in there because it didn't have a shower, they wouldn't put them in for any of the trailers in the park. In the very back was the bed. So, that's how we started out.

We stayed there about a year-and-a-half, and then a bigger trailer came up for sale, a twenty-four foot by ten-foot wide trailer. I was paying thirty-five bucks a month to pay our trailer off, so I went up and made a deal with the owners of the trailer park to buy that trailer from them. They took over the title of our trailer, gave me the equity I had paid in and applied it towards the deal of the new trailer. I'll never forget it: Our new home cost $1,800.

We were in that trailer for about a year or so when a house came up for sale. In the meantime, the hotel I mentioned earlier had been transformed into a savings bank. The house was maybe five or six blocks west of the Products on Cummings Street, with deserted railroad tracks going past in front. John Thompson was the president and loan officer of Tecumseh Savings Bank. Patty and I were pretty uptight when we went in to get a loan, particularly with no credit. Having a job at "The Products" was the key. And so, we got it, so we owned our first home!

It was a duplex with two stories on both sides, and we rented out the larger side to roomers at $5 a week. We had six to seven roomers that worked at The Products in there all the time, which helped make the house payment. We lived on the smaller side, with the bedrooms upstairs.

When I took my instructions to practice the Catholic methods, I wasn't sure I had been baptized Catholic, as we never could find the baptismal papers. I later asked my dad about that, and he said, "Yeah, your mother and her sister snuck you off, and they got you baptized without my knowledge." That was news to me.

Of course I'm in my twenties by that time. Because of the rhythm method that the Catholic Church prescribed, we did not use any other type of birth control. Well, do you know what they call people that use the rhythm method? They call them parents. And man, we started having kids one after another after another in a short period of time. "Franny," Frances Vernon, came along on September 27, 1951, and then a year later and one day earlier in 1952, Mark came along, September 26.

During that period of time, I was very enterprising with making money: Rototillers were new on the market, and most people had never heard of one. I went to Sears and I bought a rototiller. We owned a station wagon that we had traded the Ford for, so I bought a flatbed trailer and got a hitch on it, and bought a trailer. Now I was in the gardening business! I went out and rototilled gardens as everybody wanted a garden but nobody had any equipment to do it with. Well, I made a killing! I did that for a couple of years.

In the springtime I was working until after dark, even though I didn't have lights on the rototiller. We'd put a nice garden in at our house, and when the gardening season was over, I got a job at a gas station and at the Pontiac Dealership. I'd pump gas in the mornings, and went to work at the Products in the afternoons. I'd get up, go to work at 8 o'clock and pump gas until 1:00, then I'd come and have lunch, and then I'd go to the next job. Patty was still working 8:00 to 5:00.

About the time that Mark was born, Patty stopped working because the kids were just too much. I read an ad in a paper from Consumers Power Company that they were hiring a stationary engineer. Well, I didn't know what that meant, but I drove to Adrian, and I applied for the job.

It consisted of running a hydroelectric plant in Tecumseh, which sat on the Raisin River. I learned the plant had two generators and two exciters. When the water was high on the river, you'd turn the hydroelectric plant on, and the water would go through and turn the turbines and generate power. You'd phase them into the whole consumer power grid of southern Michigan. They served hundreds of thousands of customers.

So, this gentleman explained all this to me, what the job was about, what it would pay, and when you had to be there to work. As a Relief Operator you worked every Saturday and Sunday without fail. I had to have a license in order to do the work, so they gave me a book and I studied it. I went to Lansing, Michigan, the capitol, where their headquarters were, took the test, passed it, and I became a hydroelectric operator.

Now I was working Saturdays and Sundays. You had to take readings every eight hours, three times a day within each twenty-four hours, and record what time you were there, and record the reading in a logbook.

If the water got high enough while I was on duty, they had taught me how to get those exciters going, and the exciters pulled the belts down to a long, long room. The floors were painted grey, and they had to be mopped, and cleaned absolutely dry, clean from any kind of oil or dirt that would splash around. When you phase the generators into the consumers' power line, you had to be very careful with it because they're locked in under oil. Once they were going, if they're going too slow, they wouldn't go in, and if they're going too fast, they'd put a surge and line which went all the way through the whole grid. It was pretty technical, but it was fun.

And I worked – to finish my story – I worked seven years without a day off. Between working at the factory five days a week and sometimes Saturdays, and working at the hydroelectric plant, I worked seven days a week, so, we didn't go anywhere, we never went any place, and we were busy raising kids.

When I eventually stopped working every single day, and I was working for Consumers Power and at the Products, once or twice a year I would go to University of Michigan Ann Arbor to see the Wolverines play. Because I had grown up in Ohio, my favorite team was always the Ohio State Buckeyes, and I always wanted to see Michigan get beat, which they rarely did during the late '40s; '48-'49 had some excellent teams.

I also was a Cleveland Indians fan from having a little bit of connection with my Uncle Knox Chamberlain in northern Ohio. He was an avid Cleveland fan and listened to them on the radio all the time. There were a couple times that another worker at Consumers Power and I would drive down to Cleveland from where we lived in southern Michigan. He was an avid baseball fan, and offered to drive down and see a doubleheader game on a Sunday. They had huge crowds at Cleveland Municipal Stadium for the Cleveland Indians, who had a very, very good team at that time.

While working at Tecumseh Products and living in the duplex at 312 West Cummings Street, my uncle from Cedar Rapids, Iowa wrote me a letter to tell me that Lucille, my mother, had cancer and was dying. Well, it didn't bother me to hear that as I had no connection at all with the woman who had birthed me, but Patty, said, "You've got to go see your mother." I said, "For what? I don't know her. She's never done anything for me." Patty said, "You've got to go see her, she's dying." I said, "I don't want to go," and we had a two or three day argument. She prevailed, so after work one night at midnight we took off in my '41 Ford, and we drove all night on old U.S. 30 as there were no interstates, and got to Cedar Rapids the next day.

I knew Lucille lived on First Avenue, two houses away from the Stewart Funeral Home. We walked past the three houses with big old, elm trees out front, walked up to the third floor, and knocked on the door. A man answered the door and said, "Yes, can I help you?" I said, "Yes, my name is Danny Reed, this is my wife Patty, and I understand that Lucille is not well." He said, "Come in, come in." This fellow, Carl Evans, was a sales manager for Allen Chevrolet and for years made good money. I guess they lived the good life, though I don't know for sure. They were married for quite a few years.

Lucille was sitting in a big, big room; it was a big apartment. She was in a chair way across the room in a corner, and she acknowledged that we were there. Patty and I sat down on a couch across the room in a corner that had to be a good fifteen feet across from her. Lucille had her arm in a sling, and her husband sat adjacent to us.

We tried to have a conversation to the best of our ability, but Lucille wasn't having it. She wasn't into it, and although Carl was being gracious and a nice host, she never warmed up, so after about forty-five minutes I turned to Patty and I said, "Patty, it's time for us go, we've got to get back." Nobody had any problem with that because it was an awkward situation for all of us. We got up and left and we drove all night and half the morning and got back to Tecumseh. That was the second and only other time I remember being with my own mother.

8.

We had made friends with people in Tecumseh, and every now and then we'd go to card parties and play cards all evening, or dance, or do both, and we kind of rotated around. We never had them to our house, but they were always generally at the same house in Adrian. That was our social outlet.

In the meantime, Patty had gotten a job part-time with the city's leading attorney, James Beardsley, and his wife, Anne. Patty worked down in their home, which was a big, old two-story, prestigious, colonial home. She worked in their office for two or three years, and that's when I saw my wife really begin to change. She started drinking a lot of wine with Jim and Anne, and she'd get home late. By this time I had gone on day shift as a foreman.

In the Products factory, as mentioned earlier, I was a steward for two years, and then I ran for the Union Board, and though I wasn't elected, I came in sixth. Everybody in the plant knew me and liked me, and after I was defeated for the Union Board, Red Wilson, the plant's work manager, called me into his office one afternoon, and said, "Dan, I have been watching you, I watched you arbitrate here with us. You're very fair, you're pretty clear-minded, you get along with people, and you're tough to deal with." He said, "I think you should come to work for the company." I said, "I do work for the company..." and he said, "No, I am talking about becoming a supervisor with us." I said, "Well, let's talk about that."

He explained what the pay was, which was good, and that I would take over as a foreman in the day shift on the Admiral line in Plant 2. That was a thrill for me to hear. He said, "I don't want you to say anything until you make up your mind, and then let us make the announcement." I said okay.

I went home and talked to Patty, and we were both thrilled. So at about age twenty-six, I became a supervisor in the factory, and the very people that I had fought for, worked with, and so on, they became my responsibility. And we got on well. We broke all kinds of company records because I treated them fairly, and they knew it.

I was a daytime Products foreman, and weekend Consumers Power engineer, and during that period of time Patty started drinking a lot, drinking wine at her office after work. It upset me, because I was working all day, then I'd be at home with the kids and she wasn't even there to make supper. We got into a few quarrels about that.

One night, she didn't come home. I put the kids to bed, but she didn't come home and didn't come home. Finally, about 2 o'clock in the morning on a bright moonlit night, here she comes driving in. She was half-plowed from drinking wine, and just plopped in the bed and went to sleep.

The next day I got all over her about coming home so late. Patty told me she had a confession to make, and said, "Last night Jim and I went out, and we were drinking and we went out east of town." There was a farm out there by the river, and so they had an affair at midnight or so, and that's why she got home late. But she told me about it, and she begged my forgiveness.

And, at that young age my ego was so hurt, so crushed, that I would not forgive her. That started what would become our ultimate divorce because she went back and continued to work there. I was just so crushed I couldn't stand it. And, then, a few months later, she gave birth to Greg, our youngest son. It was 1955.

A good buddy of mine, Jack Dull and his wife, Lou, had gotten hold of a United Agency farm book sale in which they posted farms for sale all over the United States. They felt that they could make a lot of money if they bought a farm and started raising sheep, so I became convinced of that, too. When I lived there in my teens with my dad, he had some sheep and he sheared them. They had twin babies and all that, and I thought he was making money with it, so it sounded good to me.

We collectively went to Missouri and looked at farms, and we found two farms adjacent to one another that we both liked, so we decided to buy them. Still working in the factory, I went back to Tecumseh and the first thing I did, to get ready to have a farm, was buy a big ton and a half truck, an old Chevy. Then I bought a tractor, a plough, a mower, and went with the tractor and loaded the mower up onto that truck.

At one time I took off by myself and went down to Weaubleau, Missouri. On the way down there, it was election time and I remember listening to the radio that Adlai Stevenson was running for president. A wheel bearing went out in Springfield, Illinois, so I had to stop there, and I was there for two days while they got parts and got it fixed. That slowed me up. Then I drove and drove and drove and drove, and was way down by the Lake of the Ozarks in Missouri, down there by Ha Ha Tonka, and it was dark. It wasn't pitch dark, but it was dark. The lights went out on that truck as I came over a big hill. I had that truck loaded down with equipment, it was heavy, so I was putting on the brakes and trying to get this thing to stop.

There were no lights on the roads and they didn't have the markers like they do nowadays. I got stopped as I was going through a bridge across a river, and got over on the berm, and there were still no cars out there. I got out and I discovered a fuse below the steering wheel had blown out, so I replaced it, and voila, I was on my way.

I got there and unloaded all the farm equipment, I took the truck back to Tecumseh, and I went back to work. Patty and I had an old wooden station wagon. We sold the house, we loaded all the stuff we could, and I moved everybody lock, stock, and barrel with that truck and the station wagon to Weaubleau to a 160-acre-farm.

So there was Patty and the kids in Missouri, and there I was working up in Michigan. That was the first dumb mistake I made during this time. I went down to visit them a couple of times, and Patty and I weren't really getting along. In about 1958 she sued me for divorce.

SALES AND PROMOTION

9.

I made a mistake, and I wouldn't do that again at my age. I could have forgiven her and we could have got it together, but I didn't and we didn't, and so she went her way and I went mine. She stayed down there with the kids, and I got a room with a couple that had a boarding house.

Up until that time, there'd been just one girl, one woman, in my life, so now that I was single, I started on a real campaign with women. I started chasing women, and I was very good at it, yes, very, very good at it.

I was foreman on days at Products, and worked at Consumers Power on weekends. A guy got a hold of me that knew me pretty well, and he was the manager of the Tecumseh Country Club. His name was Raymond White, a graduate from Michigan State, and Ray wanted to know if I would come out there and learn how to tend bar and work for him in the evenings. It was an opportunity to make more money, so I said yes.

53

I started working for Tecumseh Country Club, and I tended bar for all of the bigwigs at Tecumseh Products who lived in all the upscale areas. I learned how to make all the drinks and everything, and tended bar there for two or three years, which leads me to a very interesting part of my life.

While I was tending bar there, Ray came to me one evening and he said, "Dan, we're going to have a big meeting here tomorrow and I need you here at lunch, I need you to stay here in the afternoon." I said, "Well, I'd have to get off work." He said, "I've got to have you. I just have got to have you here." So, I said, "Okay, I'll take off a half day at work."

That half-day at the bar was one of the highlights of my life. The Ford Motor Company was run by Henry Ford, the President of the Board. The C.E.O. of the company was a fellow by the name of Ernie Breech. Ernie Breech and Walter Reuther's union, the United Auto Workers, had gotten into some real big problems, and they were negotiating on their contract. Walter and his brother decided to attack Ford first out of the big three automakers for their demands. That started back in 1948.

They were having some difficult times, so the Ford Motor Company decided to have a board meeting in Tecumseh to get away, that way nobody would know what was going on. The whole board came to Tecumseh and went upstairs into the private large dining room and met with Henry Ford. His son, Edsel, was too young to be there at the time but Henry Ford, Jr. was there. I was serving them all drinks, whatever they wanted, and the ladies were serving them lunch at this important, closed-door meeting.

That went on until four o'clock in the afternoon, and then they came downstairs to the bar to have drinks. There was a parking lot in front of the club, and right beside the bar where the golfers came in there were two cars, and one was a big black Lincoln parked in a small parking space. It was Henry Ford's.

He looked at me and they all said, "What are you going to have, Henry?" and he said, "I want a bourbon and branch. Wait. Put the branch back. So that's bourbon up, I'll swallow her back." I said, "Yes, sir." I got him his drink and then I got everybody else their drinks.

They were all standing there talking. The room was full, with chairs all around in front of the bar. I'm behind the bar, which could seat about ten people, but the whole room was full. And so Henry Ford had his bourbon, and then he said, "Well, boys, see you tomorrow," and went out the door and got in his black Lincoln. And it whined and whined, and it wouldn't start.

He comes in and slams the door, and someone asked, "What's wrong, Henry?" He said, "Oh, it's just a goddamn Ford." Those are exactly the words he spoke.

They all just laughed and went out there. At the time the Lincolns were made with the hood that opened from the back, and the back doors opened the wrong way; the front doors opened the usual way. So there's all these Ford executives in their white shirts and suits, down underneath the hood of this Lincoln trying to figure out what was wrong. It was a vapor lock. They got it fixed and running, so off he went. That was my encounter with Henry Ford, and I have always remembered that.

During that period of time I was tending bar and working at Consumers Power on weekends. It wasn't necessarily bad work but you had to be there at corporate times, so it limited what you could or couldn't do, but I worked around that.

One Friday afternoon, a guy came into the bar who I'd seen before but not very often, and he ordered a drink. We started talking, just he and I, and his name was Jim Garrity. He owned Stubnitz Green which was is a big factory in Adrian, Michigan, he owned the Adrian Country Club, and he owned seven TV and radio stations across the United States, the largest one being in Miami, the smallest one being in Adrian, a radio station only.

After awhile he said, "You know, you big bozo, I've come in here a few times and I've observed you. What are you doing tending bar?" I said, "Well, I'm making some money." And, he said, "Well, you don't belong behind the bar. You should be selling. You're a salesman." I said, "Really?" He said, "Yeah. This is my card. I am giving it to you and I want you to take it and I want you to call and make an appointment to see Don Dean, the radio station manager at WABJ in Adrian. You go and see him and tell him I sent you, and he'll know you're coming."

In the next couple of days, I called and set up an appointment to see Don Dean. I went up in a shirt, tie, and suit. It was winter time, and I had an overcoat on. I was ushered into Don Dean's office. He was this little skinny guy with a lot of bushy hair on top, and he said, "Where's your hat?" I said, "Sir?" He said, "Where's your hat? You're not dressed if you don't wear a hat." I said, "Well, I don't own a hat." He said, "If you're going to work here, you're going to own a hat."

He interviewed me and said, "Well, Jim Garrity thinks a lot of you, and he wants me to hire you, so, we'll hire you and we'll give you the city of Tecumseh to start selling." I said, "Well, what am I going to sell?" He said, "You're going to sell radio time." I said, "Oh, I never sold radio time." He said, "Well, I'm going to have you ride with some of the guys for a while then we'll turn all these big accounts there over to you, and you will get more accounts. And if you get enough accounts, we'll open up a radio station in Tecumseh." I said, "Really?" He said, "Yup."

So, I quit my day job as a foreman which I'd been on for a few years, and I took my seniority and I bumped onto a midnight shift that did lab work. You might work an hour and a half out of the whole eight hours. It was the cushy job, and I had enough seniority to go on it. Nobody understood why I was giving up my foreman job, but I did.

In the meantime, I was running around with all these different women.

10.

There were two places in Tecumseh that sold liquor: the V.F.W. and the American Legion; there were two beer joints in town that sold beer but no liquor. The third place, which you had to be a member of, was the Tecumseh Club, which was upstairs above the Lyric Theater. The Tecumseh Club was comprised of business people, the chamber of commerce, things of that nature, some of the big wheels of Tecumseh Products, so being in the Tecumseh Club you could go up there, and you could buy liquor. That was it for buying alcohol in the city.

I tell this story for a reason. I had met this gal, Mary Hewlitt, at the American Legion, and started dating her. She worked in a big furniture store in Tecumseh, and she liked to drink, liked to dance, liked everything that people in our age group liked. After a while we decided to get married, and so then we had to get a house.

Because I was making good money, I contracted with a local builder there. He built a home for us out in River Acres. It was a modest home but it was located out where all the bigwigs lived. Even the owner of the Tecumseh Products lived out there along the river in a big home; I had tended bar a couple of times at his home parties.

We got the house built and we got married in our home by a Baptist minister, Reverend Bayshore. Mary had two children, a son and a daughter. She had been divorced for a number of years and then she married a guy that worked in a factory, a farmer. They were married one week, and then she divorced him. We went together for about a year before we got married. That was a mistake, something I never should've done. But I did.

So, now I'm working on third shift. I go to work at eleven at night, get off at seven in the morning, come home and shower, put on shirt, tie, coat, and hat, and go to Adrian and learn how to become a time salesman. I worked at that for about a year, and I got pretty doggone good at it. I had good contracts.

They bought me a car, a little Metro, black and white, with "WABJ" printed all over, and I had to fold my legs over twice to get in the dumb thing! It was so small, but I ran all over the place with that dumb little car. My biggest competitor was a local newspaper, The Tecumseh Herald, run by Tom Riordan who was from Pennsylvania, and a real redneck. He just hated the radio station because that was competition to him. So in turn, he hated me.

I worked there for about a year or so and I had so many contracts that they decided to open up a radio station, and so now I was going to do a morning radio show remote from Tecumseh.

They took up the Lyric Theater, which had closed, and they rented out of the front of the building. They set a whole operations room up where I broadcast from, which meant I was right on the street looking out the windows. Cars would go by and they'd honk their horns. I'd have them honk and wave and everything. And so, Tecumseh had its own radio station, and I was the radio man.

I came on at ten and went off at noon. I played all the latest songs and made a lot of talk, which I was becoming very good at. And so I ran a radio disc jockey show, and it became very popular, particularly in Tecumseh, although there were a lot of listeners in Adrian, too. We ran all kinds of contests and things. And then, I got a brochure one time about something called "Moonlight Madness…"

First, however, while I was working at the radio station, I got to be friends with fellows by the name of Stan Terry, Lloyd Price, and, Jerry Keil. They started a company called TPK Enterprises, and they came up with this idea about selling advertising signs that hooked on to bowling alleys. Bowling was a big sport then. When the bowling pin clearer would come down to sweep the pins, there would be a name like "Price Real Estate" or a car dealer, or some business like that on the clearing mechanism for people to read while they waited for the pins to be reset.

Well, that was a heck of an idea. They made me their vice president of sales. I went all over southern Michigan to where the bowling alleys were and I convinced the owners of the bowling alleys to allow me to bring in revenue for them by selling advertisements. We would put the signs on, we would do everything, hook them up and all, and they would get revenue from the advertisement. Well, that was a novel idea, way ahead of its time, and I just sold the living daylights out of signage at bowling alleys.

I had them all over southern Michigan, from Jackson to Lansing, to Detroit, to Ann Arbor, to Grand Rapids. I had bowling alleys loaded with those signs. That's what I was doing on weekends when I wasn't working at the Consumers; it was about the time I was close to quitting there. Anyway, we were just making a ton of money. And as vice president of sales, I was making really good money.

All of a sudden, we got a call from an owner to take the signs off. I went to Clinton, Michigan, the first town north of Tecumseh to talk to the guy, and he said, "We leased this bowling apparatus from Brunswick, and they own it. And they've declared us as violating their contract in leasing, so the signs have got to come off."

Well, guess what? 90% of the bowling alleys had Brunswick lane clearers, and all of them took their signs down, and so we were out of business. That's an example of some of my enterprises and how it went sometimes.

So anyhow, back to radio, I got this thing in my head about Moonlight Madness. Down in Indiana a radio station convinced the small town of Goshen to close all their stores during the day on a Friday, the biggest day of the week, and open up on a Friday night at six o'clock, and not close until one o'clock in the morning, and they called it the "Moonlight Madness Sale."

AUG 1960

Well, that looked good to me, so I went to Don Dean and I told him about this. He said, "Okay. You want to try it in Tecumseh, try it." By this time, I am now a member of the

Tecumseh Club because the radio station paid for my membership as I had a lot of advertisers who went there. I had worked the job for a year at the Products, and I finally gave it up in 1960 after thirteen years of seniority.

So in 1960, I was working full time for the radio station, and along came this Moonlight Madness idea. I went up and I convinced all the store owners and the business owners in Tecumseh, including the taverns, to close down on Friday during the day and open up at six o'clock Friday night. It took a while, as that was not easy to do. But we did it.

I rented those great big searchlights that go up in the sky, and I put those around at the main entrances to Tecumseh, east, west, and north; there wasn't any for the south. We got the State Patrol to come in and close off the highways so you had to detour through town because the whole downtown area was closed. Two blocks north and south, four blocks east and west, closed. People started coming into town at six o'clock, but they couldn't park their cars there. They had to park them outside the barricades. And, I'm telling you, it was something: We were on the radio talking about it, and WJR and WJBK in Detroit picked up on it and they had their people there with television cameras and all putting it on the air, and there we were!

The place was absolutely packed. It was a total winner. What a promotion! I was in seventh heaven. So, I'm standing down in front of the Tecumseh Savings Bank, which was the old original hotel, and who's standing there with me? Maynard Mulvany, the guy from the old hotel who gave me a room my first day in town, and the president of the bank.

Maynard looks over at me, and he said, "You've come a long way, haven't you?" I said, "Well, you helped me get started here in Tecumseh." And he just laughed. By that time, I had a good line of credit at the bank, and everybody in town knew me as I had a very high profile. The stores sold almost down to the bare walls. People came in from miles around to come to Moonlight Madness, and it was a great success. That was the top of my career in Tecumseh.

I kept on selling radio time. In the Tecumseh Club there were two brothers that came in all the time. They were both bachelors and they owned an aircraft company just north of Tecumseh called Meyers Aircraft. They built single-engine lightweight airplanes, and they also built boats. They were sitting at the club one night, and the older brother came over to me. "Dan, can you and I talk a little bit?" I said, "Sure." He said, "Gentlemen, if you'll excuse us," so I moved over to their table.

He said, "You know, everybody knows you in this area. You've done a really great job. You're the talk of the town, and we've lived here all of our lives." He said, "We've got an airplane factory out here and we're building boats. But we think we could build more boats." I said, "Really?" He said, "Yeah, we take the aluminum parts that we don't use for the planes and we buy aluminum and we make boats. They're all small boats, and we've got a good salesman here in Michigan, and he sells a ton of boats, but we think we could be selling boats all over the Midwest." And I said, "Really?" He said, "Yeah. And we'd like for you to become our boat salesman." I said, "You're kidding me." He said, "No. We'll pay you a salary of $30,000. We'll buy you a car. We'll pay all your expenses. And we'll give you commissions override on the boats you sell." I said, "Let's talk seriously about this. I'll be out there to see you next week."

I went out to meet with them, and everything they'd said was true. Well, in 1960, when I quit the factory and was selling radio time and working at Consumers, it was the first year ever I'd made a five-figure income. I'd been working towards that for a long time. I'll never forget it. That was the first year that I paid income tax on five-figure income.

Meyers Aircraft had built a plane that broke the single engine distance record the year before with a pilot from San Francisco, Peter Gluckmann, who flew nonstop for a new world record. So their aircraft business was doing great. The boat business was doing well, but they wanted it to be great, too. They did everything they said, so I quit my job at the radio station and went to work for Meyers Aircraft Company. They gave me any place I wanted to work in the United States, except Michigan because somebody was already selling Michigan, though I learned he actually didn't work much.

We were building boats and they were good, small fishing boats. I was free to go sell wherever I wanted to. They built a trailer that held a boat on each side, one on the bottom, and then a flat-top pram up on the top of the station wagon. I'd haul that trailer with me, and I'd use those boats for demonstrations. I went around to boat dealers. Indiana was the closest so that's where I started. There were quite a few lakes in Indiana so I started selling boats in Indiana. Then I went to Iowa. Then I went to Wisconsin. And that was where I hit the golden nugget.

Way up in northern Wisconsin there were two brothers that owned a place that was out in the boonies. There were no towns around it. The only 'town' that was there was their business, and they had a tremendous business. People drove in from all over Wisconsin and northern Michigan, too. They drove in there and bought all kinds of goods, like a hardware store, an outfitters' store. It was a precursor to the big stores that are now in existence like Cabela's or Bass Pro.

The brothers up there did a heck of a business so I went up there with my boat trailer and my boats. They didn't do business unless both of them were involved, so they came out, looked at my boats, and they liked them. They weren't stocking boats but they liked them and they said, "We'll take some of those boats. We'll try them and see how they go. How many can you get on a truckload?" I said twenty or twenty-two. They started working on their pricing, and I had to call the factory and talk to them about how much of a discount they would take off the price. They all agreed to it, and so I sold them boats.

I left the models there, took the empty trailer and started back to southern Michigan from northern Wisconsin. And before I even got back they changed their minds and they ordered two more trailer loads of boats. Well, that was the biggest sale that they'd ever had at Meyers Aircraft! So that's three truckloads, but they only had one truck so they had to make three trips up there to deliver all the boats. But they did, and they sold them, and they started reordering and reordering and reordering, and that turned out to be the best customer we ever had.

It was so doggone good that they had to put a second shift on at the Meyers boat factory, and about thirty-some people were hired as a result of the sales that were made. And of course, I kept on selling. I was getting an education on how to really start making money.

So I'm out selling boats and now I'm over to Illinois. I went down into southern Illinois clear down to Cairo, down on the confluence of the Ohio and Mississippi rivers. I sold boats down there, and one time I was dragging an empty trailer back up U.S. 37. At that time that was the main drive between Chicago and New Orleans because the interstates weren't built yet. I'm going up through there on a foggy, foggy night, and I'm having a difficult time driving, and it's ten, eleven o'clock at night. I came up on some hazy lights and there was a big fluorescent light out there that said "Mardi Gras."

11.

I whipped that station wagon and the trailer off the road, and I pulled into a gravel parking lot and went into the Mardi Gras. There were a couple people sitting at the bar. It was big half-round bar, which seated about thirty people. I sat down next to a guy in a white shirt, a white starched shirt. He had the cuffs rolled up, was smoking a cigarette, and he had jet black hair and oily skin, and he was an absolute twin brother of Basil Rathbone, if you remember him from the movies. He looked just like him, thinned mustache, sitting there smoking a cigarette and nursing a drink. I ordered a scotch and soda, and the gal behind the bar set it up. I think it cost about fifty cents, so I put a dollar down and I took a sip and started looking around.

It was dimly lit, and sitting back in the corner behind me was a couple of gals at one table and a couple of gals at another table, and a gal in the middle. The guy turns to me and says, "You want to stay over and have some entertainment for the evening?" I said, "No, I don't think so. I've got to find a hotel. He says, "Well, I got a motel but it's not open for business, for rent, but you can have a room for the night there as long as you want it, and you have company." And I said again, "No, I don't think so. Thanks."

Just about that time the door burst open and in came a sheriff. The guy was about six foot three, with a big flat-brimmed sheriff's hat on, and there were two deputies with him. He walks up to the bar and says to this guy who's been talking to me, "Okay, Taylor. This time, you're done." Taylor said, "Okay."

Taylor Pennington was his name, and he had married the daughter of the guy that was the head of the mafia for Capone in Chicago, Buster Wortman, and he was also the head of the mafia in St. Louis. His daughter had married Taylor, and they operated two clubs out there, the Mardi Gras Club and the Curve Inn Club.

The Curve Inn was a drive-in for trucks on Highway 37. They could pull up to a drive-up window and get themselves a pint of liquor, and then go on down the road towards New Orleans, or head north towards Chicago. It was a podunk bar, strictly redneck, while the Mardi Gras Club was a nice, nice club, it was upscale and new, and it was really pretty. That's where Taylor hung out and that's where he operated with his girls.

Well, it turns out he had done something, he'd been in jail twice before that and he'd had his license taken away from him. The thing about Taylor Pennington was that he owned two liquor licenses, and in that whole county in southern Illinois there were only five liquor licenses.

The way he got those liquor licenses was by going up to a little town, Buncombe, just north of where he was, and building a school, and so he got the mayor and the council to vote him in for two 24-hour liquor licenses, the only 24-hour liquor licenses within a hundred miles in any direction, and he had two of them. The other three liquor licenses were owned by the sheriff that was in there locking him up. So Taylor turns to me and he said, "You want to buy this place?"

I looked at him and I said in my sarcastic manner, "Yeah, sure, that's exactly the reason I stopped in here was to buy this place." He said, "Well, it's for sale. They busted me and I'm not coming out." He says, "I can't earn anything so it's going to be closed." And the sheriff said, "You're damn right it's closed. It is closed down. You guys get out of here."

I said, "Where's a motel so I can get a room?" The sheriff said, "There's Scenic View right at the top of the hill. It's a nice clean motel run by good people, got a good meal there. Go up there and they'll put you up." The Sheriff took Taylor away, the girls went back to the hotel, the lights went out, and I went up to the Scenic View Hotel and got a room.

It had been awfully foggy that night, so when I got up and walked into the restaurant the next morning, I looked out on the most beautiful view you've ever seen; it's called Scenic View for a reason. It looked out all across southern and eastern Illinois to the Illinois River that separated Illinois from Kentucky. It was just a beautiful view.

Jim Henshaw owned the restaurant with his wife. I got a nice breakfast, and I said to them, "You know Taylor Pennington down the road?" He said, "Yes, we know him. He's a good friend of ours." I said, "Well, he's in jail." Jim said, "Uh-oh." I said, "Yeah, he's in jail. And I don't know why, but he tried to sell me that place last night." And Jim said, "Well, he's going to have to sell." I said, "Well, why don't you buy it?" He said, "No, we've got a good business going here. We don't want any part of that." I said, "Okay" and paid my bill and drove back to Michigan, which is a long drive from southern Illinois.

I got back to Michigan and there was a place called the Racetrack Inn, which was a family-style restaurant and bar. All the bowlers and local people went there. Paul Snyder and his wife, Doris, ran it. They leased it and they'd been running it for years and had a good business. I went out there that evening for dinner and I told Paul about this place for sale. Paul was smoking a cigarette and he said, "That sounds interesting. Is it for real?" I said, "Yeah, it's for real." He said, "Well, why don't we get a hold of Fritz?" Max Walz, known as "Fritz," owned the Tipton Tool and Die Company in Tipton, Michigan. Paul said, "Why don't we get Fritz, go on down there and look at that? He's got the money. Maybe we can get into it and run it." I said, "All right. You line it up."

So he lined Fritz up. He was German, just as German as could be, and the next weekend we drove down there in Fritz's brand new Oldsmobile 88 to look the place over. It was locked, of course. We went down to the county jail which was six miles away, and there Taylor was sitting in jail. I said to him, "You said that place was for sale." He said, "Oh, you remember that." I said, "Yeah. Been thinking about it." I said, "These are my friends. This is Fritz Walz, and Paul Snyder. And we want to know how much you want for the thing." Taylor said, "I'll give you one price and I won't budge."

65

He said, "It's a low bottom price. $64,000 for the 10 acres, the motel, the inventory except the beds, you can't keep the beds, and two houses, there's a house behind the Curve Inn, a four-bedroom house, and there's a two-bedroom house an eighth of a mile away from the Mardi Gras." He said, "So the houses go with everything. $64,000." Paul and I looked at Fritz, and he said, "I'll buy it." Fritz said to us, "You guys want to come run it? We're full on partners." We looked at each other and said, "Yeah."

I had to quit my job selling boats, and they were not happy. But I was going to be a night club owner and make myself a ton of money with our partner, and we had total freedom to run it. Of course, I had tended bar so I knew all about that, and Paul and his wife had managed a bar and a restaurant so they knew all about that.

We decided they would move into the big house with their four sons, and I would move into the little house because I was alone. Mary and I weren't divorced but we were fixing to, as we'd been split for a while. And that begins a whole new saga, if you will, of my life, in a totally different environment. Everything was going to be different in southern Illinois.

DREAM CHASING

12.

To go back a little, while Mary and I were married and living in Tecumseh, and had a nice home, Mary had a girlfriend that was pretty promiscuous and lived down the street from us. They had been friends a long time. Her husband had worked for me on the line at the factory. One day, I think during the time I was selling boats, I came home early for some reason, and he was there in the house having lunch with Mary. I was courteous to him, but she was nervous as could be.

After he exited as gracefully as he could, we got into it, and I said, "It's just not right having some man here in our house. So what might be going on at night when I'm gone?" And she just said, "Oh, nothing like that." I said, "Well, I think we need to get some help. We need to talk to your pastor" though I actually never went to church nor did she. She said, "All right, we'll get him to talk to us."

We met with the pastor at our house a couple days later. I told him about what was going on, and that I'd call her at night and she wouldn't be home (we didn't have cell phones then), and I couldn't figure it out. This Baptist pastor, who had known her all her life, couldn't see anything wrong with it and thought I was jumping to conclusions. I said, "Okay, if that's the way you feel, all right." But that was the beginning of the end. There was more to the story, but I'll leave it at that.

One Sunday morning, her kids were running around playing, and we were in the backyard on a concrete deck that we had poured. She was having coffee, smoking cigarettes and reading the Detroit Free Press. At some point she said, "I've got to go get cigarettes." I said, "While you're out, get me some."

We usually bought cigarettes by the carton. She bought Camels, I bought Luckys, and at that time there was no such thing as filter cigarettes. There was a long cigarette out called Pall Mall, and there was a menthol cigarette out, too. She went out and she brought back the cigarettes, and opened hers up.

I'm reading the paper, smoking my cigarette. I opened my pack up and took the wrapping off, pushed the cigarette up, and went to light the cigarette from the cigarette I was getting ready to put out.

I looked out in the yard, and there is the cigarette I had thrown away earlier still burning from when I lit the one that was in my mouth, and here I'm reaching for another one. I looked at her and I said, "This is the dumbest damn thing anybody can do." She said, "What's that? You seem to enjoy it, you smoke a lot of them." I said, "Yeah, there's one out there in the yard burning. And I'm starting one before I even have this one finished. I'm getting ready to throw it all away. When I smoke this cigarette, it's the last damn cigarette I'm ever going to smoke in my life, period." She said, "Are you serious?" I said, "I'm serious." And I did exactly that. I lit that cigarette, flipped the other one away, smoked that cigarette, flipped it away, and that was it.

Now, so the people reading this in the future can understand a little bit about me, I am extremely pragmatic, dogmatic, set in my ways about certain things. And one of the things is

CONTROL. Nothing – I made up my mind at that time – nothing's going to control me, and those cigarettes were controlling me. They were a habit. And I was done.

I was still working at the factory when all of that happened. I was a foreman on the day shift and we wore blue shirts, and I had worn the pockets out of those blue shirts reaching for a cigarette all the time.

Everybody in the factory smoked, they either smoked or chewed tobacco, but most of them smoked. They laughed at me because I was a foreman and I was quitting smoking. They would blow smoke in my face. It was two or three years before I got over wanting a cigarette; I admit I wanted one every day. I'd be driving down the road, and I would smell a cigarette, and thought, "Oh, it smells so good," but I did not smoke another cigarette. I said I'm not going to smoke another cigarette, and I didn't.

At that time, you went to a cigarette machine, you put in two dimes and you got back a pack of cigarettes with three shiny pennies inside the pack with those cigarettes. There were no such thing as filters, and there was no warnings about your health. Nothing like that. For me, it had nothing to do with it: It was all a matter of mind control. I quit smoking, and I never went back to smoking again. And through all the years, the people I was around that smoked made fun of me, and I didn't really care. I had quit.

So, I was to be a bar owner. I packed my clothes and everything I could, I put it all in the car and I drove, just me, to southern Illinois and I moved into that house beside the Mardi Gras. I bought some dishes and things, bought a bed, some furniture, and set up housekeeping. I was now in the nightclub business. I was going to run the Mardi Gras, and Paul was going to run the Curve Inn.

The Curve Inn was doing a super business and the Mardi Gras didn't do any business, so we decided that we would start a whole different routine for the Mardi Gras. We had what we called the "Shit-kicking Music" going on with the rednecks at the Curve Inn. It had tables and could probably seat about a hundred people. It had a big dance floor but no bar. Once you came in, you got served in the bar but you had to carry your drinks up the couple stairs into the dance hall.

The Mardi Gras did not seat as many as the Curve Inn, maybe eighty or so people. There was a large half-circular bar that you could seat maybe twenty people, and behind the bar was an area for the music, the bands. We decided to refer to them both as the "Southern Illinois Dance Land," and we used that when we started buying ads in all the major newspapers around the area, in Carbondale, Herrin, Cape Girardeau, and Paducah.

We started buying full-page ads about dancing on Saturdays and Sundays. We had dancing on Sunday nights and had three bands come in on Fridays and Saturdays. They played until 6:00 or 7:00 in the morning because everything in Missouri closed at 1:00 A.M., and everything in Kentucky closed at midnight. It was forty miles from Paducah to our place, and it was thirty-five miles from Cape Girardeau. They closed at 1:00. And so at 2:00 and 3:00 in the morning, our place was blasted, I mean, it was jumping, it was so busy you probably couldn't get in the door. We had a two-dollar door charge at the Mardi Gras; we didn't charge at the Curve Inn. We had high quality entertainment.

There was a waitress at Curve Inn named Margaret, and she was really good looking. One weekday night, there were about six guys hanging out at the Mardi Gras, and Margaret came in. I set her up a drink on the house. Everybody knew her, and there was small conversation going on. About that time, she bet everybody $2.00 that she could go outside and pee higher on the vertical concrete foundation than they could.

Well, the guys thought that was an easy win! So they made their bets, and we all went outside, and she lifted her skirt, dropped her panties and peed about four inches above the ground on the foundation. They all thought that was funny. Margaret said, "Okay, now it's your turn." The first guy stepped up, and unzipped his pants, got a hold of himself, and that's when she said, "Oh no, no hands!" Well, that was the end of the charade. We went back inside, she picked up all of her winnings, said goodbye and left. She had done that before!

The entertainment at the Curve Inn was just local, and at the Mardi Gras I had some bigger names coming in. I had Jerry Lee Lewis there half a dozen times after he had gotten kicked out of

England for marrying his young cousin. Margaret would wear a red dress when he was booked, and everyone would go nuts when he sang "Whole Lot of Shakin' Goin' On" and especially when he sang the line about the red dress.

I had Bill Black, and Merle Hay. They were all well-known artists at the time. Our booking guy was Tiny Ford. "Tiny" weighed over 300 pounds, and he was from Cape Girardeau. He was a wholesaler, a whiskey distributor salesman and a good one. He carried good lines of whiskey. We bought all our whiskey from him and I did all the entertainment booking with him. Paul did a lot of the booking for the Curve Inn with local people, and Tiny had booking fees. I would pay to get the good names in there.

After I'd gotten all my booze purchased from Tiny, I would take all the proceeds from the weekend in cash, and would head down to the basement. Unsafe as hell, but then I'd take all that cash and drive to Anna, Illinois which is about eight or ten miles away in a different county. I did my banking over there because I didn't want the sheriff knowing what was going on in my county, as he had the other county liquor licenses, and I didn't want them tied in.

Tiny is there one Monday and said, "I got a singer that's really good. Women just love hearing him sing, he's a heck of a singer. I suggest that you book him in here for a month, because I'll tell you what, he is just going to bring the crowds in." He told me his name, and I said, "I've never heard of him."

He lived in Paragould, Arkansas, a family man with six or seven kids. Tiny said, "Now there's nothing I can do about this because it's not in the contract, and I can't put it in the contract, but he won't play anywhere unless you pay for his gas money, and he's going to ask you for cash for his gas money every time he plays." At that time, gas was about twenty-six cents a gallon, so I said, "That's no big deal." Tiny said, "Well, I just want you to know in advance." He said again, "Book him in here for a month." I said, "No, I'll take him for two weeks." He said, "You should really take him for a month," but he then said okay. I booked him for Friday and Saturday for two weeks. He came in on a Friday evening, people paid the two bucks at the door, and I had about the same crowd I generally get. And of course, after midnight, it filled up, and the crowd went nuts with him.

He played three sets. When he got done playing, after 1:00, as I was getting some of the later crowd showing up, he came up to me and he said, "Have you got my gas money?" and I said, "I sure do." It was two or three bucks, something like that and I paid him.

Funny thing about this guy: Most entertainers, when they take their break, they circulate through the crowd and drink with them and sit with them, talk to them or introduce themselves. Not him. When he took a break, he went out to his car, rolled the windows up, turned on the radio and listened to Christian music. He was just different.

I paid him his money for the night, and he left, and he came back the next night, and we went through the same routine, and had a bigger crowd earlier the next night, and I filled the place. The next weekend, I knew I was going to have a big crowd so I bumped the door charge from two bucks to three bucks. It was packed in the first set and through the second set, it was just absolutely packed, both Friday and Saturday night.

Monday came, and Tiny came to get his order for the whiskey and I said, "Listen, I want to book this guy for another month," and he said, "You're too late. He's going to Vegas." I said, "What?" He said, "Yup. He signed a year contract in Vegas." I said, "You're kidding me?" He said, "I told you. I tried to get you to take him, but he's gone."

Well, he went to Vegas and he became extremely popular. The end of the story is he was known as the Grey Fox, and two of his most popular songs were "Behind Closed Doors," and "The Most Beautiful Girl." Charlie Rich was his name.

I would go to Southern Illinois University in Carbondale and hire guys from the football team to be bouncers for me. We had no phones in the place, none in the whole place. We never wanted to phone for help because I didn't want help from the sheriff. So, I hired bouncers. I always wore a white sport coat that was like a summer tux with a red bow tie, a white shirt, and I had a little 38 that I carried just at the top of my black pants so they could just see that it was there. I never used it but that's the way it was.

We had no food in the Mardi Gras so if they wanted to eat they had to go next door to the Curve Inn. We didn't do any credit cards at all and still we were taking in tons of money. I opened up a bank account for us under the company name at the Anna State Bank in Anna, Illinois.

The parking lot out front of our place was all gravel, coarse gravel, maybe two inches of gravel, all the way down. It was a huge, common parking lot in front of the Curve Inn and the Mardi Gras, and it took up a lot of road frontage. And there were cars parked all over the place, all over the grass, behind the clubs, and everywhere.

Jerry Lee Lewis was over at the Curve Inn one time, and so I went over there to help Paul that night because I knew we were going to be busy. It was one of the few nights we charged a door charge there. At the first break, Jerry Lee came up to Paul and me, and said, "Listen, there's a bunch of guys sitting over at that table, and I've told this one guy to shut up when I walked by and all he did was give me a dirty look. You guys need to get him to shut up or I'm going to beat the shit out of him." I said, "Well, where is he? I'll speak to him." I went over to talk to the guy and said, "Hey, cool your jets a bit. Jerry Lee's got a short temper."

Then the break was over and Jerry Lee went back to playing, and this guy started to loudmouth him again. Right in the middle of the song Jerry Lee stopped, got up, went over and grabbed that guy out of his chair, dragged him across the dance floor, down past the bar, out the screen door, onto that gravel parking lot, and kicked the hell out of him, kicking, I mean, literally kicking his side. Jerry Lee Lewis was a boxer in the army, and he was a good boxer. He just beat the living crap out of that guy, put him face down on that gravel and dragged him face down for about thirty feet, and the guy was bleeding all over. Jerry Lee walked back in and said, "I told you guys to take care of him and you didn't." He went over, sits down, and started playing again. So, that was one of my episodes with Jerry Lee Lewis.

13.

I used to go into Anna to the bank on Mondays, and I'd make the rounds at all the bars and buy some drinks to do some advertising for us. I didn't drink all that much. then I'd go bowling on Monday evenings. I would generally stop and have dinner at some restaurant in Anna, and all of a sudden there was a gal and her name was Ruby, and Ruby was a knockout. She waited on me and was also giving me the eye and all that. So I started making time there at the restaurant, I'd have dinner before or after I went bowling. Pretty soon we were dating, and she would come over to the Mardi Gras and sat at a special place at the end of the bar all night long, just watching what was going on, enjoying herself.

One Monday night after doing my banking in Anna and bowling, I stopped as usual about 10:00 p.m. in Brownie's Tavern to have a drink before driving twelve or fourteen miles to my house by the Mardi Gras. Brownie, the owner, was a big, affable guy. Many of his regulars would come to the Curve Inn or the Mardi Gras on weekends, so it was good business to buy these people a drink.

Unbeknownst to me, a guy named Sam Casper, Ruby's ex, was having a drink with his new flame, who never liked me because, as good looking as she was, I never gave her a second glance. While I was having my drink at the bar, she convinced Sam to get a tire iron from his car trunk. He did and he snuck up behind me and hit me in the back of the head.

I remember trying to hold onto the bar as I slipped off the stool and onto the floor, bleeding all over my clothes, my hands, and the floor. I barely remember Brownie coming over the bar to deck Sam, kick him and the woman out, and ban them from ever coming back.

Meanwhile, people got towels and were trying to clean me up but my head was bleeding badly. They were trying to get me to go to a doctor, which I refused because I had no insurance and didn't want a doctor and a hospital bill. After a lot of ice and consolation for about thirty minutes, I took an ice pack, got into my car, and went home. I changed ice packs a couple times before falling asleep.

When I woke up in the morning and sat up, the pillow was stuck to my head from bleeding all night. I went over to see Paul, my partner, and he knew all about the incident. His wife cut my hair and shaved my head, and bandaged me up, and so I was back working with a throbbing headache, which lasted for days.

That night, Ruby drove over to see me, which was unusual because she would usually only see me at the bar on Saturdays when she would sit at the end of the bar all night. I paid a pretty good price for her company which lasted about a year. After I left Illinois, about a year later she married a guy named Boswell who owned the other tavern in town, and they had a good marriage. Her sister, Dorothy, who has been a good friend of mine for years, took very good care of Ruby even after she got dementia and was put in a nursing home, where she died. Ruby was a great lady, a good person, and I was fortunate to be a part of her life.

One time I was on the way to do my banking on a Monday, and about a mile across the county line at the state park, there was the sheriff alongside the road, and he motioned me over into that state park. Well, he had no jurisdiction over there, so I drove in. He gets out of the car and says, "Dan, how you doing?" I said, "I'm good and well, thank you. What's going on?" He said, "Well, you guys seem to be doing pretty good up there, and, you know, we've never bothered you a bit. We've never been up there to check on anything, we just keep hands off." I said, "I appreciate that. We're not doing anything that needs a business permit." He says, "Well, a lot of your customers are coming out of there pretty high when they drive out of the Curve Inn or the Mardi Gras. And we've been kind to them, and we'll keep on being kind to them if you just want to stop here and meet me every Monday and put a few dollars in my pocket."

That's the South. That's the way the police system works in the South. I said, "What are we talking about, 'a few dollars?'" He says, "A hundred dollars. It's good protection." And so I made a big mistake. I reached in my pocket and I took out a hundred bucks, gave it to him, and went on and did my banking.

The next Monday, it was the same thing. The next Monday, it was the same thing, and this went on for months. One day, I stopped by there and he said, "You know, I think you guys are really doing good up there and we haven't bothered you." He said, "I think maybe the price of your protection went up a little bit." He said, "Let's just double it." I said, "That's bullshit." And

74

he said, "No, I think you need it. I think you need to pay me $200 a week." That was pretty good money then. I said, "I'm not going to do it." And he said, "Okay."

So, I went to Anna and he went back to Vienna, Illinois. I didn't pay him, and a couple weeks went by, and then on a Friday night when people started leaving our place, blue lights came on about a mile on either side of us. We didn't see the cars before that. The blue lights came on and people got tickets, and that went on all Friday night, and that went on all Saturday night.

The next weekend you could have shot a gun down through our place and had a hard time hitting people. Nobody was there. He had destroyed the business.

Well, three weeks or so later, the sheriff is sitting out there again at the park. So, I started paying him again, but now it was $300 - it went from two to three hundred! I paid him $300 a week for the rest of the time I was there, in cash. Of course, Paul knew it and Fritz up in Michigan knew it. But it was the beginning of the end for us.

The sheriff came to the Mardi Gras just one time. We'd hired a kid that had worked for Paul in Michigan. I used to bowl with him, and he was a heck of a good bowler. He never had any money and he drank a lot. He was a little short kid, and he was our bartender. His car had broken down, so he wanted to borrow my car. I had a Lincoln (I'd gone up in the world), which I had before I moved down there to southern Illinois. He borrowed my car, went to town and got drunk, took it down to the Country Fairgrounds and was racing around the dirt track - and he rolled it. When the sheriff found it, he said, it was wheels up in the air. The car was pretty well damaged. It wasn't totaled but it was damaged. It cost me a lot of money to fix it up. Of course I never saw that kid again. He got out of jail and he went back to Michigan. But that's an example of the stories you learn about human nature as you go through life.

If I didn't go down to Anna on Mondays, which I usually did, I'd go down to Paducah on Tuesdays and make the rounds at the bars and invite everybody to come to our place. I was there at the Holiday Inn in Paducah, and there was a nice bar in there, and a good looking gal tended bar. (Seems like all these gals in the story are good-looking, doesn't it?)

But anyway, I got a couple of drinks, and in walks a guy and he sits down two stools away from me and ordered a Grandad and Branch, Old Grandad, straight Bourbon. He'd been coming there and he started talking to her, and they talked quite a while. She introduced me to him and we had an afternoon there just really enjoying it. His name was Walter Brennan, and they were making a movie down in Southern Illinois called "The Winning of the West." He was starring in that movie and he was staying there at the hotel, and that was how I got to meet the great actor Walter Brennan, which was one of the highlights of my life.

The nightclub business kept going downhill for some reason or another, I don't know, but it kept petering out and I wasn't making enough money there. They were putting Interstate 57 through so I got a job working for the union, working with my back in labor again, helping build the interstate.

In the meantime, it cost me too much money to get my car fixed up so I bought another car, an old Plymouth '47. I drove in there driving a three year old Lincoln and drove out driving a old beat up unpaid-for-car, making $37 a month payments on it. So that's ridiculous, but that's my story about southern Illinois, and it ends another chapter in my life.

14.

During this time, I had given Patty a check for $1,500 after our divorce. At one point, I had been behind nearly $3,000 in what I owed her, then I was all caught up, and then I got behind again. They couldn't do anything about it in Michigan, not that I was trying to beat it, but I just didn't have the money. But, finally, I had caught up on all my back child support.

The next few years, for reasons that will become obvious, were pretty scattered in my mind. When I left southern Illinois, I went back to Michigan and saw my kids. I hadn't seen them in a long time. I got a job working for a wholesale drug company delivering pharmaceuticals in northern Ohio and northern Indiana. It was a lot of driving, and it was low pay.

I was having breakfast at the Commodore Perry Hotel in downtown Toledo one Thursday or Friday morning, and as I was reading the newspaper ads there was one that said, "Action!

We're now hiring two preneed counselors at Ottawa Hills Memorial Park. Apply in person, Saturday Only."

I said to myself, 'how could there be any "action" in a cemetery business?' So I went there, and I was introduced to a man who was doing the interviews. It was the first time I'd ever been in a cemetery like that. I did the interview and they said if you're ready to go to work, we'll hire you, and you start on Monday.

I went to work on a straight commission job, no bennies of any kind, no base salary of any kind, no guarantees of any kind, no hourly rate. They gave me forty leads a week that had been telephoned to see if there were three things that qualified them: If they considered themselves to be permanent in the area, if they were over the age of twenty-one, and if they as yet owned their cemetery property. If they answered no to all that, which 95% of the people did, it was a lead. And they gave us leads right down the street.

Toledo had a lot of row houses like Philadelphia. I went through my training, I went into the field, and watched a man named Paul Withrow make a couple presentations. Jim McClauslin was my sales manager and Fred Jewett was his assistant manager, a nice elderly man who had been there for years. John Vogeli ran the operation, and Frank Amerhein was an owner, a man in his late 80s or early 90s who walked around with hands full of cash and dropped it by mistake on sidewalks and in the offices and everywhere. Frank Amerhein owned the Fort Wayne Pistons pro basketball team, which later became the Detroit Pistons.

I got to work for this beautiful cemetery in a nice suburb of Ottawa Hills, which is on the northwest side in Sylvania, Ohio. They taught us to wear a suit and hat, shirt and tie, and you had a little book that was about four inches wide and about five inches long and maybe two and half inches thick and you put that in your side pocket. In the inside coat pocket you kept a map of the cemetery, contracts and a receipt book. You would knock on the door, and you didn't go to set appointments, you went to go in the door.

I would start at 4:00 or 4:30 in the afternoon and I was supposed to knock my way into two doors a day, make two presentations a day. And if you were good at closing, and you made two presentations a day, that was ten a week and that would result in two sales which would make you between $110 to $200 a week. The customers' payments were $10 or $15 a month.

Armed with that, you went out and knocked on doors with the lead card in your hand, and you were taught to say "My name is Dan Reed, may I come in please?" and you walked right in. You sat there and went through a "warm up" which they called the "prelude." You got them warmed up, and then you'd move to the kitchen table, and then you'd come out with a packet with a little book, and say, "Folks, I'm here to talk to you about Ottawa Hills Memorial Park."

At the door you did not identify yourself with Ottawa Hills, just your name, because most people thought you were a minister calling them from a church or something. Well, they'd just go aghast, and then you'd open up your little presentation book and you go through a fifteen minute presentation, and you would attempt to close on selling two cemetery lots. That was truly creative selling!

If they had enough money, you could add a bronze marker to the book, which was $10 a month, and the others were $5 a month. It was very low ball, and I made good sales. They had seven salespeople, and I was never the number one salesman, but I was never below a three, I was always third or second. A Jewish fellow, Sol Rappaport, who had his hair cut real short and always ran his hands through his hair when he got exasperated, he was always the number one salesman. He was a dynamic closer and he just twisted people's arms and practically beat on them until he wrote business; they did so mostly to get rid of him. His brother was a good salesman but not as hard a closer as Sol, and I wasn't a good closer, but I was a hard worker - does that surprise you? So, I made lots of calls, lots of presentations, and got a few sales.

Because I did pretty well in the cemetery sales they gave me an opportunity to go to Cincinnati, Ohio. I had never been there before in my life. I got a room in a nice home in a nice area of Blue Ash, a suburb. I got the Yellow Pages, and I looked at the all the stores to familiarize myself with the area. I went to work on the grounds at the cemetery on Memorial Day. Well, Memorial day is "Christmas" in the cemetery business, so I was out there patrolling all the grounds, getting leads, and I got lots of leads, and I went back out and sold those leads in Cincinnati. I did pretty well.

They called me back to Toledo and said they had a sales manager position open for me in Youngstown, Ohio. Well, I had never been there in my life, so off I go and get an apartment and I'm in business as a sales manager.

There was a guy there named Jim McCain, and he wrote all the bronze business and made lot of money. I was a sales manager charged to hire and train people to sell cemetery lots, and we didn't make a lot of money. At the time I went down to Youngstown there was a sheet and tubes steel processing plant. The other six foundries in Mahoning Valley in Youngstown had been on strike for over a year. Nobody was working, you could hire people all day long, though dirty fingernails never sold a thing their life. We would go out and knock doors but nobody had any money, so I just went broke, again. It just seemed like I never learned.

There was an ad in the paper in Conneaut, Ohio, north of Youngstown up on Lake Erie, the first town in Ohio when you come in from the western Pennsylvania town of Erie. They were looking for a night radio announcer. Well, guess what, I'd done that before. So I go up to Conneaut and meet a fellow by the name of Lou Skelly, and he interviewed me. He owned a radio station in there and one in Erie. He had quite a bit of money, had a big flashy watch, and he made fun of my Timex watch. He said, "How long have you had that expensive watch?" I said, "Oh, about five years." I never was one for a lot of jewelry, and spending money. If I made money I was trying to save it.

He hired me. I went to work at 6:00 o'clock at night, I'd be done at midnight, when we had to go off the air, and I would lock up the station. I rented a place up on Lake Erie, a little ramshackle lake house.

DEAD END

15.

About that time, in June 1962, I got a call that my first wife, Patty, my son Franny, and my niece, Mary Applegate, had been killed in a tornado. I went back to Michigan to the funeral service, went to the cemetery and the little funeral home in the little town of Cone. I don't remember much about it, but, I remember the caskets being open, and Franny's head was misshapen, and he was all bruised. I was shocked and just screamed and yelled at the funeral director to close Franny's casket, and all the caskets. It was traumatizing.

It was a very difficult time. I went back to work in Conneaut. I'd get off work and I'd have a fifth of Jack Daniels and I'd drink that until it was gone. I'd fall into bed, get up the next day, hang around until 6:00 o'clock, and go to work again. That went on for about a month or two.

When I got off work sometimes I'd go to one of the local taverns, and I'd start drinking. It wasn't a very big town, and was right on Lake Erie, and there was a bunch of pipeliners working there as they were putting a pipeline through the area. I got acquainted with them. They were fixing to move to Washington, Pennsylvania, south of Pittsburg, to start on a pipeline down there that was going to go all the way through to Delaware. They said, "Come with us, we'll get you a job and you don't have to worry about this. Come on with us."

Pug Tyler, who was from Oklahoma and wore a big cowboy hat, convinced me to interview with him. He said that he wanted me for his swamper. He was an operator on a D7 or D8, a big Caterpillar. A swamper is the lowest-life job you can get on a pipeline. You clean all the mud off the cleats on the rig, you do all the oiling before they get there, you oil the engine up, you gas it up, you make sure that everything is in working order, and then all day long you carry brush or trees, you get them out of the road, out of the way. If there is mud you clean the cleats every hour or so. At lunchtime, when they stop to eat, you've got to clean them again.

It was hard, dirty hard work. I started work at 7:00 o'clock in the morning, I worked seven twelves, seven days a week, 7:00 to 7:00. At night we'd go to town, get supper, and start drinking. I lived in beat up motels and hotels and all of that, all across Pennsylvania and into Maryland.

Welders on the pipeline wore polka dot caps, and operators wore cowboy hats. Most of the operators were from Oklahoma, Arkansas, and Tennessee. Welders were from all over, but welders and operators didn't mix, it was like oil and water.

We were in downtown Frederick, Maryland in a Chinese restaurant one Saturday night, and it had paper maché dividers. There were eight or ten of us operators and swampers there, and in came about eight or ten welders. Well, they saw us there and we saw them there, and they were behind the paper maché dividers and they start with the wise remarks about this, that, and other. Before you know it, we're in a big fight, and I mean a big fight, and that Chinese restaurant was torn to pieces, everything, and the cops came and we were all thrown in jail.

In those days in the South it was segregated. They had one big cell for all the black men and they had smaller cells for four white men, two bunks in each one, one on top of each other. I got a bottom bunk. And, so we were in the doggone jail.

Apparently the blacks in there at the time began raising cane about 5:00 o'clock in the morning. They started rattling on things because they wanted to get their breakfast, because they were in there every weekend for fighting or gambling or whatever. It was just a mess and we didn't get out of there until 9:00 or 10:00 o'clock. All of us got hell when we got back to the pipeline because we had missed a third of a day. There was no union there. I worked for the Williams Brothers Pipeline Company, and they did not have unions. They do not hire local people, so when you sign on, they expect you to be there.

The Williams Brothers Pipeline Company was one of the biggest pipeline companies in the U.S., operating out of Texas. We started in Pennsylvania, and we put that pipeline in all the way through to Delaware. Winter was coming on when we finished, and everybody was dragging up and going home for the winter. Pug said, "I'm not dragging up, I'm going to Texas." We had worked together most of the winter, and he said, "Come on with me," so off we went in our cars to east Texas down around Mount Pleasant to start on a pipeline down there.

We always worked on what they call the "big inch," which is a thirty-six-inch pipeline. We were digging the right of way, the clear way so people could come in and dig the ditch, and then they'd lay the pipe down in the ditch and they would level it out with cribs.

I did part of that when we were in Pennsylvania. Those cribs are four feet long and they're made out of oak and they're triangular, and you'd take those cribs out after they got the pipelines welded. After it was welded, they lifted the pipes up, and you'd take the cribs out and throw them over to the side for the trucks that would come by to get them. It was just a dirty, hard work job. I worked up there all summer. I was drunk most of that year I was on the pipeline, that why it's all kind of hazy in my mind. I don't think I drew a sober breath. I wasn't real proud of myself.

It was a day or two before Thanksgiving, it was raining, and I was down in that ditch. I was trying to get a chain around that pipe so that a worker could lift it up so I could put the cribs underneath it. I had on hip boots, had water running down into the crack of my butt, it was muddy, slimy, dirty, and it hit me.

I took hold of that chain and I pulled myself up out of that ditch. Pug was startled and said, "What are you doing?" I said, "I'm dragging up." In pipeline vernacular, when you "drag up," that means they have to pay you within forty-five minutes - and you can never come back to work for them again because now they've got to find somebody to do your job. So I dragged up, and I went and got my pay.

I had that old Plymouth that I was still making payments on, and I was out there by the warehouse where I got the gas every morning. The gas came in flat, ten-gallon cans. In the morning I went there before anyone else, and I filled my trunk as full as I could with those ten-gallon cans of gas. The trunk was so heavy the car had the hind wheels down and the front wheels up, and with that I took off to Michigan to see my kids.

I drove a while, and when the gas got down to about half a tank I'd stop somewhere on a side road, I'd take those gas cans, and I'd pour them into the gas tank and then I'd throw those things away. Eventually the car was leveled up, but you talk about a dangerous thing driving down a road with a trunk full of gas - that was awful. I drove to St. Louis, Missouri.

I had never been in St. Louis before. I stopped and got a cheap motel room and got a St. Louis Post Dispatch, and started looking at ads. There was an ad in the paper from a cemetery in St. Charles, Missouri looking for salesmen. I had sold cemetery plots in Toledo, Cincinnati, and Youngstown, and I thought, "What the hell, maybe this is better than what I had." So the next morning, I answered the ad and met a fellow by the name of Fred Newman, who became my lifelong friend.

I told him I was reading the ad in the paper, and he said, "Where are you?" and I was down somewhere in south St. Louis, a ratty part of town, and he says, "You stay right there, I'll buy you dinner and we'll talk." And, I said, "Okay, sir." A couple of hours later we went to lunch, and I went to work for Fred the next day.

BEGINNING SUCCESS

16.

I went to work in St. Charles, Missouri at the end of 1962. Fred Newman and his partner, Ray Humphrey, had started a cemetery called St. Charles Memorial Gardens. All I did was what I had been trained to do, except I didn't have any leads, so I just went around and knocked doors. Across Interstate 70 were two subdivisions, Mark Twain One and Mark Twain Two. They were middle-income homes. I went over to that subdivision and I started knocking doors. I worked it, I sold a ton of cemetery lots, they liked it, the terms were right, the prices were right, the cemetery was new, and so here we go, starting a new career in St. Charles, Missouri.

Pretty soon they promoted me to a sales manager, and I recruited, hired, and trained salespeople, taught them how to go out and knock on doors and make a living. A guy came in the office one day, a great big red-headed fellow by the name of Red Schumer, and Red was from Arkansas. He had come over there in response to my ad and applied for a job. He was a tremendously good salesman, but he did not know how to prospect. So I took him into the field with me and taught him how to prospect and how to make presentations and he was really, really impressed. Red hung around there for awhile, but he didn't do much. He might have made a few sales, but I remember he didn't do too much.

What I didn't know was that he had been sent over there by a fellow named David Coates. David Coates was running a water conditioner sales organization in St. Louis and he had quite a few salespeople, but they were having problems getting leads so he'd sent Red over there to see how I was going about knocking doors and prospecting. It paid off handsomely for him, and I did not know this at the time, but it went on about five or six months. I continued to sell and hire and train, doing the right work, and even had traded cars to a newer '56 model Lincoln.

All of a sudden this David Coates shows up at the office with Red Schumer, and he introduces himself. He was a big, tall, good looking guy, and he said that he had been watching what I was doing, that he had sent Red to learn how to prospect, and that he'd like to have me join his company as a sales manager. I listened to him, and I as nicely as I could deferred because I really liked Fred Newman, I liked working with him, he was just a great guy, treated me super well and became a long time friend; he was best man at my third wedding. So I deferred the proposition and went on about my work.

A few months went by, and I was doing quite well. I was in buying a brand new Buick when the news came on that President Kennedy had been assassinated in Dallas..

About that time Dave Coates came back to me and said, "Dan, I've got a real good opportunity for us, it's in Iowa and I'd like for you to come up to be a sales manager with me. I've got two sales managers, Red Schumer and Don Dickson, and you would be the third sales manager working for me. We're going to open up the state of Iowa, which has very hard water. We're going to open offices all over Iowa, hire and train salespeople and sell the heck out of water softeners." And, he said, "This time around I'm going to offer you $250 a week salary and overwrites plus good commissions when you make your own sales. But I'm not interested in you making sales as much as I am in you building an organization in Iowa."

Well, that really appealed to me, $250 a week guaranteed plus overwrites on salespeople and the offices I opened. I talked to Fred about it and Fred said, "Well, it's something you've just got to decide." He said, "You know I don't want you to go, I want you to stay here, but I understand if you want to improve yourself and you think you will."

I packed up my car and left Fred in St. Charles. I had been living in an apartment in Clayton, Missouri, the county seat for St. Louis County, with a Federal Aviation Administration guy. He'd come home all beat up, emotionally exhausted from work. I also left a girlfriend behind. She was a hostess at the best restaurant in St. Charles built right on the Missouri River called Three Flags. She was good looking, a tall, statuesque blonde in her mid-thirties. We'd been dating for about a year and got along just great. I left her, took all my stuff, and I went to Cedar Rapids, Iowa.

Now that's interesting, because Cedar Rapids was where my mother was from, and all of the relatives on my mother's side lived there, and I didn't know any of them. I did remember that my half-sister lived there. She'd married by then and her name was Evelyn Oujiri. She was several years older than me, and her maiden name was Werner, as my mother had first been married to Charles Werner, but they divorced after a couple years.

It's important to note that my mother's parents had raised Evelyn; Lucille didn't want her, either. History repeats itself: My mother had two children, and raised none.

I got to Cedar Rapids, got a room, and went down to the offices that were just opened to meet the millionaire owner who had a huge dry cleaning business in a number of towns around Iowa, four or five in Cedar Rapids. His name was Bill Wheeler, and he was just a nice, gracious man. How Dave Coates had found him I don't know. But we were going to start selling Lindsay Water Softeners.

I met Don Dickson, and saw Red Schumer again. Dave had brought quite a few of his sales people from St. Louis to the Cedar Rapids office. I didn't know anything about selling water softeners so the first thing they had to do was teach me. Don

Dickson got the responsibility for teaching me, and he was good. He was a tremendously good salesman and he taught me how to sell water softeners, and I went out and started opening up offices.

I opened an office in Washington, Iowa, which is in southeastern Iowa, I opened an office in the Dubuque area and one in Decorah, both in northeastern Iowa, I opened one in Des Moines, central Iowa, and that all took a bit of time, hiring and training sales people, and getting set up. .

17.

During that period of time I decided to track down my sister, Evelyn, whom I had never really known except for seeing her a few times.

The first time I remember meeting Evelyn as a kid was when I went to Cedar Rapids with my dad. My grandparents on my mother's side owned a grocery store in the southwest part of town called "Bohemie Town" for all the Czechs and Bohemians that lived there; now it's called Czech Village.

I met Emma and Joseph Nejdl, my babi and děda, pronounced "bubby" and "gedda," Czech for grandma and grandpa. I met Evelyn, and she had a tricycle which we rode it up and down the store. It was a long store with wood floors, and had all kinds of provisions in it. They didn't do much business, and they lived in a house attached to the store at the back of the building.

The second time I met my sister was as a kid living in Montana, and my dad had brought her out there to visit. I remember Evelyn as just being a beautiful, beautiful young woman.

Now, back in Cedar Rapids, I wanted to see her. Don't ask me how but I found her, I called her, told her who I was, and she just screamed on the phone, "Oh my gosh!" She was so excited. I said, "I'd like for us to meet for lunch."

There was a shopping area called Lindale Plaza, which was, incidentally, right next door to a big memorial park cemetery called Cedar Memorial, located on First Avenue, the main thoroughfare through Cedar Rapids, just as you went into the next town of Marion. They had a Bishop's Cafeteria, and so we met there. I described myself, she described herself, and we met, sat down and started talking.

The hour went by far too quickly. She had to get back to work, for an attorney or an accountant. But that started a love affair between the two of us, brother and sister reunited, and that was an excellent, excellent, excellent part of my life. I just adored her and it was so neat to have a real-life sister; I never thought of her like a "half" sister. We shared something so important: Our mother had given us both away, Evelyn to her grandparents, me to my grandmother on my father's side. And, we were raised totally, totally differently. Evelyn was raised Roman Catholic, I was raised in half a dozen different religions and none of them stuck.

At one point Evelyn and I would meet for lunch weekly. I remember that as I talked about the stress I was experiencing, she would reach over and uncurl my fingers from the fists they were in.

While I was in Cedar Rapids, I worked in all these different offices, I hired sales managers and trained sales people and everything and we were doing "do-wa-ditty," really well. I was running all over and we were making a ton of money. We were the 3Ds: Dan, Dave, and Don.

The 3Ds became pretty prominent, and we were selling two hundred fifty water softeners a month. We became one of the biggest dealers in U.S. for Lindsay Water Softeners, which were manufactured up in Wisconsin. To this day I have a water softener, and I've never been without it ever since I got in the business. I love it.

Don Dickson was always the first one in the office, and he was the first one to disappear in the afternoon. But one day, he was in the office, and said, "Have you heard the bad news?" I said, "No, what are you talking about?" He and Dave looked at each other, and he said, "All of these water softeners we've sold are leaking out there." "What?" "Yup, we got people calling with in basements filled with water, garages running over with water. They're leaking, they're malfunctioning." Well, there went the end of my dream of making a whole ton of money on a long-term basis with Lindsay.

During that period of time in Washington, Iowa I had hired a sales manager by the name of Don Schwartzendruber who was Amish. He had been an All-American playing at the University of Iowa, even played in the Rose Bowl, and he was a heck of a nice guy. He had a beautiful wife and a nice family, and we would meet and have lunch every time I went to Washington.

One day at lunch his wife said to me, "Dan, you're single." I said, "Yes." She said, "I've got a very good friend who's a widow and she is just a princess of a lady. I love her dearly and I don't know if you'd be interested meeting her or not. She is a good looking lady. She's got three children and she's been a widow for about three years now. But," she said, "I'm going to tell you something. If you touch her, if you lay one hand on her I will haunt your grave for eternity. She is a lady through and through and through." I said, "Okay, okay, all right."

I had had a few girlfriends around Iowa by that time. Incidentally one time I flew one gal to St. Charles on Ozark Airlines from St. Louis, as we were having a big Christmas party. She got off the plane, and there she was in a glittery, long gown, low cut, just drop-dead gorgeous. People went nuts over her. It was a big Christmas party and everybody knew that I had her on my arm. I tell you this because I had a reputation and I was dating three different women in Iowa at that time. The weird thing is that their names were all a variation of Betty: Betty, Elizabeth and Liz.

And then I meet this new Betty, and so that made four! It was crazy. Don's wife told me to wait until she called me, after she talked to Betty to see if it was all right to give me her number. So she did, and I called Betty, and we set a date and went to a really nice restaurant called The Ranch in Iowa City.

Betty drove up there from Keota, Iowa and I drove down from Cedar Rapids. She was sitting there in the foyer when I walked in. She was very pretty, wearing a beautiful gown, she had jet black hair, and nice big smile. She was of German descent, her maiden name was Greiner, and her married name was Jaeger. There were a lot of German Catholics in that part of Iowa.

We met and we started dating. We dated for quite a long time, and then finally I told Evelyn about Betty, and she said, "Why don't you have Betty come up for dinner?" So she came up and met Evelyn and her husband, Al, and their daughters. We had a nice evening. A few days later when Evelyn and I met for our weekly lunch, she said, "This gal is a keeper." I'll never forget the words. She said, "You better not let go of her. Don't you lose her." I said, "Okay, I'm listening to you."

In the meantime Lindsay Water Softener Company and us had split ways. The machines didn't work, and all of us were out of our jobs. Leo Blevins was the factory man for Lindsay for the states of Iowa, Nebraska, and Kansas and we were his biggest dealer. Of course with the machines going corrupt, he was hanging on for a job, too. He went job hunting in the industry

89

where he was well known, and he went to the Water Refining Company in Middletown, Ohio where he talked to the guys that owned it. They made a water softener called Miracle Water Softeners, and had a few dealers around the Midwest, but not much of a big sales force. They had a good product, a heavy duty product that looked good, and worked well. Leo became regional vice president for the Water Refining Company. He brought the three of us Dave, Don, and myself along as sales managers, and we went through an all day meeting with the two brothers that owned the company.

Now you talk about coincidences, this has been going on all my life. It turned out these two owners and I had gone to school together in Glasgow, Montana where they were from! They were older than me, in the upper grades of school when I was in the fifth or sixth grade, so it's a small, small world. I will say that didn't me cut a lot of slack or anything, as this was a job, and it was what we had to do.

We got to pick territories, and of course Dave Coates nailed Iowa right away. He and Leo had been friends for years so he got Iowa so that he could get back to all those dealers and switch them over. I drew Indiana and Illinois, as Ohio was taken by Larry Higdon. For me, that meant I had go to drive for a week and then come home from Indiana and Illinois.

18.

Betty and I had been dating for maybe a year or more, and we decided to get married. We were wed on July 11th, 1964. Patty and I were married July 31st of 1948. I forget when Mary and I were married; that was a joke but it wasn't a joke, it was a disaster.

At the time, Betty was living in her deceased husband's farmhouse that belonged to her in-laws, who lived right across the road. She had two boys and a girl, and there never had been any work except on that farm. Before we got married, because she was Catholic, here we go again, we had to go through those instructions about Catholicism, which I did. Four kids and two divorces later, I finally wised up.

I had seen a big billboard while driving to Des Moines one day, a huge billboard with two doctors on it, and it said, "Vasectomies Performed," contact so and so and the address and a phone number. I didn't know what a vasectomy was the first time I read the billboard, but I had been going down past there for months, and I saw that again and I thought, "What the heck?" So I learned what it was, drove to their office, and I said, "What do I need to do to get a vasectomy?"

And they looked at each other and they said, "Are you married?" And I said, "No," they said, "Are you sure you want to do this? It's irreversible." I said "Yes." They said, "Well, it's going to be painful for you, but if that's what you want we will do it. We expect you to pay cash before the operation." It was around $300, and I said, "I have to have a vasectomy."

So I had it done in Des Moines, and I remember when I came out of the ether they said, "Where do you live?" I said, "Cedar Rapids," and they said, "No, no, no, you've got to get a hotel, you can't be driving, you're going to be all swollen." So I went down the road a little bit, and I checked into a Holiday Inn. I told them I wanted a room close to the ice machine, which they gave me on the first floor, and it was just a door away from ice machine.

I've got to tell you, folks, you talk about swelling up, they understated it. I was so sore, I'd go get ice and I laid in bed for two days with ice packs on me. I could hardly move, and my legs were black and blue, clear down to my knees.

When I checked out of the hotel, the first thing I did was drive back to Keota to Betty's house. We had supper there with the kids. They went to bed after a bit, and when we went to the living room, I pulled my pants down to my knees and showed her my legs. She said, "What has happened to you? Have you been in an accident?" I said, "No, I think I am an accident."

I said, "You don't have to worry about any more children. You've got three, and we decided we're going to raise my three, too, so that's six. That's more than enough for the two of us." And there was a look of relief all over her face I'll never forget, because she knew she didn't have to worry about getting pregnant and or worry about more kids.

When we got married, we bought a brand new home in Cedar Rapids in an area called Sunland to the southeast. It was a nice home, a multi-level. When you walked in you went down the stairs to the ground level, which some people would have called a basement except it was finished off. There was a bedroom and big recreation room down there, and down below that was the basement. Down the steps and up to the right there was the garage, and then up the steps halfway was the main level with the living room, dining room, and kitchen. Up another set of steps was the third level, as it was called a tri-level, and up there were two bedrooms.

My kids joined us for the wedding. I remember that the boys had their heads shaved by their grandfather, and they were there with all these people they didn't know. This would be a totally different experience for them having been raised by their grandparents for a number of years. Betty and me and the six kids moved into our new home.

I was working for the Water Refining Company, and went to Indiana and Illinois setting up dealers. We all did pretty well, we worked at that about a year or so, and then out of the pure blue sky all of us were terminated. They tore the whole marketing down and the four of us were out of the job, Leo, Dan, Dave, and myself.

What to do now? Well, I didn't know for sure what it was I wanted to do. Betty had a close girlfriend whose husband's name was Don Fosdick. He lived in Keota, and he was a salesman. He sold farm products, and he sold a lot of farm products around Keota, which was big farm country, hog country, and had really good farms. I mean just rich, deep, deep black soil. We ran around with Don and his wife, and two or three other couples and they were Betty's friends, and we just had a great time socially.

One time Don says to me, "Dan, I don't know what you're doing and I don't know how much money you're making, and I don't want to know. But there is a new company starting up here in Iowa called Hawkeye National Life Insurance Company and it's going to be big. It's backed by numerous bankers around the state of Iowa and they're going to start selling stock and it might be something you'd want to look into. The president's name is

Titus Shrock and you can get in contact with him in Des Moines. If you want to know more about him, I'll put you in contact with my banker, who's down in Mt. Pleasant." He was president of the bank there in a town that was bigger than Keota. He said, "I'll hook you up, and you can go talk to him about it."

So he did, and I did, I met this guy, and damn. We spent a couple of hours together, and he said, "I can really help you out with banks all around Iowa. There's twenty-five pre-incorporators to this Hawkeye Life Investment Company, and there's going to be two and half million dollars of $2 common stock sold. When we come out of escrow, we'll then form the insurance company and the pre-incorporators will have their stock and they'll look for proceeds from the insurance company." So, that's how the whole thing was going to work and that was my introduction to stocks because I had known nothing about it. And now, I had to get a securities license to sell stock.

I went to Des Moines, got the book to study, and took it home. I studied it for a few weeks and studied how to pass the test. It was quite a lengthy test, a lengthy study, but I then went back to Des Moines and took the test on a pre-assigned day. I sat next to Titus and got a higher score than he did, which made me feel pretty good. I got my license, and I thought, 'Well, now how am I going to go about making money when the stock issue breaks in a couple, three weeks?' There were 178 registered security licenses in the state of Iowa at the time; I remember that so vividly. Then, I got a brainstorm.

I called the licensing bureau and I said, "Have you got any kind of a registry for the licensees in the state of Iowa in securities?" The lady said, "Yes. We have to keep it on file here." I asked, "Actually, what kind of a file is it?" She said, "Well, it's in a book." I asked, "Can you get copies of it?" She said, "You can get copies for twenty-five cents a page." I said, "Thank you very much." Boom! Back to Des Moines I drive. I paid my couple bucks, and I got pages of all the licensees, names, addresses, and phone numbers. Now I'm getting in business. That's my entrepreneurial spirit.

I went back home and I got on the phone and introduced myself to all of the licensees that would listen to me. They didn't want to do it because some of them had people working for them. I told them this deal was coming out, and they acknowledged they knew of it, that it was going to come in two to three weeks. I said, "I'd like to have you write with me." To do this, they assigned their license number to you so that you got an overwrite on commissions. I hired seventy-some licensed security agents, and here I've never sold a piece of stock in my life! That was the beginning of a new career for me in February of 1965. I was in business.

In the meantime, I had gone back down to Mt. Pleasant to see the bank president, and he gave me a check for $25,000, which was a big, big, big check for stock, believe me. We had a kick-off meeting in Des Moines at the Holiday Inn right where I had stayed after the vasectomy. The room was full of people, just packed with people. And Titus was up there at the front with the officers of the Hawkeye Investment Company sitting with him, and Titus was telling us all about it. Then he said, "Okay guys, let's go and get it!" Everybody rushes out the door to go sell stock because it's legal starting at 10:00 a.m.

I walk casually up to the front and hand the check to Titus, and I said, "Here's the first check for Hawkeye Investment Company." Two or three of those guys got up out of their chairs to have a look at that check for $25,000. Titus looked at me and he says, "Dan, if this company goes the way it's starting off, it is going to be a winner." And, I said, "It will be, you watch." So that was my beginning with Hawkeye Investment Company.

We start selling stock for the Hawkeye Investment Company, which was soon to be the Hawkeye Life Insurance Company. The banker I had met in Mt. Pleasant had suggested to me that I go see some banks around the state of Iowa, that he would give me names of people that would be interested in investing in the stock.

I will never forget this. I was in Webster City, Iowa, it was colder than the devil, there was a clock on the main street, and it was noon. I was in town and had been calling on businesses to see if I could sell some stock, and I think I made a sale or two. I hadn't been out in the countryside yet. But, it was noon, and I thought, 'Well, what do I do? Who can I call on? I guess I'll go have lunch. No, no. I don't want to take time for lunch. Time is too short. These things are going to sell out. Who can I see?

Bankers. Ah.' So I walk into the bank in Webster City, because presidents of banks are always there at noon. That's when their top customers come in.

I asked if I could see the president of the bank. I gave the employee my card, and pretty soon he came over and offered for me to come into his office and sit down. He said, "You are with Hawkeye Investment Company?" I said, "Yes, I am." He said, "I've heard good things about them." I said, "Well, I can help you, because I'm selling the stock." He said, "I'll take $5,000 worth of stock." Well, with $2 commission, that's a pretty good sale. So I wrote up the contract, and while I was doing that he said, "Excuse me, just a minute."

He went to the lobby as there was a local car dealer from town standing in line; you could always tell a car dealer because they wore a big wallet in their back pocket with a chain attached to it. All of a sudden he brings the dealer in, and he said, "This is Dan Reed," and introduced me to the dealer, and said, "He's interested in some of that stock." And I said, "Well, that's just fine. Let me help him out. I'll just finish with yours here. All you need to do is sign it."

He came up to me and said, "That's good. $10,000." And it had been five. I then explained what the stock was about to the car dealer, and he said, "Well, I'll just match him. I'll just take $10,000, too." Well, that was a nice run for me! About that time the banker said, "Just a minute." And he got up and went out again when he saw the local lumber store dealer doing his banking. He brings the lumber dealer in the office. He said to me, "Here, Dan, come on. Take my chair. You sit over here and help these fellows out. I'll just sit on the side here."

There I was sitting at the bank president's desk on a lunch hour that I didn't take, and writing business. I wrote $25,000 worth of business, two tens and the banker's original five. I wrote $25,000 in forty-five minutes. Then I went and had lunch. Well, they all gave me the names of people to call on, and it was now a high referral business. And I mean referral. I hate that word with a passion, but I followed up on them, and I called on turkey farmers and hog farmers, and I sold stock.

Instead of going home to Cedar Rapids and mailing that stock, I called Betty and said, "I'm not coming home. I'll be home in a week or two. I'm going to stay out here selling." So I got a hotel room, and I drove through the morning, and I carried that stock into Titus's house, and gave it to him personally. I was concerned that if you oversubscribe an issue that's coming out of escrow, for the last ones in they get their money refunded to them, guaranteed. That's part of the sale.

I drove my stock in for the next few nights, and sure as the world, within two weeks we sold that out. My guys were making sales for me in addition to me making sales, so I made a ton of money in a short period of time, just in a month. That was a good way to spend the winter in Cedar Rapids, Iowa. I took stock and put it in the kids' names and gave it to all the kids, all six of them. I gave them a hundred shares of stock. I gave it to them at separate times and their eyes got as big as saucers. They were really somewhere. They owned stock in Hawkeye Investment Company at $2.00 common.

That's the end of my stock story. I made good money, and I can't remember exactly how much it was, but I know I made somewhere around $50-55,000 that month, which was very good. I was starting to get my education process put in place, and all that education was starting to pay off for me.

GROWTH

19.

I wondered what I was going to do next, and I then got a call from Fred Newman. Fred had been to Denver, Colorado that fall to a national convention which I had never been to, the American Cemetery Association (A.C.A.). He got talking to a man named Dave Linge, whom Fred knew from belonging to Central States Cemetery Association as an owner. Fred asked me how things were going, and I told him what had happened with me and the stock deal, the water refining deal, and all that had gone down. He said, "Well, things change in a hurry, don't they? You are welcome to get back in here anytime you want to." He said, "There is a guy in town that I talked to about you. Dave Linge is looking for a sales manager at Cedar Memorial in Cedar

Rapids." Cedar Memorial was the nicest, prettiest cemetery I'd ever seen, and a lot nicer, a lot bigger, and a lot older than St. Charles Memorial Gardens.

Dave Linge called me and said, "I've heard about you, and I would like to meet with you. Let's meet for lunch." I said, "Okay, where will we meet?" He said, "I have to go to Sears there in Lindale Plaza. I'll be in Sears, and I'll be smoking a pipe." I go to Sears, and I find him, and he said, "Let's go to Bishop's for lunch."

I went through the interview with him. He had me talk about myself, my sales experience, and my sales management experience, and so on. He knew Bill Wheeler from Lindsay Water Softeners; I gave Bill as reference, which was good. Dave then said, "We need to get together. Give me a few days. Why don't you and your wife come to my house for dinner and we'll discuss this in further detail?" and I agreed.

We made a date, and Betty and I went over to his pretentious old home in an old area of southeast Cedar Rapids. We had a nice dinner, we had a few drinks, and he produced a contract.

Dave said, "Dan I have taken the time to put this contract together for you, and here is what I've got to offer for you and Betty." Betty and his wife, Audrey, were getting along famously, and they were doing small talk while we were talking business, all of us sitting in their living room by the fireplace. I looked at the contract, and he was going to pay me a salary, about $1,100 a month, and an overwrite at different levels of production would be 3%, 5%, 7%, all the way up to 9%.

I read it through while he was sitting there smoking his pipe, waiting on me while the three of them were talking. I laid it down and I said, "Dave, this is a very generous offer," I said, "You've put some thought into it, and I appreciate it. I'm going to have to reject it though, because I think I can do better for us than that contract."

Dave about bit his pipe in two. He said, "How is that?" He was obviously a little upset, a bit annoyed. I said, "Well, what I'd suggest we do is for me to come to work for you for six months on an overwrite basis only. At the end of the third month we will review what's been accomplished and if neither one of us like what we've got going, we'll review it. At the end of six months, if we both like what we are doing we'll continue with it ad infinitum, no ending to it, just keep on doing what we are doing." And, he said, "Then I don't pay you a salary, I just pay an overwrite for sales?" I said, "That's it." And he said, "What's the overwrite?" And I said, "It's 10%." And he said, "Well that's fair, that's reasonable. I don't pay you any salary?" I said, "No you furnish all the office equipment, you furnish me a secretary, but no salary for me."

He stood up and walked across the room said, "Dan Reed, we've got a deal," and he shook my hand. And so everybody was happy, we had an after dinner drink, and went home. When we were on our way home Betty said, "Why did you do that?" I said, "Do what?" She said, "He offered you a salary, and a good job." Understand that Betty wasn't sales-oriented, she wasn't into promotion like I was, and so to her a bird in the hand is worth two in the bush, and she liked that security idea, for us with six kids. I said, "It will work out, just trust me, have trust in me, it will work out." "All right," she said. So I went to work for Dave Linge.

At Cedar Memorial, there was a home on the grounds where Dave was raised. It was off to the side away from the grand entrance to the cemetery, and it was up on a hill. That's where they stored all the equipment for the maintenance shop. It was hidden behind bushes and trees. Dave decided that it would be a good place for my office as opposed to being in the cemetery office. They moved everything out of the basement underneath the house, they got all the cars out of there, and put up walls. I had desks made for two people sitting at each one, four desks, for a total of eight people, and I got a big blackboard at the front of the room. Down the hallway from that there was a side office where I sat with Betty's sister, Loretta, whom I hired as a secretary. She and I started going through records.

The records at Cedar Memorial were about 8,000 strong, and they were all paid up property owners, people who had bought cemetery property over years and years. What we were going to do was go out and sell these people prearranged funerals. Dave's ambition was to take the home that I was in and convert the whole upstairs into a funeral home. He kind of got the cart ahead of the horse. I had Loretta going through and writing down the

98

names on three by five cards of all these property owners. We didn't do it alphabetically. I started with the Ms and worked backwards; it was just a thing of mine: I didn't want people thinking they were going to be called alphabetically.

I started recruiting, and I hired eight people. I told all of them, "If you don't do your job, somebody is going to be here to replace you, because this is what I expect you to do on a monthly basis." They said, "We've never heard of that, we've never had minimums before." And, none of them had been in the cemetery business.

The only guy I hired who was already working for the cemetery was a guy driving a flower truck, a nineteen-year old kid by the name of Ron Heldt. Ron didn't know anything about selling. He was a good kid, and he was excitable as could be.

Again, I told them all, "If you meet your standards, I will not have more than eight people in this room. When the room is full of eight people meeting their standards, there won't be any more hiring. Your job is going to be safe, but you are going to have to maintain standards along the way." I had written up job standards for what they had to do, which were reasonable to begin with then increased incrementally as they got more adept at what they were doing.

One day in downtown Cedar Rapids I was coming out of Commerce Bank. Jim Smith was on the corner talking to some folks, and he waved me down and said he wanted to talk. Jim had been sheriff of Linn County for thirty-plus years and knew a lot of people. He had been involved in the capture in Oklahoma of Bonnie and Clyde along with a posse of sheriffs from all over the Midwest. He had a very high profile in Linn County, and in 1964 when Lyndon Johnson and the Democrats won the election he was voted out.

Jim and his wife had prearranged their funeral with us at Cedar Memorial, so he knew me. He said, "Dan, you have a good thing going and I would like to be a part of it." So I hired Jim and attempted to train him, but the 'vaccination' never took. Jim didn't know much about selling so he would go to people he knew and tell them prearranging "was a good thing." He did write a lot of business, and mostly I just left him alone.

One day Jim came to me and said "Dan, I need your help." He had a family to see in Vinton, a small town thirty miles from Cedar Rapids. I went with him to Vinton on a gravel road going up and down over rolling terrain. We topped a hill and I saw a group of sheep, probably about fifty. I said, "Look, Jim, those sheep have just been sheared." Jim looked past me out the window and said, "It would appear so from this side." I sat there thinking of the logic he had just imparted to me. The longer I thought about it the more I realized the impact of his words. POWERFUL!

We got to the farmhouse he was calling on and I helped him get his sale. That ride to Vinton had a tremendous impact on the rest of my life, namely that things may not always be the same from a different point of view. I sincerely hope this may have an impact on your attitude about life. Jim Smith and his simple philosophy did on mine.

Loretta would make appointments for these fellows from the leads, the paid-up property owners, so they were happy as the devil to be at Cedar Memorial. We would have telephone appointments for these guys, and that was why they were hired: They'd go out and run two appointments a day. I put presentation books together for them. I had never sold funerals. I went to the field, and I wrote three or four funerals while I was recruiting and hiring, and I said, "Good gosh. This is a piece of cake compared to what I did selling cemetery property." We were going to set up preneed funeral trusts and that's how we started, funded at 100%.

When I said Dave Linge got the cart ahead of horse... when you start selling preneed funerals and you have funerals that people are depending on to be taken care of, you've got to have a funeral director. Dave tried to hire a funeral director, and all the funeral directors in the State of Iowa, 568 of them, hated Cedar Memorial with a passion, because we were selling preneed funerals.

There was a very, very active funeral director in Cedar Rapids who owned three funeral homes, John Turner, and he lived right across the street from Dave Linge. John did fireside chats on the news every evening at six and ten, and he started advocating that preneed funerals are the worst thing a family could do. So that was our competition.

We went ahead and pretty soon Dave found a retired funeral director that would come in and take the job. Now that we had a funeral director, we had to put in a whole prep room upstairs in the home. It became a beautiful home for funerals.

Then it got more tense. The laws about this in the state of Iowa at that time were ambiguously written, and could be interpreted a couple of different ways. Dave had a flock of really good attorneys that investigated all this thoroughly before he decided to go into the preneed funeral business, and his was the first funeral home in the state of Iowa to do that. We started making sales, no one knew how many sales we were making, but it became the talk of the town. The more sales we made, the more John Turner was doing advertising against us. Then he got a funeral home in Waterloo that joined him, and he got one over in The Quad Cities to join him.

The next thing you know every funeral director is getting together, 568 of them, and they started running full-page ads in nine major newspapers in Iowa proclaiming the same thing: "Beware of suede shoe salespeople knocking on your door attempting to sell you preneed funerals. Deal with a reputable, responsible funeral director in your hour of need..." Da, da, da... Those ads went on for months, but we kept selling for months.

I weeded a few guys out that weren't making the cake, and I had sales people calling me, wanting a job. The best doggone sales people in Cedar Rapids called me, so I wound up with a really, really good sales force, and I still needed help. I reached out to Dave Coates and said, "Dave, I need help, I need you to come in here and help me. Not to train or anything, but to manage these people and get their schedules made on a day-to-day basis, take care of the paper work, do all that. It's just overwhelming." Dave Coates came to work for me, and I paid him an overwrite, and so Dave was back in my life. I don't know what Don Dickson was doing, but he did not come to work for me. We kept on going, kept on going, and all of a sudden, as the old saying goes, the shit hit the fan.

20

We were enjoying soliciting to sell prearranged funerals, the key word being "solicitation." The law was ambiguously written about that. A sheriff came to my home one evening. The eight of us were there sitting around the table in the dining room, the six kids and Betty and me. I knew him, he'd been a sheriff for quite a few years, and he served a warrant on me to cease and desist from solicitation of preneed funerals. He said, "Dan, have you got guys out in the field?" I said, "Yes, I do." He said, "You have got to get them off the street," so I said, "I'll go get them." Well, I didn't know where they were right then and I didn't care to. The next morning at the sales meeting I said, "Fellows, you're out of work."

Dave Linge had a houseboat, and belonged to a country club. He took my eight salespeople and had them all playing golf a couple days a week, and also had them down in his houseboat at the lake in Iowa City. We were keeping them occupied. They weren't on salary or anything so Dave and I decided we'd pay them one hundred fifty bucks a week until we got the lawsuit settled.

The court date came up and we went to Grinnell, Iowa, the home for Maytag in Central Iowa then. We went there for our district court hearing, and lost, so we appealed to the Supreme Court. We got on the docket for St. Patrick's Day the following year.

We couldn't resolve our case, and we couldn't settle, so we were out of business. We decided to take the guys that we had and start selling lawn crypts, which I'd never heard of, and Dave was the first one in the state of Iowa to sell them. We took the sales people and put together kit books, and trained them how to sell a lawn crypt. Well, they didn't like that at all. That was a lot different of a sale, trust me; knocking on doors, going after and selling cemetery property is five times harder than selling a preneed funeral.

In the meantime Dave Coates had vacated because he said he couldn't exist on $150 a week. He had six kids at home, and next thing I know Dave Coates was in St. Louis with a huge cemetery there, and he was going to sell mausoleum crypts. And, he took my sales force except two men who didn't want to move their families to St. Louis.

I was left with two salesmen, and they were the weakest of the bunch, Dave took my sales force, moved his family, and went to work for a company that was owned by Cliff Zell called Valhalla. So, we have no sales force, no promises for getting anything done, we're waiting to go to court, and Betty's on pins and needles.

We'd been making good money, and I mean good money. And we'd been at that for well over a year. The first year there with Dave Linge I made $78,000. Now that's in 1965, and that was a ton of money. My sales people were making between $50-60,000 a year. That kid Ron Heldt that had been driving a flower truck, he even bought four new cars in one year, and he kept upgrading and finally at the age of nineteen he owned a Lincoln outright. He had a girlfriend in Oelwein, Iowa, his hometown. Years later, he moved to Colorado and had a bunch of kids, and got into a wholesale dealership and ultimately became a millionaire who had two airplanes, and all kinds of cars. He was a good kid, as honest as could be.

I had always subscribed to Playboy Magazine; I always hid it so the boys wouldn't find it. Playboy would always do an article on how movies were made, and in one issue they had one about how they made a pirate type movie in the Caribbean that was out at that time. There was some advertising going along with it, and there was an ad to come to the Caribbean and sail. You could lease or charter sailboats, different sizes, different voyages, and different lengths of time, and so on.

I always gave Dave Linge my Playboys to read. One day Dave called me to his office, and said, "I was going through this magazine and what would you think if we went together at our own expense and did a cruise in the Caribbean? I said, "I think it'd be great." He also said, "Well, I'm thinking it would be a little pricy." He and his friend Bob Kabrick owned a cemetery down in Clinton, a small town on the Mississippi River in eastern Iowa. Dave called Bob and told him about this, and he said, "Yeah, that sounds like it will be fun." The six of us went together and chartered a 62-foot Ketch, two-master. We were to fly in to Antigua, get on the ship, and sail from there to Grenada, then fly back to Barbados and then back to Cedar Rapids.

We had our tickets all lined up, and we flew into Antigua, and stayed there a night. We got on the ship the next day, and we started sailing for seven days. Our cost per couple was $400, or $200 a person, and that included the trip and all the food, but it did not include the booze so we went together and stocked up on booze, and took it on board the ship. It so happened that Dave and Bob were both Scotch drinkers, so it worked well for me. We got vodka for gimlets, which the women wanted.

We took off and we sailed past the Pitons. All these people were bridge players, but I was not; I never played bridge and still don't. They were playing bridge as we were sailing past the world famous Pitons on the south end of Saint Lucia, and I said to them, "You guys are missing all the scenery here!" Everybody just kept playing bridge, and missed all that beauty. We started in Antigua, then to Saint Lucia, and then we went down to Saint Kitts and picked up our chef, a black French chef, and boy was he good, he could just cook anything. We'd catch fish, and he'd make that up. He'd make tuna salad for lunch, and we had steaks in there, too. It was fabulous. We were king of the world. There were three people staffing the ship. The captain was from England, his first mate was from Switzerland, and his wife who was a Miss Player Cigarette champion of the world; Player was the big cigarette in England. It seemed liked she changed bikinis on the hour; she wore bikinis the entire trip.

We got into Grenada, which was the end of the tour. In the meantime, we had raced another ship all day long from some little island in that whole string of islands in the Caribbean. We stopped on the island and we went up on the shore. There was a Scottish guy who owned a ranch there, and he took us in as he did all the tourists passing through. He had a beautiful, beautiful home, and he served us goat. We didn't think goat was going to be very good, but it was delicious.

So, in Grenada, after racing all day long, we got stuck on a damn sand bar taking a shortcut, and so there we were. We couldn't get the quarantine flag down. It's a yellow flag, and it's got to come down every time you go through customs so then you can go on shore. But we were stuck out there in that sand bar until the tide came back in the next morning. We decided to drink, and we were about out of ice, but we decided to just party and stay on board.

Well, after a night of drinking, everybody had gone to bed, and Dave and I were up on the deck. It was a dark night, there was no moon. I couldn't see him because it was so dark. He was smoking his pipe, sitting in a deck chair across from me, we were drinking Drambuie and had two or three of them. Dave said, "Dan, there is something that I just really respect and admire about you." And, I said, "Tell me what that is." He said, "It's your infallibility, not swerving from whatever it is that you are going to do. You just have so much tenacity, I never saw a person with the tenacity you've got." I said, "Well, I guess so." He said, "Well, let me tell you. I'm envious of you. I'm jealous of you, and I'll tell you why. I'll tell you a story."

He said, "I own a big ranch out on the western slope in Colorado. I got about one hundred fifty registered Black Angus on the western slope. Well, a couple of years ago they got diseased and started dying like crazy. I lost two thirds of the herd. I was pretty morose over it because I lost a lot of money. Come tax time, with all the other incomes I had..." (he had other numerous incomes besides the cemetery and the ranch, he owned a lot of land in Cedar Rapids, and sold all the property out, got a good lease out of it all) "...I did it as a write off, and it saved me money. Everything I touch turns to gold. Everything I touch."

He then said, "You are just the opposite. This is the first time you really ever made any good money in your life." I said, "That's true." He says, "You had your best friend steal your sales force. You didn't say anything about him, you just went about recruiting, started hiring, started rebuilding. You take knock after knock, and we've got this case coming up in the Supreme Court, we don't know how we are going to do." He said again, "I just admire your tenacity." Well, I thought that was a really, really great approval from a superior of mine, and a trusted good friend.

Many years later I was in Milwaukee, Wisconsin and heading to Seattle and I called in to check my phone calls. Betty said I got a call from Dave and was supposed to call him in Iowa City, so from a phone booth at Mitchell Field in Milwaukee I called him. He said, "Dan, I've got the big C." He said, "I'm not coming out of this hospital alive. I doubt if I'll be here another week. I want you to come to Cedar Memorial and run it. I got an idiot wife that's an alcoholic, I got sons that are incompetent, and you're the only one I trust to run that. I want you to come and be president and run it." So, before I get into that story, he did lose, he lost just one time and it was a big one, and that was good of him to say all that to me.

So, we're in Grenada, we've been drinking all evening, and Dave went to bed. We were maybe a hundred yards out from the town. The music was playing and people were out milling around on the sidewalks, and I thought, "Hell, I'm going over there."

So I climbed down off the boat and I got into a little Tender which was tied on the boat, and I rowed and rowed and rowed some more, and I had gone nowhere. I had forgotten about the damn rope that was tied to the back of the boat, as I was smashed! I unhooked it, and I finally rowed over there, and there is a big wall about five feet high up above me. I get ready to pull myself up the wall because I'm going to go have myself a nice time, have some drinks, and do some dancing or whatever. Just as I put my fingers up on that wall there were two really shiny pair of black shoes looking at me. I looked up and there were khakis and I look up further and there was a guy standing up there with his arms folded. He said, "Hey mon, where are you going?" I looked at him, I looked at his shoes. I said, "I'm going right back to that boat." I got back in the Tender and I rowed back to the boat. And that was my Grenada experience.

It got worse the next day. We were to fly out of Grenada, and there were hardly any hotels there. Grenada had a little airport out in the country up on top on the hill, and it had no windows, no doors. A commercial airplane came in once a day and then took off to Barbados. We all had tickets for that plane to go to Barbados. We took the van ride out there, lurching around all of those terrible roads. The six of us got our luggage, we go to check in at an outdoor counter, and the booking agent said, "We have two seats left in this plane, it's oversold." We looked at each other and said, "What do you mean oversold? We've had our tickets forever." He just said, "Two people from your party can go on this plane, period. You decide who it is."

Dave had to be back to meet with his attorneys to be ready for the court hearing, so we immediately agreed that he and Audrey should be the ones to get on the plane. They take off, everybody leaves the airport, all the cabs leave, everything, and we are sitting out there in this big block building about twenty-four by twenty-four feet with a table in the middle of it looking at each other and wondering what are we going to now. There is no hotel so how are we going to sleep out here?

About that time, a plane comes circling in, comes down and makes a landing. It's a single engine monoplane, and it says "Jimmy's Weather Flying Service, Waco, Texas" on the sides. I look at Bob, Bob looks at me, and we were running out there before that plane's engine shut down at the end of the runway. When he taxied it in we were there and ready to talk to the pilot. He turned and said, "Hi fellas." We said, "Hi, are you Jimmy?" He said, "That's me." We said, "Jimmy, we need your help." He said, "Well, what can I do?" We told him our story. He said, "Well, I came down here to pick up Susan Hayward," a very accomplished movie actress at the time. He said, "Tomorrow morning I got to take her to Barbados." I said, "Can you run us up to Barbados? We'll pay you for it, and then come back?" He said, "Well, there could be a problem with that. There is a big storm coming up. I think I can get you there but I don't know if I can get back tonight or not... but, okay, I'll take you guys." We throw our suitcases in the plane, the four of us get in, Bob sat up by Jimmy, and we take off for Barbados, which is about 300-350 miles away.

We went through a huge weather front, but it wasn't a storm, thank God, we land at the airport and he said, "Guys, I have got to get turned around right now and get out of here." We paid him $100 each, got our suitcases, walked into the airport, and we see Dave and Audrey coming up through the main course. So we just locked arms, and we are talking like we didn't even know that they were there. They stopped, their jaws had dropped, and they couldn't figure out how in the world we got to Barbados at the same time they did.

We got back to Cedar Rapids and in March we had our Supreme Court hearing at the capitol in Des Moines. We lost that case, and it wasn't even close. We lost it, and we were out of business.

The N.F.D.A., the National Funeral Directors Association, was 30,000-some strong and had come in as a friend of the court on behalf of the Iowa state funeral directors. They brought in one of the top attorneys in the United States who was a relative of General Mark Clark, as his name was also Clark, and Howard Raether, who had ruled the N.F.D.A. with an iron fist for about thirty years, a very bombastic guy from Milwaukee, Wisconsin where they were headquartered. He stood on the state capitol steps and shook his fist in my face and said, "We're going to run your kind out of our business, we're going to run you out. You're not going to stand a prayer."

At that time, there were seven states in the U.S. where it was legal to sell preneed funerals. In all the rest it was illegal. The key word was "solicitation," and if you couldn't solicit to sell preneed funerals you were out of business. You could sell preneed funerals, but you couldn't solicit to sell them. That meant a very passive funeral director would sit in a funeral home and hope that people would walk in to buy a funeral. Well, that was nowhere.

I set out to change that over a period of years. I fought for prearranged funerals in state capitols and hearings in similar type cases. We won some, lost some, but I became a special expert witness. I didn't get paid, but I was doing it because I loved it. I loved the concept of people having a choice on how they arrange their funerals.

I went back and continued to do what I was doing, which wasn't very much, and I got call from a guy in Kansas City, Missouri. With that big court case in Iowa, my picture and name was splattered all over every trade magazine in the industry, I was either a hero or a culprit based on whether you were in the cemetery business or whether you were in the funeral home business because the two were sharply divided in ideology.

I had become a very well known figure, and in Missouri, one of the states where it was legal to sell preneed funerals, they were being sold all over the state. They were sold in the form of a trust, a preneed funeral trust, and by law you had to trust 80% of the money. In Iowa, David Linge had trusted a 100% of the money because that's what the law called for there, and he had paid me because he had deep pockets, he paid the whole sales organization out of Cedar Memorial. In Missouri, the trust files were 80/20 instead of a hundred and nothing.

A fellow by the name of Garnet Waddell, who was the president of Mt. Moriah Cemetery in south Kansas City, a cemetery and a funeral home, called me and he wanted to know if I would come see him, that he'd like to talk to me about coming to work with him, and he would pay my expenses to come down there. I told Dave Linge about this when we were at dinner with Audrey, and she said, "Oh no! I don't want you going down there. They're trying to steal you away from us." Dave said, "Well, that's what goes on in the business," and she said, "I just don't like it." I was above board in telling Dave this, and flew to Kansas City and met with Garnet and his wife Betty.

Garnet had had a person who was very well known in the industry, Frank Karnes, who owned cemeteries and did contracting for sales with various cemeteries; he did consulting, and also sold preneed funerals. He also had a fellow, Dick Link, who was his sales manager, and somehow the two got crosswise with Garnet and they left. They moved up the street about twenty blocks to a cemetery called Forest Hill and started selling preneed cemetery property there, which they were very good at.

When I met with Garnet, he made me a proposal about selling preneed funerals and being the cemetery sales manager. He had eight sales people that didn't go with Frank Karnes and company. They stayed at Mt. Moriah because it was a good cemetery and a good funeral home to represent. I decided to leave Cedar Memorial and Cedar Rapids, and go to Kansas City.

21.

In 1969 I moved to Kansas City, got an apartment, and went to work for Mt. Moriah Funeral Home and Cemetery. I hired some sales people, and my management style was different than what they were used to. I was a very strong manager, very, very strong in my ways and my methods. We had sales meetings every morning, which they weren't used to, and they were very structured.

Garnet wanted me to start selling lawn crypts as I'd done in Cedar Rapids although they had never been sold in the state of Missouri. We carved out one of the nicest areas in the cemetery, and it was mine to sell for lawn crypts. I put together a lawn crypt package, a lawn crypt presentation, I trained all the guys, started recruiting and hiring, and we all went out and sold them and preneed funerals.

We didn't have the luxury of using the files at Mt. Moriah like I did at Cedar Memorial because they'd been exhausted by then. We door knocked and I became known as "Door-knocking Dan." Now that I was selling preneed funerals and preneed lawn crypts, I started making the news in the trade magazines that I now worked for Mt. Moriah. This really put me on the map for sales more so than Iowa had. It really gave me quite a bit of name recognition because it was a very prestigious cemetery, not that Cedar Memorial wasn't, but this was even larger and in a bigger market.

I recruited three of the salespeople that were with me in Cedar Rapids, and they moved with me to Kansas City, so that was a tribute to me also. We did pretty well. We worked hard, and played hard. We kept knocking on doors, and I started getting on national programs, sales management seminars, was doing a lot of public speaking and things were going along well. We did very well for a number of years in Kansas City.

While I was in Kansas City, I had started something that went nationwide and then was in existence all over the U.S., but at the time, nobody was doing it. It's a strange story and it comes full circle later in the story with the Loewen Group in Modesto, California.

In Kansas City, my offices were in the basement of the administrative offices, at the top of the hill while the funeral home was down on the main street, Holmes Road; we had two cemeteries and two funeral homes. When you came past the funeral home, you went up the hill and then you went down a long, sloping hill, and all that area was the cemetery. One day I was in the office writing a new ad, trying to bring business into the cemetery for my salespeople, and I kept hearing 'whiz... whiz... whiz... whiz...' There were cars going by the office, and after a while it got to be annoying.

I went up through the administrative offices and went out the door, and there were all these cars lined up coming into the cemetery, past the funeral home, down over the hill, filling every road in that cemetery with cars: It was a huge funeral for one our state senators. I looked at that dumbfounded. After the service was over, the slow 'whiz... whiz... whiz... whiz...' started again. It took them forty-five minutes to empty that cemetery, that's how big the funeral was.

About that time, the manager of the funeral home came up the hill. His name was Jack Farmer, from West Virginia, a short guy who wore beautiful, expensive ties all the time, and he always gave me his ties for some reason. I said, "What in the world is going on, you've got a huge funeral." He looked at me and said, "You damn preneeders, you never know what's going on around the funeral homes and cemetery. All you do is make sales." I said, "That's right, that's my job." He said, "We just had a funeral for so and so," and I said, "Oh, I didn't know that" as I didn't read the obituaries.

I went back to my office and sat down, and I said to myself, 'You dummy, here you are writing another ad to put in the papers, spending your money to get leads, when all those leads that you are wanting are here at the cemetery and they are leaving! They were here, and you didn't even reach out and touch them!'

That hit me, it really hit me, and that's the reason family services came into existence. I am going tell you about family services, because it's a very important part of my life and the lives of others, many others, to this day.

I put my thinking cap on for a few days, and I went to talk to Garnet as we always met for breakfast on Tuesdays. I said, "Garnet, I've got this idea for marketing, and I want to run it past you and get your approval on it." I told him what it was, and he looked at me and said, "I never heard of that."

I said, "No, nobody else has either." He said, "Well, I am a little skittish about it," and I asked why. He said, "Because I am concerned that what you are suggesting will upset some of our families that we're doing services for at the funeral home." I said, "No, no, I assure you I am going hire only women, and these women are going to serve those families, they are going to serve the way I want them to."

He said, "Okay, I'll give you authority to do it. Just give me time to tell Jack (Farmer) about it, and, Dan, if my phone lights up from getting calls about people upset with what you are doing, it stops, do you understand?" I said, "Yes, sir, I do." He gave me the green light I needed to put my program in place.

I hired four women and trained them to sell prearranged funerals and preneed cemetery property, although I knew primarily they would sell prearranged funerals. These four women were all middle-aged, they'd all been in sales or marketing, and they got the opportunity to come to work for a brand new program at Mt. Moriah, which had a tremendously good profile in the Kansas City market, namely because of the marketing that I'd done.

What I did next was overkill. I went downtown and bought dozens and dozens and dozens of plastic-wrapped cups. I had those cups imprinted in green on white with "Mt. Moriah Funeral Home." I also bought about ten five-gallon coffeemakers, and two pounds of coffee for each one. We had a closet reeking of coffee, full of coffeemakers, and all these cups, and here is the way the plan went into action: When people came in to make their arrangements - and remember, we were doing over six hundred funerals a year at that time at Mt. Moriah (and were trying to crack that hundred mark in North Kansas City) - and when the funeral directors were nearly done, they called the office at the cemetery, and one of the women would come down and meet the family. They would then grab one of those coffeemakers with the two pounds of coffee in it and a bunch of cups and carry them to the family's car, put them in the trunk, and say, "This is compliments of Mt. Moriah, it's part of our service so you have coffee for all the people who are coming to your home for the next few days. After about five or six days, I'll come by and pick it back up."

I thought that was pretty clever! And guess what: it worked. When they stopped back out to pick up the coffee pot, they made an appointment with the family to come back in the near future at their convenience to help them arrange their funerals. And with their families with them, brothers, sisters, parents, children, whatever... It was unbelievable.

The amount of excitement that this created with these women resulted in everybody wanting to work in the family service department, but I locked them out, I kept it to four as four could handle it. They were on a rotating basis and would be in the family service office two at a time and on days they weren't there they would be out in the field selling. It was "do-wah-ditty." We just sold a ton, and the women were all over me, they were crazy about me because they were making hellishly good money. I could see that I had really opened up a Pandora's box.

About that time I went to a Toppers networking meeting, and there was a new program that was just beginning to run across the U.S. called the Veterans Program. Dick Herbert, from Clemson, South Carolina, was instrumental in making the Veterans Program work. His sales manager, Chuck Gaudreau, from Virginia, had come up with the idea: A veteran would get a free space in our cemetery and then his wife would purchase an additional space, or we gave his space away, and we sold the other space, and then we would sell lawn crypts; of course we give them credit for space in the lawn crypt or if we were selling spaces side by side, we would then sell them a companion bronze marker.

So, I went to the Toppers meeting and introduced my family services program, and I tell you what, you could hear a pin drop by the time I was done. These Toppers, all marketing and sales guys, just jumped out of their chairs. Dick Herbert said, "Danny, Danny, you have got to come to Clemson and see me. I want you to introduce this program to us. In exchange for it, I'll give you our Veteran's Program, everything we are doing on it." So we made a trade. I got the Veterans Program, he got the family services program, and it was wonderful for both of us.

Our family services became the standard in the industry for sales and lead procurement. It worked marvelously well, and is a mainstay for most cemeteries and funeral homes today.

I began to become active in the association work, and we really expanded the sales force so much that we didn't have enough space at the cemetery, where I was working in the basement. It seemed like I was always in a basement!

I moved my offices to Troost Avenue, which was about fifteen blocks away, and I rented a big office there. It was a nice space, and I hired more women to work in the office. I had a contract there, they didn't provide me with anything, I had to do everything myself, but I had a good contract and was getting fifteen percent on trust sales, and thirty-five percent on cemetery sales, and then I had to pay my salespeople, the sales managers, my office help and all. I was growing a company and becoming more and more well known in association work speaking at conventions.

We did real well in Kansas City, just really well, so well that after a few years Garnet decided that we should build a new cemetery and a new funeral home on the north side of Kansas City, up where the big new airport was being built.

We went out there and searched for land and found it. During that period of time, Dave Coates was at the state meeting at Lake of the Ozarks, Missouri because he was working for Valhalla. He and his wife wanted to have dinner with us, and I said, "No, Dave." That was the first time I'd talked to him in a long time, and I said, "Dave I'm not interested." And, he said, "Dan, we need to sit down and talk. Don't be like that, don't be bull-headed. I made a mistake," and again he said, "We need to talk."

I talked to Betty about it, and she thought maybe we should meet with him, so we all went to dinner. He sat there and begged for forgiveness for what he did to me, for stealing my sales organization. It was the second time in my life I'd had somebody beg for forgiveness.

The first time I refused him and it made me sort of sick, and the second time I decided I wouldn't, so over our steak dinner we shook hands, became friends again, and I said, "Now, if that's behind us, when things go to hell at Valhalla, and they will, come back with me to Kansas City." He said, "I'll do it in a heartbeat. I won't wait for things to go to hell, I'll come back." So he came back to work with me, and he brought Don Dixon, so there were the three Ds, together again.

22

I was building a big organization. I put an ad in the paper for a sales manager for the new cemetery and funeral home, and I got a fellow named Jerry Roberts, from Ohio. We had grown so much that I couldn't fit in my offices on Troost anymore, so I moved downtown to Union Station, which is huge, and leased the east half of the second floor for two dollars per square foot. Oddly, Union Station wouldn't give me any longer than a monthly lease even though they didn't have anything to do with the building because the trains were hardly coming in anymore.

Half of the sales group would come from the north and half would come from the south, and there we were in central Kansas City. We were in these huge offices upstairs, big old-fashioned railroad offices, and they were done up first class. They had big doors on them, and there were six small offices adjacent to one another on one side of the hall. When you came to the top of the marble stairs you walked in and there were all my office women, the 'ladies forum.' They had big windows looking out on South Main Street across to the World War One Monument with the Indian up on top of the hill.

There was a restaurant down below called Ralph Gaines, a very prestigious restaurant with a big business lunch and dinner business. I had quite a large office, and there was an office next to me that Dave Coates and Jerry Roberts shared. On the eastern side of the hall was an office, which went the width of the building and it was big and could hold fifty or sixty people, which it did every Friday when we had a meeting. The managers held their meetings daily during the week. I didn't do that anymore because I had gotten into consulting.

From a marketing standpoint in the cemetery funeral business, I owned the Kansas City market. If somebody would come to town to try and start a sales organization, I would give all my people bonuses, I'd put a contest up, and I'd have them going all around and knocking on doors for a month. People would come in and say, "Boy this place is sold out. Dan Reed has got everything covered," so that was my marketing scheme, and it worked.

I'd made such a good name that I was travelling the U.S. and consulting with cemeteries and funeral homes all over. I started a separate arm of my contract with Mt. Moriah, called Midwestern Cemetery Consultants, a consulting firm that was strong on marketing. I had contracts all over the U.S. and it just kept getting bigger and bigger and bigger. All the educational years had paid off handsomely for me.

One time at Union Station a guy came in and introduced himself as Dick Gardner, the President of the National Association of Sales Education (N.A.S.E.). He was promoting himself and nationally known speakers that put on one-day seminars all over the U.S. I invited Dick to come back on a Friday to do a meeting for us, and it was excellent. He did a reading of Dr. Seuss as part of the program, and all our people, including me, were really impressed. I told him I would like to use his presentation and he had no problem with that.

At that time in my career I was involved in numerous seminars nationally. I bought the book, "Green Eggs and Ham" by Dr. Seuss, and found a t-shirt with "Sam I Am" printed on it, and added wearing it to my repertoire. It was a huge success because I married it to the psychology of closing sales. Being the big ham I admittedly am, the crowds really liked it since the book was popular. I went to a studio in Kansas City and made an audio cassette and sold a lot of them nationally. The A.C.A. had a sales management seminar in Atlanta and I was the main speaker for one day. I did my "Green Eggs and Ham" along with my baseball analogy of managing a sale and handling objections, and I got a standing ovation, which was a first for an A.C.A. sales management seminar.

I flew back to Kansas City after a great day in Atlanta and got to an Italian restaurant downtown for the big dinner the evening before my daughter Celine's and husband-to-be Dan's wedding. All of Dan's relatives from Chicago were there, and it was a great evening. Dan was managing the Playboy Club in Kansas City and was just a great guy. I loved him then and still do to this day. They had a nice service in a Catholic church and started living close to us in a little house in Grandview.

A few years later Celine and Dan bought a farm in Raytown. They did a lot of work on the old farmhouse and made it really modern. Then along came a son, Daniel, my first grandson. A couple of years later, they had a daughter, Celine, my first

116

granddaughter. I really regret I didn't see more of them. I was living close by and could have and should have done better. I did go see "Cee Cee" play soccer, and she was really good!

To jump way ahead, and give away some of the plot lines, if you will, many years later, after getting divorced from Betty and when I was living in Seattle and dating a woman named Sherry, there was a big Navy Day Celebration, with a parade, lots of ships and so on. I had talked to Celine and Dan about it, and they decided to take a vacation and bring the kids to see it. We all had a great time. We went over to the ocean and spent the day picnicking and swimming. That was the first time the kids met Sherry. Now, Celine is very inquisitive and she learned some things in conversation with Sherry that put Celine on guard. I had felt the time spent in Washington with Sherry was good, but I should have learned more about women's intuition and listened a bit more closely. I respected Celine's then and still respect her wisdom about many things in life.

Also many years later (and to add a new plot line), Pat and I went to Cee Cee's graduation from Central Missouri State in Warrensburg. She was an honor student, inherited the inquisitive traits from her mother, and good judgment from her dad. After Pat and I got together, she pushed me to visit Raytown more often and see my family. Cee Cee and I became very close, and still are to this day. Daniel had a stellar career in the Navy, but unfortunately we grew apart due to a number of factors.

Back to N.A.S.E., Dick Gardner and I had become very good friends socially as he lived nearby in Mission, Kansas. He called me about a year later to tell me of an upcoming seminar in Kansas City. I put up a contest with my people to go see Zig Ziglar, the motivational speaker and author of the best-selling book "See You at the Top." (Most of them won, as I expected.) I had never met Zig, and really looked forward to hearing him. About a week before the seminar, Dick called me to make sure I was going. The seminar was to be all day long at Roe Bartle Hall.

The whole time I was in K.C. I was an avid, and I mean a very avid Chiefs' football fan. Their teams were having a good amount of success. The day of the seminar, Dick came out to the audience to take me backstage to meet Zig personally. That was a great experience! He also introduced me to Willie Lanier, a middle linebacker for the Chiefs, and wow, that was another great experience.

During a break in the seminar, Dick announced that I was the Kansas City Sales Executive of the Year! There were people in the audience from all over the Midwest - Omaha, Tulsa, Little Rock, St. Louis - and it was quite a large crowd. All of that added quite a bit of flavor to my year. My good pal Dick Gardner sure surprised the hell out of me!

That should be the end of that story, but there are two more endings. Dick loved old classic cars and he had gone to California and bought a collector car from Dean Martin. Two weeks later, Dick was killed when that car hit a tree in south K.C. That was tragic, as he was only in his forties. Years later, I had Zig Ziglar come to Portland, Oregon to do a seminar for my western division of the Loewen Group. As usual, I ran a month's contest and the winners got to meet Zig personally and receive an autographed photo with him. I also had my sales managers and me in photos with Zig, which he signed. Unfortunately, a few years later one of the greatest motivational speakers of all time passed away from dementia and Alzheimer's. .

23.

I started working in Kansas City in 1969, and was there for twelve years. In 1970 Betty and I bought a home there, a big, long home out in the country but still in the city limits, on ten acres, and it had a full basement underneath it. I contracted carpenters to wall off the basement, stucco it, and we made a nightclub out of it with dim lights and a big bar. I could sit twelve people on my bar and I stocked it with booze and everything needed; I didn't know until years later that my kids were drinking all the time down there! I had a fireplace and a big TV set.

Upstairs there were four bedrooms, a sunken formal dining room, another family room with a fireplace in it, and a big kitchen and dining room adjacent to it where we could seat eight people. We really made it a nice place. We had a big fireplace out in the back yard. Once a year at my company picnic I would barbeque a whole hog. We would have about ninety people every year, and it was quite a time. Betty always had a big garden, and the girls had a barn and some horses.

One time a snake had gotten in the house somehow and had a bunch of babies, and we had snakes crawling all over. They were only black snakes, thank goodness, but they would be down in that deep pile rug in the basement, and they were little bitty devils. One morning, Betty's daughter, Cindy, opened up the kitchen closet to get some cereal and there were two snakes up there. It scared the daylights out of all of us. So they were crawling around the floor and the ceiling and everywhere. We got an exterminator to come in and I think they killed a dozen small snakes and never did find the mother.

We lived next door to Bob Johnson, who was well known in Kansas City. Bob represented a catalogue company and sold all kinds of stuff. He was a good salesman and he did a lot of entertaining. He had five acres and a big home. He also was known because he rode the horse with war paint at all the Kansas City Chiefs games. He got me involved with Chiefs games, so I bought season tickets for Betty and me, and we went to the Chiefs games starting in 1969 and '70. They had good teams, really good teams, and we got to see them play at the old municipal stadium at 22nd and Brooklyn.

In '70 and '71 the Chiefs decided to build a big stadium called Arrowhead. If you had season tickets at the old stadium you got first dibs on seating preferences in the new stadium. When they got the stadium built up far enough to where you could see where the seats were, I went there to walk through it with a guide. I picked my seats, front row in what they called The Golden Circle which is still there to this day. The seats were on about the twenty-five yard line and were just excellent, excellent seats. I watched some great games, and never missed one in twelve years. I saw some great teams, and some lousy teams. I sat through horrible weather and nice weather, but I never missed a game.

I also got season tickets for the Royals when they built their new stadium, Kauffman Stadium, which opened up adjacent to Arrowhead. I shared those with two other couples for about ten years, so we'd go to about every third game.

Because I was an avid fan, a lot of the Chiefs used to come to my house on Saturdays during the off-season, and they would play golf on a course that my neighbor and I put up. One of the Chiefs wound up instructing my son: Emmitt Thomas, an NFL Hall of Famer, taught Mark how to play safety.

One time we were all talking about racquetball; none of them played. And they said to me, "You ought to play Hank Stram" Hank was the coach that took the Chiefs to the Superbowl twice. I said, "Is he a racquetball player?" They said, "Oh, he's an avid racquetball player. We've got two racquetball courts down at Arrowhead." I think it was Freddie Arbanas who said, "I'll line you up for a game with him." And so, he did, and I did and we did, and I played Hank Stram in three games of racquetball, and he beat me in all three.

Hank had been a tremendous athlete at Indiana University. He had lettered in numerous sports, was possibly a five-letter student athlete. And here is something I will not forget: When you're playing racquetball, the secret is holding mid-court. You stand in the middle of both sides and in the middle of both ends because wherever that ball goes, you're in a better position to get to it. So I was crowding the middle of the court, and Hank didn't like that, so, man, he hit a screamer right up in there and it hit me right in the kidneys. I mean it left a black and blue mark the size of that racquetball for about three weeks. I turned around and looked at him, and he just turned and looked at me and said, "If you want the mid court, that's what you get." I didn't give up the mid court, but I got a lot of shots in the back that day.

Going back to my office in Union Station, six small offices held six divisional managers, and I got a bright idea one time. I don't know where, but I found a monkey for sale and I brought the monkey into the office in a cage. The women all started screaming and hollering. I sat that monkey down in my office, and I brought in my two sales managers, Dave and Jerry. I said, "Now guys, you've got divisional managers and they've each got an office. I am giving you this monkey and at the end of the first week whichever divisional manager is lowest on the ladder on production has to feed and take care of this monkey for a week. If they want to get rid of it they need to get off the bottom."

Well, that created mayhem, I'll tell you. There was that monkey in one of those six offices and everybody was trying to get rid of it, because whatever you feed a monkey you then have to clean up later, and they left a smell on things in a room. You would walk into one of those offices, and my God, the odor just hit you. The women just hated that monkey.

The end of the story is that one day somehow that damn monkey got out of its cage and had come out to the area where we had floor to ceiling windows. They were fifteen, eighteen feet high, all draped. That monkey got up in those drapes and pulled all those drapes down. The office women were screaming and hollering, and they ran and opened the door, and the monkey ran out, down the steps and into the restaurant.

The restaurant manager didn't know where that monkey had come from, and he ran to open the door, and that monkey hopped right out of there. The last we ever saw of that monkey it was going up Main Street just chirping and hollering. The monkey was gone and everybody was elated, but that was one way I motivated salespeople to get the monkey off their backs.

I had my own newspaper in which we told stories about the staff's families with pictures. I had my own TV room, because if you came to work with me, you had to be able to give an acceptable presentation on videotape before you could go out in the field. Most people hated that. Some people would walk out when they were told that, but we built a dynamic sales force and were selling all over the Kansas City area and we did really well. I built my marketing company, took on contracts, and things went well.

I went to a convention in Hannibal, Missouri one time. The World Series was on and Cincinnati was playing Detroit. I was sitting there having a drink and talking to bunch of guys that I knew in the business in the state, and Fred Newman was among them. He was always so proud of me. He was president of the State Convention one time, and he had me speak for him, do presentations, and he raved about me, what a great sales man I was, and I so always got my ego fed pretty well by him.

A guy comes up to me and said, "Dan I'd like to talk to you when you have time, would you mind?" I said, "Sure, I'll take time right now" so I got up and we move over to a table. He introduced himself, said his name is Monte Lamontagne, lived in Leavenworth, Kansas and had a little cemetery he started over there on his own, about seven acres. He was doing well with it, but he and his wife wanted to retire. They were just tired. He did all the grave openings and closings, he did the sales and maintenance of the cemetery. His wife did the bookkeeping, and they lived in a house trailer on the cemetery. He wanted to sell it, so I said, "Well, I'll come look at it."

I went over to see it, it was just a little cemetery, and so I asked, "How much do you want for it?" He says, "I'll take $25,000 cash." I said, "I'll have a check for you within the week." And so, I became a cemeterian, and for the first time I owned a cemetery.

I went back to Iowa, and I got hold of a guy who had been a really good salesman for me named Cy Christiansen. Not only was he a good salesman, he also was a tremendous piano player and he played piano at the Hotel Roosevelt restaurant in downtown Cedar Rapids every Saturday night. Cy's wife's name was Jeanne, and they had six or seven kids, though most were out of school and had graduated from Regis High School. I called him and said, "I got a proposition for you. You always did a pretty good job selling lawn crypts. I bought a cemetery and I would like to make you a partner in it. I'll move your family to Leavenworth, Kansas, but you're going to have to get your own housing. I'll get you a membership in a country club there, and you'll become my partner. Every year that you produce a hundred sales, you get 10% of the stock of the company, and you become a 10% owner. Then you can become a 20% owner, and in five years you'll be at 50%. We would have an agreement that's called a 'put and take' agreement. When you become 50% owner, we will make an offer for the remaining stock. What we'll offer is you put or you take, you don't negotiate. So if you say, "I'll offer the stock for five dollars, you have to either sell it or you have to take it, so we drew up a contract towards that effect. They moved to Leavenworth, and I'd go over occasionally and try to play golf with him, which was a farce, but he did his job, and he did a good job there for five years.

At the end of five years, I said to Cy, "Well we've got a contract coming up on the stock. It's a put and take position. Do you want to mention the stock value or do you want me to do it?" He said, "I'll do it." He mentioned the stock value and he had no choice. He would either take it or I had to sell it. He gave the figures for the stock and they were reasonable, so I said, "Okay Cy, you can have a job with me over in Kansas City. I'm buying your stock." He was a little flustered because he really wanted that cemetery, but he said, "Okay, that was our deal" and I bought the cemetery. He came to work with me in Kansas City over on the north side as it was across the river from Leavenworth.

I got a guy that had been mowing and maintaining the cemeteries for Newcomers in Kansas City to come and manage that cemetery for me. Newcomers owned six or seven cemeteries, and Duayne Huitt was working at one of them one evening at about 6:00 o'clock, a half a mile from my home. Cemeteries are hot in summertime when you're mowing. I took him a six pack of beer, and I said, "Here, have a beer with me." He said, "Okay," and shut the mower off, and got down off the tractor, sweating profusely. I said, "I got a job offer for you." He said, "What's that?" I said, "I'd like to make you manager of my cemetery in Leavenworth. You manage it, you run it, I'll get a sales force over there and you can manage them." He said, "I don't like selling, Dan," and I said, "I know, but I'll pay you a good salary and you can manage the cemetery. We've been selling lawn crypts, and I've got a sales force, though it's not very big, just three or four sales people." He said, "Okay, I'll come to work for you." He gave his notice and came to work for me, and worked for a couple or three years.

During that period of time, the advertising firm that I had created for making video systems about selling all over the U.S. came to me and said that they had a deal that they thought was pretty good. It was called "Green Up" and it would fit into the cemetery business: Because we've got trucks and equipment, why not go out and maintain people's yards? Well, that was the beginning of another business.

We named the company Beauty Up, and I bought a brand new truck, put the name on the back, got all kinds of equipment and pesticides and insecticides. I hired two really good-looking, gorgeous gals, one was a blonde, the other was a redhead. I put them in polka dot tops and short skirts, and they went out and knocked doors. I paid them a salary, and I paid them a bonus for every customer they got, so they went out and knocked every door in and around Leavenworth. They built a customer base of nearly two hundred customers who wanted their lawn sprayed; we didn't mow. Duayne Huitt managed it, and I made him a partner in that company.

All of this was going really well, and a guy came to me who owned a whole flock of vault companies in Oklahoma, Missouri, Arkansas, Kansas and maybe Nebraska and Iowa. He was big in the vault business, manufacturing and selling them to cemeteries. His name was Courtney Sloan and he headquartered in Kansas City. He came to me and said, "Dan, I'd like to buy your cemetery." And, I said, "Well it's not for sale." He said, "Well, you've got a good business going here with the truck. I've been watching what you've been doing, and paying attention to you at the meetings." By this time I had become president of the Kansas Cemetery Association, so I knew all the cemeteries in Kansas. I had a contract with a cemetery in Topeka and one down in Wichita. Courtney said, "I'll give you $300,000 with a third down and the balance over five years." I accepted that, and I really thought I had done well, "caught a fat hog" as the old saying goes, and I did, I had done very well. The end of the story is that four years later he sold that for $2.5 million. So, you can't ever lose what you didn't get.

NATIONAL RECOGNITION

24.

All those education years were really paying off for me and I always felt good about that. Incidentally, during that period of time Duayne and I built a chapel on the grounds of our cemetery and scared the devil out of the funeral directors in town because they thought I was going to build a funeral home out there, which I wasn't. We built a nice, non-denominational chapel so people didn't have to go out and stand in a tent. When we had burials, they could get inside and have a really nice interment chapel. It was a big building and I commissioned a kid who was going to Rockhurst College in Kansas City to build a large plaque for the front to let people know it was open to all denominations.

Getting elected to the Kansas Cemetery Association was really huge for my career. I made a very high profile in the industry. I achieved that and numerous other things during this time. In the late 1960s the conglomerates had come into the industry, and a number of large corporations became even larger, publicly held corporations. Ones like Service Corporation International out of Houston, Texas (S.C.I.), Stewart Enterprises out of New Orleans, the Loewen Group out of Vancouver, Canada, they all came into existence and they started paying outlandish prices to swallow up different funeral homes across the U.S. and cemeteries and cemetery-funeral home combinations. As a result, it really gave a lot of opportunities for expansion and growth.

The time that I spent in Kansas City was a time of evolution for me. First I became president of the Kansas Cemetery Association when I was at the Cemetery of Leavenworth, Kansas. Then I was asked to join a group called the Cemetery Management Council, which was a group of cemeterians and sales managers from the East Coast, all over New Jersey, Pennsylvania, Maryland, Delaware, New York and that area. It was quite fruitful and a good learning experience because we shared an expression of ideas with no punches pulled, and that's what it was supposed to be all about. They were no dues to pay, and we met once a year.

As a result of that group, I became very involved in the national Prearrangement Interment Association of America, the P.I.A.A., including quite a bit of speaking at conventions. I made quite a few friends in the P.I.A.A. I became president of that national trade association in 1971, which was quite an honor and very, very enlightening and educational. I traveled all over the eastern half of the U.S. Before I became president, I was the first chair for their first-ever convention to be held on foreign soil, in Malaga, Spain on the Gold Coast. For the registration, the airfare and the hotel the total cost per person was $479. We ended up with three planeloads, two out of Cincinnati and one out of Pittsburg, and it was filled with people. We had a good time in

Spain, and Betty and I got to do quite a bit of sightseeing in southern Spain including Ronda, which is my favorite city of all cities in Spain.

I did my stint as president of the P.I.A.A., and about that time the Toppers organization was in the same situation as the Cemetery Management Council, except the only thing that we met for was sales and sales marketing. We would meet at exotic places around the East and West Coasts, we had two or three meetings in Bimini, and I chaired one in Barbados. We had one in Tampa, some in California, Arizona, and we had one in Ixtapa in southwest Mexico, which is about one hundred fifty miles north of Acapulco.

I'd never been to Mexico before. Our good buddy Steve Ragland from Mississippi chaired that one as he owned a home there. We stayed in a hotel right on the Pacific Ocean. I fell in love with that place, it was really beautiful. A year later Betty and I went down to Mexico and we wound up buying a timeshare, which I still own to this day, although not the original one. At the time we bought it they only had four buildings, and today it's a monstrosity of a place with golf courses and seven restaurants. It's really grown and I have grown with it in that I have upscaled my two-week timeshare there.

I got to meet a lot of people while I was in The Toppers organization, and I met Cavett Roberts, who was an attorney from Arizona that got into the cemetery business and marketing. He was a very, very fluent speaker, and wrote a nice book. I had run into him in the airport in Cincinnati, Ohio years later and he wanted to know how it was going, and he was having some tea, and he gave me a book that he had written, "What To Do After You Retire." I need to read that book!

I was with Dick Herbert one time, a good buddy of mine from Clemson, South Carolina, and he asked if I had ever met Napoleon Hill or heard of him. Well, yes, I've heard of him because I had read his book - everybody in sales has read "Think and Grow Rich!" Dick said, "Let's go up and see if he is there."

We drove maybe forty miles up a mountain somewhere in South Carolina, and here is this little guy out there in Bermuda shorts and straw hat whacking away at some hedge along his home. It was a beautiful home sitting up on top of the mountain with a view for miles and miles and miles, and he graciously invited us to come in and have some sweet tea.

We sat down and talked to him and he gave me three autographed books of "Think and Grow Rich." I gave them to my two sons (they have probably lost them!) and I've still got one and it's a fond memory of mine.

During that period of time in Kansas City, I decided to get a houseboat. Betty and I went down to Gibson Manufacturing in Tennessee, and we picked out our boat, our colors, the fabric, the interior, everything, and they brought it up to the western end of the Lake of the Ozarks. Now we could drive down in just an hour and a half from Kansas City to spend time on our boat. We generally left on Friday afternoon and came back on Sunday night. It was just a great thing. As the kids got older, they were raised on the boat. It could sleep a bunch of people up on the top deck, it had dual controls, top and bottom, which I always used up on the top deck. The first guest we ever had on board was Jack and Janice Frost, my dear friends from Georgia, and there's a lot of memories with that. Betty kept a log of everything that happened on that boat. I still have it with my souvenirs.

VOL. 3 • OCTOBER, 1970 • NO. 4
A PUBLICATION OF THE PRE-ARRANGEMENT INTERMENT ASSOCIATION OF AMERICA

forward

"...help them make tomorrow's decisions...today"

New PIAA President Elected   Officers -1970

DANIEL E. REED
PIAA-PHEA President for 1970-71

Dan Reed, President of Midwestern Cemetery Consultants, Inc., Cedar Rapids, Iowa. Age 42. Married, six children. Was employed 13 years as a factory production worker, Union representative and Company Supervisor. Has been active in various sales fields including radio, real estate, boats, water conditioners, insurance, stocks and securities and cemetery sales.

Started in the cemetery field nearly nine years ago in Toledo, Ohio. Within three months was promoted to Sales Manager at Youngstown, Ohio. Following this began cemetery sales contracting in Iowa and Missouri. Is currently Director of all sales at Cedar Memorial Park in Cedar Rapids, Iowa, Kansas City, Missouri, Sunset Memory Gardens in Leavenworth, Kansas and Mount Moriah Cemetery in Kansas City, Missouri.

His continuously expanding company has 30 employees in three states. Dan is a firm believer that salesmanship is a profession, which requires constant self-improvement and credits his success in ever striving towards that goal.

President
DANIEL E. REED (1971)
Mount Moriah Cemetery
Kansas City, Missouri
Vice President-Administration
FRED W. MEYER, JR. (1971)
Memory Gardens Management Corp.
Indianapolis, Indiana
Vice President - Meetings
JACK FROST (1972)
Atlanta, Georgia
Vice President - Sales
ROBERT J. McCORMICK (1972)
Jefferson Memorial Park
Pittsburgh, Pennsylvania
Secretary-Treasurer
EDWARD P. CANNON (1971)
Memorial Gardens Assn.
Minneapolis, Minnesota
DIRECTORS
CHARLES BELL (1972)
Floral Hills Memorial Gardens
Florence, Kentucky
DAVID L. BOYD (1972)
Lakewood Memory Gardens
Chattanooga, Tennessee
ROY DEMANES (1972)
Memorial Consultants, Inc.
Peoria, Illinois
DALLAS E. DOHERTY (1972)
Consolidated Industries, Inc.
Littleton, Colorado
PETER O. ERNST (1971)
River Hills Memorial Park
Batavia, Illinois
F. WAYNE GAINER (1972)
Hixson Hills Memory Gardens
Nashville, Tennessee
DONALD COIN (1972)
Kankakee Memorial Gardens
Kankakee, Illinois
GEORGE HARVEY (1972)
Worcester County Memorial Park
Paxton, Massachusetts
CHARLES C. KIRKPATRICK (1972)
Rosewood Memorial Park
Virginia Beach, Virginia
JACK REDDEN (1972)
Memphis, Tennessee
RICHARD T. SMART (1972)
Sunset Hills Burial Park
Canton, Ohio
GEORGE F. STOECKLEIN (1971)
Penn-Lincoln Memorial Park
Irwin, Pennsylvania
RALPH STUBBLEFIELD (1971)
Marshall Memory Gardens
Huntsville, Alabama

In '72 when I was president of the Central States Association, which was made up of seven states in the Midwest, Fred Newman was president of the Missouri Association. He asked me to chair a convention for him at the Lake of Ozarks at Tantara. We had maybe a hundred twenty-five people sitting at the tables having dinner, and because I was chairing it, I was up on top at the head table. I finished my dinner and I was getting ready to start introducing various speakers who were at the head table with me when I thought I should take care of nature before we get started on an hour and half long program.

While I was in the men's room, in comes the governor of the State of Missouri, Warren Hearnes. I recognized him right away, and I said, "Governor, you've got a lot of constituents out here, cemetery owners from all over the State of Missouri, would you take the time to go speak to them?" He had just come from a trip down in South America, and he was on the way home with his entourage. He said, "Sure I will, a good politician never misses an opportunity to speak to an audience."

I took him up on the dais, and nobody was paying any attention, everybody was talking, glasses were clinking. I rapped on the mic and I said to them, "Ladies and gentlemen, hello, hello, hello, ladies and gentlemen. It's customary for an audience to stand when they're going to be spoken to by the Governor of the State of Missouri." They stood and applauded, and he made a few good remarks and then he was on his way. That was coup de grâce for me.

I got involved in a lot of conventions all over the United States, either chairing them or speaking at them, and my profile was growing bigger. One time I chaired the National Convention in Kansas City and set up in an outstanding place downtown. I had everything in the can, everything was done by remote, and nobody even saw me the whole time it was going on because it was a state-of-the-art upscale audio-visual kind of hotel. In fact, I cut spots and the hotel put them on every morning. People attending would wake up in their rooms and there I was on their TV telling them what the schedule was for the day, what was upcoming for the ladies, what they could do, and so on. It was kind of neat.

I chaired a convention in Los Angeles, a nationwide sales management seminar. It was at the Century Hotel in L.A. and I had all the staff come in. I called it "The Olympics of Sales Management," and they put brochures out across the United States which showed a picture of a guy running, and as you opened it up it showed me coming closer and getting bigger and bigger. I had five different speakers besides myself, and I had everybody, men and women, dressed in track uniforms, in sweats. When introduced, they would run down through the crowd, and then up on the stage with me where we had a torch burning like the Olympics, and it was just a fun thing.

Ted Nuckolls, President of Loudon Memorial Park in Baltimore, a part of Stewart Enterprises, had invited me to speak at a couple of seminars and we really hit it off. He was an avid reader, a very good speaker, and I learned a lot just by being with him. I remember him telling me one time, "Dan, guard against allowing your beliefs to become convictions." That was sound advice that I use to this day. He was being groomed to be president and was always very supportive of me when I was in the same position a few years later.

I had everybody come in a day early because one of the guys in my program, Walt Woods, owned a 38-foot cruiser, and he kept it at Newport Beach. We all went down there, and I had the president of our association, John Bailey, and Hugh Keatley, one of my closest, dearest friends in my life with me.

Hugh drank a lot, and he had been drinking Jack Daniels all day. At about two o'clock in the afternoon, after going through Newport Beach and seeing all the huge ships and cruisers (that's where the all millionaires keep them), we came idling up to a really nice estate which sat on a hill just down from the beach. It was on a sloping hill, with a sidewalk going up to it and a huge manicured lawn.

Out came a guy with two black Labradors, and he began walking down the hill. Somebody said, "Hell, that's... that's John Wayne!" Walt sidled the boat up to the dock, and John Wayne came down there with the dogs. Hugh, who is full of pop by that time, shouted, "Hey Duke! Hey Duke, come on, let's arm wrestle, let's arm wrestle!"

Well, John Wayne was so gracious. He went down the side of the boat and he asked the names of every one of us individually, spoke to us, wanted to know where are we from and wished us all the best. In the meantime, Hugh was still popping off about arm wrestling with him! John Wayne was very kind, and he addressed everybody individually by name as he was saying goodbye, he casually did that salute that he was famous for, and then he sauntered back up the winding sidewalk there to his home. It was quite a story, and one of the highlights of my life. I'll never forget that.

There was another meeting that I chaired for P.I.A.A. in Tampa at the Playboy Club. I got a lifetime membership in the Playboy Club for putting on that convention, which became useful years later. Five of us decided to go fishing, so we chartered a boat and went kite fishing, which was a new experience for me.

With kite fishing, you really have to work at fishing. The boats go up and down, and the kites are different colors and made out of silk in different densities. The color denotes the density of the silk and is contingent to how fast your boat is running and what the winds are as to the kind of kites they put up. Attached to the kite, up in the air behind the boat maybe fifty yards, is a line coming straight down with live bait on it. You sit there with the line coiled between your legs so you can pull it up and down so the bait skims the ocean, just skims the top of it. With the waves and the boat going up and down and the wind blowing, you work efficiently to get sailfish. We caught five sails that day. I put the whole thing together, and everybody got a sailfish but me. One gentleman, Jack Frost, got two. The skipper flies flags for how many fish they've caught, which is common down there in Biscayne Bay.

We were coming back in from being out on the ocean about ten miles and all of a sudden here comes a PT boat across Biscayne Bay with sirens blaring and lights flashing. A guy on a megaphone said, "Shut that boat down, shut that boat down! The President is coming!" So, we shut down and are drifting, and we've got these five flags flying. So here came President Nixon, and he had his boat come over next to ours, and he said, "You guys have done a great job today. Five sails!" he said, "that's unusual, that's really great!" and then he gave us his famous signal with two fingers on both hands raised, his arms extended in the air, and then off he went. That was my encounter with President Nixon.

I don't know why all of these things always happened to me. They just happened out of the blue. .

25.

During the mid-70s, I was still working in and speaking at numerous conventions for different associations, state, regional, etcetera. One time I spoke at a convention in Chicago and I didn't know it at the time, but there were some attendants there from France. After I was finished speaking, they came up and handed me their cards and wanted to know if they could talk to me later, so I said sure.

Herschel Auerbach, another great friend of mine, was there also. He was President of the A.C.A., from Chicago, Palatine, and he owned a Jewish Memorial Park there. Herschel was aid de camp to the Nuremburg Trials and was in Germany for two years. I asked him to go with me because they said they wanted to talk business.

We had lunch with them, one was French and one was English, and they represented the largest company in France, O.G.F., which owned insurance companies, all the power companies in France, shipyards, they owned everything. They had heard I'd been speaking about preneed funerals and wanted to know if I would come to France and show them how to do preneed funerals. I agreed to a one-year contract, and so I traveled to France bimonthly.

O.G.F. owned 2700 funeral homes in France! The funeral homes there were not like the ones in the U.S. Most 'funeral homes' were walk-in stores that had coffins (they didn't call them caskets in Europe), made out of wood not metal, and ran from the sublime to the ridiculous in price. They were leaning against the walls in stores, with little artificial flowers on them.

In France at that time there were only two or three real honest-to-goodness funeral homes. Funerals were held in the churches, not funeral homes, and in Paris they would have six or eight funerals going on simultaneously on a certain floor in the hospitals. They didn't do any embalming, so the funerals were held right away the next day. They would partition these huge hall-like rooms for all the different families depending on number of people, and then after they would put the coffins into an ossuary.

People don't own cemetery lots in the cemeteries in France, they lease it for period of years. When the lease is over, the remains are removed from the chambers in the ossuary and somebody new goes in. They could lease them for ten or twenty years or however many years they wanted.

There were forty million people in France and O.G.F. was doing about 65-70% of all the funerals, and they wanted to do all of them, so they decided to sell preneed funerals. One of their fellows came over from France and we worked for a couple weeks teaching him about preneed funerals. I would go over there every other month to Lyon or mostly Paris. Their employees had extensive expense accounts and it was "Katie bar the door" when we went to lunch because it was the top of the line French cooking at the best restaurants.

One time I was there they invited the U.S. Ambassador to France, Mr. Howard Baker, who was very prevalent during the Reagan years, to have lunch with us, so I got to meet him. He was from Nashville, Tennessee with a big family, and was just a nice, nice man.

At Midwestern Cemetery Consultants Incorporated (M.C.C.I.) in Kansas City, not only did we have about sixty to seventy salespeople, we built a new funeral home so then we had two cemeteries and two funeral homes, one on the north side and one on the south side. We were hiring all the time because I would place people out on contracts. Dave Coates was in charge of that and would take the contracts on site in Maryland, Arizona, Oregon, or wherever it would be. He would take all our newly hired sales managers and train them, and then we would move them to the sites for a year or two based on the contracts. If the company had a sales manager already, then we would bring them to Kansas City and teach and train he or she how to do our methodology, which was really working really well.

M.C.C.I. became very well known nationally. I was making audio-visual tapes and selling them across the U.S. at different operations. Then I got the bug to cut an audiotape and I decided the speaker that was essential for me to get was Earle Nightingale, who was up in the suburbs of Western Chicago.

Earle Nightingale was the most heard voice on the radio for years. He was on about six hundred stations internationally every day for fifteen minutes: He was the voice before Paul Harvey. Earle Nightingale had a tremendous voice, and he was a prolific writer and had written numerous books. I had the audacity to drive my Lincoln from Kansas City to Chicago unannounced and went to his office and asked if I could see him.

I gave the receptionist my card, and she wanted to know who I was and what I wanted. I said, "I have something to propose that Earle and I could work together on collaboratively." She said, "He will take the time to see you because he does accept visitors," and I was ushered into his office.

It was a dark, dark, office, full of books. I never saw anything like it. I had never seen that many books in a library. He was sitting at a very ornate desk and on it was a model of a schooner, a sail ship, and so I found the common denominator between us to talk about.

He invited me to sit down, and I asked him about it. He talked about how much he likes sailing, and I told him about my sailing trip down through the Caribbean on a ketch. A ketch isn't as big as a schooner, but they are faster, and there are generally three masts on a schooner. And so, we had a common bond.

I didn't know it at the time, but he was a speed-reader, and could read 3,200 words per minute. He told me, "You don't read words, you read thoughts." I was so impressed with that I went to a class and learned to read at a rate of 1,100 words per minute. I learned that the average reader reads at 600-700 per minute.

I explained my concept to Earle, something that I had always wanted to do, and he said, "Well, sure I can do that with you.

You write it, and I'll edit it, I'll clean it up for what I think it should be, and I'll put it on a tape." My proposal to him was that we would sell the tapes nationally. He would get a royalty or a stipend, whatever which was normal for him to get in that kind of business then.

I left and wrote up and sent him the written script, and he cut a tape, which I've still got to this day. Earle talked about selling prearrangements, and I sold those all over the U.S. as a prospecting tool.

We were having a convention in Philadelphia and I got him to come speak to the association. The association paid him $3,500 plus expenses for a thirty-minute oration. We were in a hotel on the Schuylkill River, and I had a very, very well positioned booth with cut-out cardboard photos of Earle and I standing beside each other, and Don Dixon selling tapes. Earle spoke his keynote, and we sold a ton of tapes. A side note, Earle had all expenses paid, but didn't have cash for the cab fare, so I paid it and told him he owed me $7. Of course I never got it, nor did I ever care.

During the mid to late 1970s a fellow from Warren, Pennsylvania who owned a vault company called me. George Ferver was a great big, tall guy and he sold vaults all over the eastern U.S. He had a flatbed tractor trailer that they would load twelve at a time, and they would carry them to Pittsburg or wherever in Pennsylvania. He had quite the clientele. Many of them were C.M.C. members I had mentioned earlier. He offered me stock in the company to become president of the vault company, and the reason he did it was because of my high profile, my name, and he knew I could go out and sell to people that he wouldn't be able to. And so I did.

They had the assembly lines, and because of my background working in the factory and on the assembly lines, when I came in we started a second shift building vaults. I went out and called on a number of the people that I knew from C.M.C. and others from association work, and I sold a ton of vaults for our company.

Because I was on an accrual basis for my commissions with M.C.C.I, I got paid for all the sales I made as the money was collected. So, I introduced an automatic withdrawal plan to the industry, and spoke about it in Indianapolis at a meeting. I wouldn't accept contracts from anyone unless they agreed to what we called autopay. For autopay we'd get a voided check. There weren't any banks that would touch it in Kansas City, except one black bank. They saw the future of it. At the zenith, we had over 6000 active customers paying for prepaid funerals on a monthly autopay basis.

As a result of being on an accrual basis on income, and my sales people wanting to get paid every Friday, I had a tremendous cash flow problem. I went down to Commerce Bank with Garnet (the president of Mt. Moriah who had been banking there for years), and he introduced me to a fellow by the name of Charlie, and he set up a separate credit line for me. I started off borrowing about $12,000-18,000 a month at 5% and 6% interest.

During the time I was at Mt. Moriah, my sister, Evelyn, became cancer-stricken and we lost her in 1975. What a beautiful lady cancer destroyed, and she left behind her husband and four daughters. I was extremely sad to lose her. I had cherished having a sister as wonderful as her.

July 4th, 1976 was the country's Bicentennial and the day I started my beard, which I still have to this day.

26.

As the years went by and Jimmy Carter was President, I had borrowed almost a quarter million dollars from the bank. I had a standing credit line that at any one time would have been between a $130-150,000, borrowed for cash flow between my sales people and my help and everything. Things were paying off pretty handsome then.

He makes funerals easier on families

A trend by cemetery owners and funeral directors to combine operations has prompted the recent formation of The American Cemetery/Mortuary Conference, a division of the American Cemetery Association.

Daniel E. Reed, the new president of the association, said the number of combined cemetery and funeral home operations had increased from fewer than 50 a decade ago to nearly 100 today.

One of the biggest reasons for the expansion of combined funeral and cemetery services is that "it's far less complex and less expensive for consumers to have all their needs met in one place," said Mr. Reed, who is national director of cemetery development for Funeral Security Plans Inc., a division of D.W. Newcomer's Sons.

The combined funeral home and cemetery concept, used by several Kansas City operations, can lessen the expense for church facilities, motorcades and additional administrative chores and staff needed when funeral and burial arrangements are made independently, he said.

DANIEL E. REED

Incidentally, on that line of credit from Commerce Bank, they called my notes after Carter had been President for a few years and the interest rate had doubled. I mean it had gone from 5% and 6% and 7% to 12%, 13%, 14% and in some places 15%. The money I borrowed I was paying back at twice a rate of interest. But my cash flow had caught up with me quite a bit through the accumulation of sales and customers making their payments, and I got the first payments as they came in, so that was helping, and my borrowing went down. Still, I paid the notes all off at a higher rate of interest... that is not good!

During this time, my good friends in Cedar Rapids, Dave and Audrey Linge, called me and wanted to know if Betty and I would like to go on a float trip with them down the Green River in Wyoming. We thought that would be great fun, so we went and we had a great time.

That led me the next year to get a group of good friends together to do this. I rented a thirty-two-foot RV and had them come to Kansas City, although one good buddy from Phoenix flew into Moab, Utah, which was where we were going to start. We took off in the RV and drove nonstop, trading off drivers. You couldn't drink anything for four hours before you drove.

We stopped in the outskirts of Denver before going up the mountain pass. We went to two or three different restaurants trying to cut a deal for dinners, and we finally got a guy that would give us a 10% discount. And we just had a party, I mean everybody was drinking beer all the way to Utah. I think there were about fifteen people in that RV.

We got to Moab at 8 o'clock in the morning, parked the RV and got on the five or six boats we arranged for floating the Colorado River almost to the Grand Canyon. We floated down to the Parker Dam. It was a wonderful time.

By this time the boys, Mark and Greg, were in Grandview High School and playing football. My days of broadcasting became useful as they were looking for somebody to call the games. While they weren't on radio, there was a loudspeaker system so for three years I broadcast all the games. Two of those years we were the city champions, and that was lot of fun.

Mark and Greg moved to a small town in eastern Kansas after high school. Mark decided to ride his horse from Kansas to Colorado, and take his dog along. At that time he was a real hippie! A few years later I went to Colorado and offered him a job at a cemetery I planned on buying in Nashville, Tennessee. Eventually, he wound up selling at M.C.C.I. in Kansas City. Then he worked in Texas and California where he started his own company after receiving his insurance license. He had a number of salespeople and funeral homes in California.

My years in Kansas City were the most fruitful of my career, from a standpoint of growth, building image, and accomplishing many different things.

I ran a sales management school about once a month, and a fellow came from Abilene, Texas, a young man, who came with deep pockets, born with a silver spoon in his mouth. His father owned a number of funeral homes in West Texas, and had convinced a number of other funeral directors there to form an insurance company called Funeral Directors Life Insurance Company. They had eight people on the board, all funeral directors, and were headquartered in Abilene. The son, the heir-to-be of the company, came to our school, along with sales managers from all over the U.S. It was practical training. Not only did they get theoretical learning in the classroom with me or Don Dixon, they also got practical teaching from having to go into the field. I charged $5,000 per person for a two week course. The son went to our school and then back to Texas, and I went on about my business.

About six months later, his father called me and wanted to know if I'd come to Abilene to visit with his board of directors. I agreed, they paid my expenses, I met with them, and they made a proposal for me to bring some management people down there. They were already selling preneed funerals, as Texas was one of the first states to start selling them. It was very big in funerals. They had started this insurance company with their own funding and were doing a so-so job. They offered me a one-year contract to sell preneed funerals for them in all of their funeral homes, and we came to an agreement.

I went back to Kansas City to make arrangements for this. My son, Mark, who'd been selling there for a year or two, actually started selling when he was just a kid. Dave Coates' son, Dan had done the same thing, and although they didn't work together, they had worked in sales, and I knew they were about the same age. I had an idea and discussed it with Dave, and we decided to send our two sons to West Texas to run this new thing for us.

I took the sons down there and got them all lined up to work. The guy who was supposed to be a sales director wasn't much of one, so I went there about every two to three months for a year, to Abilene, Lubbock, Odessa, Midland, LaMesa, all those towns in West Texas.

In Big Spring, I had a funeral director and he had two sons there. They didn't want to go into sales but Big Spring had a memorial park that was abandoned, and they had taken it over. It had been abandoned by a guy who had gone broke, and who later became the executive vice president for the Loewen Group further on in the story. That contract lasted for a year and then that was the end of that.

One other time while in Kansas City, I went to a convention in Toronto. I was up there looking for business, and although I didn't get any contracting, I heard a gosh-awful speaker named Jack McQuaig. He had created a testing system for psychological purposes and he was selling it to different industries in Canada. I was impressed with his dissertation, although he was a terrible speaker, and I learned his son, Peter, was also there.

After getting back to Kansas City, the more I thought about it the more I liked the idea. There was nothing like that going on in the industry. With all the recruiting they were doing, they weren't testing people to see if they were psychologically suited even to be in sales.

I called Peter McQuaig and got fifty or so of those tests. I wanted to go through it and counsel with all my sales people to see if we're working with the right people. I learned a lot from that: Lo and behold, the majority of the people that were the top producers fit all of the scale that the McQuaig study called for, being high in dominance and low in compliance.

The elements, "D, R, S, C," were dominance, resistance, sociability and compliance. If you had a guy that was high in dominance and low in compliance, that was a good combination of traits. All our top producers all were in the scales from top left to the bottom right. It convinced me that that was a good test.

I thought this might be something I could sell in the U.S. so I talked to Peter McQuaig two or three times. Peter was a young fellow, about twenty-five. I suggested to him that we could sell these in the U.S., and would he be willing to pay me a nominal commission on all the sales I made. He said he had to talk to his dad about it. They called me back and they agreed. They paid me a stipend, which didn't amount to much. But, I got a hold of all the people I was in the Cemetery Management Council with, all the Toppers, and some cemeterians I knew, and I invited them to come to Kansas City at their expense to hear a revolutionary way of cutting down on recruiting costs because you're not hiring the wrong people. I got about eighteen guys from all over the country to meet with me in my home. I got a good deal for them at the local motel, and I catered in the food for the meeting in my basement. We had a big party and did a lot of drinking, Peter did his spiel and he sold quite a few of them.

Although I didn't make a heck of a lot of money out of it, the McQuaig system of interviews really took over the U.S. I put him on a program I was chairing one time, and he did a bigger business in the States than they did in Canada because when it came to marketing and sales in the cemetery business and funeral business there it was just practically nonexistent.

Around 1980 I was approached by Who's Who in America magazine and they published my name. They got a donation, and so that was a nice write up to get. Then, my twelve years in Kansas City came to a sudden conclusion.

If you recall, I would meet with Garnet Waddell, the president of Mt. Moriah, every Tuesday for breakfast. One morning out of the blue he announced he had sold both of the properties and funeral homes to S.C.I. I put my utensils down, looked right at him and said, "Garnet, you have just destroyed my life!"

He reassured me how great S.C.I. was and that they wanted me. Well, due to my extensive traveling, consulting and association work and so on, I knew better, and, I also knew S.C.I. would not ever permit me to become president of A.C.A., which was a major goal for me.

Garnet advised that Betty and I go to Houston for a visit, so we set off in one of their jets. We flew to Houston mid-afternoon with drinks and appetizers and a crew of three. We checked into the Shamrock Hotel, and had dinner with the president and some executives, and it was all glitz! I was assured "nothing will change!" including me being responsible for all my employees and my own paycheck, that they would honor the remaining two plus years of the fifteen-year contract, and all would be well.

We flew back to Kansas City the next day, I gathered my managers, and we all met with Garnet in his office where he announced the sale, and I proclaimed, "All would remain status quo."

And so it was for about three or four months, until I got a phone call from one of the top execs that had been at the dinner in Houston. He directed me to meet him at the Marriott Hotel at the new Kansas City airport on Friday evening at 6:00 p.m.

Dutifully, I arrived at the scheduled time, went to his suite, and we met. There was his overnight bag and a set of golf clubs sitting beside an ornate table, which his feet with $400.00 cowboy boots were resting on.

Without any conversation what so ever, he looked at me and said, "Dan, Ben Hollingsworth (the president of S.C.I.) wants his name on your paycheck." I sat in stunned silence, then responded to the effect that was not our verbal agreement in Houston. He told me Russ Valby, the regional V.P. of sales would be in town next week with all the necessary paperwork for me and all of my employees. Again, I did not reply because I was absolutely stunned. He asked if there were any questions. I simply said, "No." He said, "If not, I'm going to catch a plane and go golfing." I really didn't give a damn where he went. I got in my car and with my mind reeling about all the things I needed to take care of, and drove home.

In the meeting in Houston I was told I must sever all consulting contracts I had and work only for S.C.I. I had accomplished that tenant, so the only source of income was S.C.I. Their compensation, due to my contract, remained the same, so for a few months I was the only contractor S.C.I. had nationwide and that word had spread quickly within the industry, which was a negative for me.

Harold Brown, a consultant from Topeka, Kansas had called me at home congratulating me on joining S.C.I., one of his major clients. We had always been good and friendly competitors. He had held a national S.C.I. meeting which I had attended (it was compulsory). The large crowd was justifiably gracious to him even though all of his materials, comments were old hat and outdated. That was the way S.C.I.'s marketing and sales promotions were. So when Russ Valby came to town, his monthly meetings and ideas were met with a great deal of skepticism. My management team and all of my sales force was the largest with S.C.I. However, in a few months, sales were down, volume was down and many of my sales team were leaving. It was a disaster.

After three or four months I had had it working for S.C.I. I drove to the airport one mid-week day, purchased round trip airfare to Houston on Braniff Air, arrived, got a taxi, went to corporate headquarters, and asked to see Ben Hollingsworth.

After a reasonable wait I went to the twelfth floor, and there was Harold Brown and Steiner, the jerk that came to Kansas City carrying the message from Ben a few months previously. Russ Valby, my upline, came in shortly, and I was asked to commence why I was in Houston.

I began by saying to Ben, "Because you are a G--D--- liar and so are most of the people that answer to you" at which time the founder and C.E.O. of S.C.I., Bobby Waltrip, came in. He said good morning to me, sat down next to me, and crossed his legs. I noticed he was wearing an expensive pair of alligator shoes. He then asked me why I was there.

The pinnacle of my encounters with S.C.I. would be to repeat what I had just said to Ben, word for word, adding, "and that goes for you, too," but I silently kept that to myself.

Immediately I said "You can't fire me because I am quitting this chicken shit organization right now. I bought and paid for my tickets, so I'm leaving" without another word being said.

The next day, my office manager of twelve years called, telling me I must have all of my personal possessions out of the office that day. Some of my sales people and all of my office staff helped me move out twelve years of accumulations. A couple weeks later I received a severance check and a reasonable fee for all of my fixtures and equipment.

The final footnote to the S.C.I. saga was that they sent out a national edict I was never to be hired as a S.C.I. employee. I wore that invisible badge of honor proudly! S.C.I. got along fine without me and I never missed them. Ever!

A secondary footnote to the story: Bobby Waltrip and I were engaged many times due to my ascendancy to the office of President A.C.A., and he never looked me in the eye and we never spoke. Of course, everyone that knew me understood my vitriol towards him and S.C.I.

28.

After I parted ways with S.C.I. I got a call from a fellow named David Newcomer. D.W. Newcomer and Sons, four generations of them, owned numerous funeral homes and cemeteries in Kansas City. They came the closest to being our competition. Although they did lot of selling, they couldn't hold a candle to us. Their sales manager was Duke Radovich and they hired him out of Rockhurst College. He came from Perth, Australia, and Duke was a great big, tall guy, about 6' 9" and he played basketball at Rockhurst. He sold for them and he did a pretty good job. They built a sales force which went all over the country, and they sold a funeral trust. Preneed funerals were in their infancy then

David Newcomer the 4th wanted to know if I'd meet him for lunch at the Kansas City Country Club so I agreed. It was in the spring, a nice day but still cold. And out there practicing on the golf course, not putting but practicing with the short irons was one of the great pro-golfers of all time, Tom Watson. He looked at me and gave me a big wave as I went by. He was a very friendly guy, though I never met him in person.

At lunch, Dave and I sat down, and he said, "Dan, you've been beating on us in Kansas City for twelve years, and I'm asking you to join us." I said, "Well, you've got a sales manager, Duke Radovich." He said, "Yes, but what I am asking you to do is to represent us and go to the state of California, which is beginning to blossom for preneed funerals, and open up to the state of California and set up funeral directors to sell our trusts."

We discussed it, and eventually we did a handshake, and I went to work with D.W. Newcomers. I started travelling and was all over California with different funeral homes. I set up a number of funeral homes, and soon I had to have a manager.

I took one of my good managers who was still with S.C.I. and moved him and his wife; I had hired him out of a bar lounge that he and his wife were running in downtown Kansas City years before. He was a heck of a good salesman and a good sales manager, and he loved to gamble. We moved him to Marysville, California, twin cities with Yuba City, and my son Mark went with him because he'd finished up in Texas. I had a funeral director out there who was also a pilot, and he used to fly me around central California on his plane. I set up a number of funeral homes in California, and Mark and the sales manager did a very good job.

It wasn't long-lived, however, because I only worked with him for a year, because during that period of time I got very involved in Seattle and Tacoma and there was no way I could continue working with Newcomers, too; they made that very clear in the beginning.

I negotiated a contract with the two largest funeral homes and cemeteries in Washington, one in Tacoma called Mountain View, and one in Seattle called Evergreen Washelli. I was permitted to do consulting as long as I maintained sales, which I always did. This resulted in my contracting with Forethought Life Insurance Company as a consultant to Fred Rockwood, the president.

At a convention one time, I had just finished speaking when three representatives of Batesville Management Services (B.M.S.) asked me if I would consider speaking for them seven times a year for two years at various locations across the U.S. We had lunch to discuss it, and I met Mike James who was a wheel with B.M.S. I agreed to their request, the stipend was good, all expenses paid, and I was on a panel with the same people every time.

Boy, I got a lot of publicity because B.M.S. advertised to the entire funeral industry (some 30,000 funeral home members), and it increased my publicity a great deal. Margaret Kubler-Ross, who started the hospice movement in England, was on the panel along with other well known personalities.

I remember speaking in San Francisco and many of the funeral directors in attendance booed me because I always spoke positively about preneed funerals. They were liberals then and still are today. The last seminar was held at the Hilton in the Georgetown area of Washington, D.C. Mike James made arrangements for dinner at a really nice Mexican restaurant that specialized in green enchiladas, a favorite dish of Fred Rockwood, whom I was introduced to at dinner. Fred had been pirated away from a top-notch consulting firm in Boston to become president of the new insurance company.

After finishing dinner Fred produced a voluminous contract and offered me a position as vice president of sales for Forethought. I wasn't expecting that, and was taken off guard. I explained I had seventy sales people in Seattle and Tacoma and was on a contract. Mike James thought I was crazy when I deferred. Fred said he was disappointed, and then we walked with him to the train station where he overnighted to Indianapolis. About two weeks later, he called me in Seattle to ask me if I would consult with Forethought answering only to him. I agreed.

I was in a meeting in a hotel south of Indianapolis with all the officers of Forethought. The board was full of figures with his projections about the average funeral, what we convert into this, and Fred had figures all over the board and the guys were all working away at their computers. I looked at him, I looked at the board, and I said, "Fred, excuse me what are you basing those figures on with your contracts?" He said, "For every sale we get, this is what it translates to and then I extend it up and gets into our profit for the company, etc." And, I said, "Fred, I got news for you. Don't ever tell the president he's wrong, but you're not right in putting those figures up there." Fred stopped, and everybody stopped, and everybody looked up.

So here's this consultant, and they were all scared to death about what I was going to do because I'm the only one who had a pipeline with Fred. All the rest of them operated together and were going to be setting up their own offices. I was a consultant to Fred only, and they were looking over their shoulder wondering what I was doing, where I was going with this.

I said, "Well Fred, you say 'sale' and then you get your figures for that. But, " and I paused, "a sale represents 1.7 contracts. In my experience that is built on years of not only selling but managing sales organizations, you average 1.7 contracts per sale." He said, "You do?" I said, "Yes. It's not one contract at a home. When you going to a home, if you're doing it right, you're going sell to *two* people. And, if you're going to a lot of homes you will get some single people, so that drags it down, but that results in 1.7 contracts." Fred exclaimed, "Whoa!" and he let out a big hoot, and he said, "Guys, just take everything out of your computers and erase the board and we'll start all over." He said, "You guys can help me out."

That made a heck of a big difference for Forethought, I'll tell you. Forethought became the number one provider of insurance products in the United States for years. Hilrom Industries wound up selling prototypes to a separate group, and they have since been sold to two or three times, but that was the beginning of the Forethought Life Insurance Company.

Incidentally, years later, one of those four in that meeting became president of a huge life insurance company in Des Moines called Homesteaders, and another guy became owner and president of a marketing firm in Portland, Oregon and to this printing is operating sales programs all over the U.S., selling a specialized product insurance fund.

A quick sideline story, I was back in Indiana at a meeting and we were getting ready to go to lunch. By this time Batesville Casket Company had a sales force of about a hundred salespeople across the U.S. and they made tremendously good money. Fred had been talking to them about a kind of a card they'd heard about that when customers purchased their preneed funerals from a cemetery, they got a card with their name on it, and it was registered, and if anything happened to them, they could call the number on the card and that was always a number of the local funeral home. I said, "Well, is it a card like this?" and I pulled out a card that I had created in Kansas City.

It was a plastic card with identification on it. On my cards we listed trusts for Mt. Moriah; we didn't have the numbers on them, we weren't that sophisticated yet. I had hunted all over for a card and found a place in Wisconsin that manufactured plastic cards and I bought them by the hundreds. We gave them to all the customers and they could write their name on it. It had the name of the funeral home to call if there was an emergency or something happened.

Fred's idea was to create these and have an 800 number for funeral homes so anyone across the U.S. could call this number regarding preneed funerals because they had to be registered with the insurance company, and each had a policy number and so we would have every one of those on file. He opened up a small office in Indianapolis, put in the 800 line, and he had it answered around the clock. That went along okay for a few months after I had suggested that and I gave him that card. I just gave it to him; I didn't charge him for it as it's pretty hard to charge for ideas.

They called this card the Lifeline Card, and it had a picture of a lifeline as on a boat and had "Forethought Lifeline" on it. They were going along fine with it and then all of a sudden they got a lawsuit. They got sued because an insurance company in New York had copyrighted the name Lifeline. They received a cease and desist, and so that took him out of the lifeline business and they had to go back to the old fashion way like I did where everybody just called their own funeral home.

Batesville Management Services led to Forethought and Forethought led to my consulting with them for a year or two, and then they brought all of their Batesville Casket sales people across the U.S. in for a meeting, and one day of it was dedicated for me to talk about helping the funeral director sell prearranged funerals. But what could you do in a day to try and explain an entire book? I did the best I could. I got to know them, and we became good friends. It comes around full circle, the friends you make as you're on the way up.

By this time, the Forethought president had hired some sales managers with the intent to go to funeral homes all over the U.S and teach them how to sell preneed funerals. One time they asked me to come back to Batesville for a week.

They have a place in Batesville, Indiana called The Farm where they would entertain funeral directors from all over. They have been doing this for years. They put them up in nice quarters, and it's not The Ritz, but it's nice. They feed them and they have meetings, and this time they wanted me to get these sales people trained.

Fred went to the brother of the C.E.O. of all the consolidated industries, Gus Hildenbrand, and asked him if we could use their house on a piece of land that was adjacent to The Farm. They were worth a lot of money and they didn't live in the house, a very ornate house, so they agreed to let us use it. My bedroom had a gigantic bed in it with a big canopy on top of it and a copper-lined bathtub.

The room of this house where I was to train twenty or so sales people who would then go all over the U.S. and train people was a big room off the dining room, which had a huge, long table that could sit thirty people. And this room was filled wall to wall, all four walls all the way around, it was filled with nothing but Red Skelton's paintings of his clowns. They were originals, he had been commissioned to paint them for this lady that loved those clowns. That was quite a training experience, to have clowns all around me.

Here's a funny Batesville story: Fred said, "We've got a meeting to go to. Gus wants to talk to the two of us about our consultants. It won't take long but we need to go over to his office." We went over to the ornate C.E.O.'s office and were ushered in. Fred had been there numerous times, but I hadn't. There was a huge, solid teakwood desk. Beside it, on about three or four pillows piled high was a big, old, English bulldog lying there snoring, and passing gas every other breath. Nobody paid any attention to or said anything about that dog as he was Gus's, and Gus just loved that dog.

We sat down, and Gus took off his silver half-rim spectacles; I remember them, they were real silver, they weren't chrome plated. He spun them around on his fingers, and he looked at me and he said, "Dan, what do you think of women?" Now, that's a pretty loaded question to get from the C.E.O. of one of the largest Fortune 500 companies in the United States!

So, I'm thinking on my feet, and said, "Well, it all depends. If you're talking about women as women in general, I'm crazy about them. I love them since the evolution of Adam and Eve. I think women play a very important role, they're just vital. Of course, if you're talking about women in the workplace, I think they're the most under-hired, under-trained, underpaid people available to us, and they do marvelously well in prearranged selling. People will listen to them more than they will men."

Gus put his glasses down, he looked at Fred, and he said, "What have I been telling you?" And Fred, also thinking on his feet, said, "Well, we're working on it. As a matter of fact, Dan is going to help us with that. We're going to get some women hired into Forethought." Gus said, "Well, I am glad to hear it." And that was about the extent of the meeting, so we were summarily dismissed and we didn't even get down the hallway when Fred said, "Where are we going to find these women?" He knew he had to get all over that.

I hired three women that I knew in the business, one in Oregon, one in Washington, and one in Texas, and they were doing right well. Two of them stayed with Forethought Life Insurance Company for years. It's just strange the way things happen, the way they unfold, and the way they come down: Be in the right place at the right time with the right people.

During the time in Evergreen Washelli (E.W.) and Mountain View Funeral Homes Cemetery, David Daly, the President of E.W., and Buck Thompson, the President of Mountain View, pledged me to join a group called the Cemetery Council, which was made up of the largest cemeteries or combination cemeteries and funeral homes in the U.S. There were about eighteen people who belonged to it, you attended every year at your own expense, and you had to come with your guns loaded, with two or three topics prepared and ready to deliver during this three-day meeting, which you had been assigned to do by the chairman of the council.

They brought me in because Eric Marmorek, who had been the leading sales expert in the industry for years, was getting ready to retire. He lived in Sharon, Massachusetts, and he had always been kind to me; every time he wrote a new book, he'd send me a copy for my perusal, and he mentioned me in two or three of his books, which I still have. I went in there as a marketing guru for these guys to listen and take this information back to their hometowns and it give to their vice president for sales or sales managers or directors.

As a member of Cemetery Council, we met at the Drake Hotel in downtown Chicago at the same time every year in the winter, cold as the devil, and the Drake was right across the street from the Playboy Club. Remember that I had been given a lifetime membership in Playboy Club which was good in any Playboy Club in the U.S., and that meant you got a big discount on their hotel rooms and food and drinks. They weren't much on food, but they were on drinks and the Bunnies, so instead of going to the Drake, I always went to the Playboy Hotel and then would get up in the morning, walk across the street, and go to the meeting. Everybody was always jazzing me about staying at the Playboy, but it was interesting. A few of the members, the same ones all the time, always planned for me to invite them over to the Playboy Club as a guest for drinks, so that was always fun in the evenings.

29.

While I was living in Seattle I became president of the American Cemetery Association (A.C.A.), which at that time was a highlight in my career, a big honor for me. That made four different associations for which I have been president: the Kansas State Cemetery Association, the Central States Cemetery Association, the P.I.A.A. and the A.C.A, which then was comprised of about 1300 members from across the U.S. and some foreign countries. Today, that association is comprised of about 3,500 members because years after I was president, they began a merger and started bringing in funeral directors and funeral homes.

I went into the New Orleans meeting as President and I went out in Nashville at The Grand Ole Opry hotel in Nashville, a great night with a big raised dais, everybody in tuxes, long evening gowns, quite a prestigious thing. That was quite an honor.

During that year as president, I got a citation from President Ronald Reagan for contributions made to the United States citizenry in helping them prearrange their cemetery needs. I took that citation and put it in our national headquarters, where is it is to this day in Washington D.C.

I had been Vice President of the A.C.A. and for some reason, was always running into famous people in that role. At one convention in Washington, D.C., the A.C.A. dignitaries were sitting at the raised table at the front of the hall. Most of these gentlemen gave brief messages on their tasks for the year. The featured speaker that I sat beside was George H.W. Bush, the head of the C.I.A. We had a good conversation about China where he had been actively involved. He was a really nice man.

Another time, I was getting into an elevator in a hotel in Maui, and there is Lee Iacocca, the C.E.O. of the Chrysler Company. I introduced myself and we had a nice conversation. He was very warm and gracious.

Years later, Sherry and I were at The Dalles on the Columbia River in Oregon about to check into a hotel, and who drives up at the same time in a chauffeured limousine: Burt Reynolds and Loni Anderson! She was a knockout. She was on the popular

T.V. show "WKRP in Cincinnati" at the time. It is funny how things happen!

AMERICAN
CEMETERY

November 1982

Dan Reed — President, American Cemetery Association

 Convention
Reports

The Magazine of Cemetery Management

Sometime in the mid-1980s, I was approached by Buck and Dave that a friend who owned two cemeteries in Yakima and

Wenatchee, Washington, and three funeral homes, one in Wenatchee and two in Yakima, wanted to become a part of our act, he wanted to join in. So I went over the 'Hill,' that's what they call going over the hill past Mt. Rainier to Yakima, and sat down with Royal Keith and Joe Meredith who had formed a company.

They wanted to get into prearranged funerals and sell trusts there in central Washington like we were in western Washington. Keith had just come out two years prior to that as president of the National Funeral Directors Association, and he was held in pretty high esteem nationally as a result. Joe was a funeral director in Wenatchee, and was a 'funeral director's funeral director.' He was absolutely against everything I wanted to do in sales and marketing, just a typical dumbass funeral director. One thing he could do is take care of families in a service, but he didn't know crap about marketing and sales but thought he did. I went to work for him, met with him monthly, and made them a bunch of money, but I did not get along with him at all.

I asked one of the ladies who was from Kansas City and working in Seattle if she wanted to go to Yakima and be the manager, and she did. Then, the best thing happened to her. She hired and trained her sister who wound up being one of the top salespeople in U.S. selling cemetery property for us. She was really good. Her name is Patty. It seems like Patricias are always good at sales: If you hired a Patty, you were going to get a good salesperson.

About that time, Bob Gordon came to me. He was a second generation cemeterian, and his dad, Bass Gordon, had very deep pockets. Bob's brother was mayor of Glendora, California, which is about sixty miles east of Los Angeles. Bass had two sons and two daughters. They were very wealthy, owned two cemeteries and a funeral home in Glendora. Bob came to me and said, "Let me explain something to you about our family."

Over lunch he explained there were two families that owned all of this wealth, and one side of the family was not in the cemetery business and they didn't know squat about it. One member was very big in the oil business in Houston, another was big in a grocery store chain in North Carolina, and, the third was apparently the dummy of the bunch, living there in Glendora.

And, these families just could not get along. They couldn't even agree on where to go for lunch and what time to have it. They couldn't agree on anything, and yet they were running a multimillion-dollar a year business.

Bob said, "We've all agreed that we're going to go to the field, go into the industry, and we're going to recruit and hire somebody to come on to be the tie breaker on the board of directors. I want to know if I can put your name in the hat." I said, "Yes." He had three names in the hat, Gordon Ewig, who became a very close friend of mine and followed me as president of A.C.A., who was big time with S.C.I. and with consulting, and a man whom I don't recall.

Bob was pretty close to me, working together in Tacoma and Seattle and he pushed for me, and I got on their board. They met once a month at the company's expense. They couldn't agree on how to settle the earnings from the company every year, but they agreed on paying themselves fat director's fees and expenses. When we went to a meeting, we all got $1,800 for the day, which lasted about five hours, we had expensive dinners at the country club, and our travel expenses were paid. Once a month, I flew to Los Angeles, rented a car and drove sixty miles to Glendora and attended a board meeting. It was a very interesting part of my life.

30.

Bass Gordon, Bob's dad, ran that company with an iron fist. Everything he did he did first, and then he'd tell the board what he did. He hired a good friend of mine on contract, David Wharmby to come in and do sales, selling preneed funerals and preneed cemetery lots. Dave had left Indianapolis, Indiana, stopped at my house in Kansas City on the way to Los Angeles where he was going to work for a huge cemetery, and whose president followed me as president of A.C.A. by about four years. He was a member of the Toppers, and just a neat guy, and then, unfortunately, he died of cancer. Dave Wharmby was working for him and he built a heck of a sales organization. He had about seven hundred salespeople at its zenith.

At Glendora, they had around a hundred sales people, and the majority of them were Hispanic, here illegally from Guatemala, Mexico, El Salvador, Ecuador, all over. They could hardly speak English, but they were all landing in Los Angeles and they all had a need for cemetery property. So Bass hired Dave to take a sales contract with his cemeteries and sell preneed funerals and preneed cemetery property. They were selling cemetery property seventy miles away from the cemetery to people who had never even seen it.

Dave was quite a guy, he was absolutely a good promoter, and he made a lot of money in prearranged sales. One time, Dave asked me to come down and do a sales meeting for his managers and I agreed. Dave had a big hall built down by the airport that could accommodate around three hundred people. It had a single stage with a podium, it had fold-up chairs, and that was it. When Dave had his sales meetings, he would wear long flowing robes in Mexican colors made out of satin. Dave would address these people in fluent Spanish so they'd understand him.

I went there for a meeting in that great big hall, and there were only twenty-five or so managers there. I went on stage and waxed eloquently for about forty minutes.

People have always told me I can't say in five minutes what I can easily say in forty-five, so I have a reputation for that.

I finished and looked at Dave. He got up and they gave me a standing ovation. And then they all left, and Dave walked over to me. He's a big, tall guy, and he put his hand on my shoulder and said, "Dan, guess what?" I said, "What?" He said, "They don't understand a word of English." So he had pulled my chain pretty good! I thought that was funny. He and I are close friends to this day, one of my best pals.

Dave made a lot of sales, lots and lots of sales. This went on for about a year and a half. Every time we'd go to a board meeting and vote on the balance sheets, and vote on the standings, and vote on the cash flows, everything was just "do-wah-ditty," everything was great because Dave was making all the sales.

Then, gradually, the sales started slowing down. I'm reading the balance sheets and I'm seeing some problems. People had been cancelling left and right. We had sold the Hispanics for five or ten down a month, and then, a month or two or three later, they would cancel, but we were still carrying them on the books. This went on for a year before I woke up to the fact that all this business on the books, about 35-40%, was no good, it just wasn't there.

I confirmed it in the board meeting, I confronted Bass Gordon about it, and I said, "What are we doing about this? Why don't you get this off the books? We're kidding ourselves." He said, "Well, it doesn't matter, we all know what it is."

Well, they did not know what it was. The other half of the family didn't know a single thing about it. His sons knew, and I knew, but the other three didn't know at all. I said, "I'm going to make a motion that you clean up your books, that you get rid of the cancellations." Boy, did he glare at me, and said, "Well, it will take a while. It's a lot of book work." And I repeated, "Well, we need to get them off." It went on about two or three months, and then it finally came off the books and the balance sheet.

During that period of time, I was investigating in a discreet fashion and asking the right questions here and there, but I didn't get much out of the office because he had that office manager really wired; she stayed with him for years. I had to go outside the cemetery to find it out, but I did discover through Dave Wharmby's organization that Bass had cut himself in on a 3% or 4% income off of all sales going on in the books. He as an individual had cut himself in with Dave when he gave him the contract, so that's why he didn't want the cancellations to come off.

When I found that out and I had the goods, and I had clarification of it, at the next board meeting, I talked to the three other family members about what was going on with their company, and they were aghast. I said, "Look, this calls for a removal of the president. This president should be removed from his official capacities. The only way you're going to do this is get four votes. Now, you guys haven't agreed on much that goes on with the Gordon family, and there's three of them on the board, and there's you three, but there's me. I'll put it in motion, and we will kick him off the board, and elect a new president." They said, "Well, who would that be?" I said, "Well, Bob

Gordon. Bob Gordon is a son. He knows the business inside and out. Elect him president."

They thought about it and they thought about it, and they talked about it, and I didn't let them go home to think about it more, I said, "We've got to have the decision. I'm not going to go in there and make a motion like that unless you guys are behind me and stand for it." So they pledged to me that they would. We all shook hands around the table on it, and we broke for lunch. They went back to Houston and Carolina respectively and didn't say a word.

The next month at the board meeting, we no sooner than sat down that I made a motion that Bass Gordon as president be removed from his office duties because… and I produced the figures and the sheets and showed them he was involved in overwrites, and that's why he wouldn't take them off the books. We voted and it was four to three. He was voted off. We voted his son Bob to become president of the board, which he accepted. We had Bass leave the building and told him to vacate his office.

Incidentally, I flew with Western Airlines all the time I was going back and forth to Los Angeles. I had a lot of miles with them and they came out with a special deal that if you join their club, for an extra hundred or so bucks you got a lifetime membership in their private clubs at the airports. I joined, and during that time Western Airlines went bankrupt and Delta bought them out. Delta honored that lifetime membership with Western Airlines, and to this day, I've had a membership with the Sky Club for free.

I went down to the board meeting the next month as usual, and when I got out of the car in the parking lot, I was greeted by Bob's sister. She said they were in a meeting and I was to wait out there until I was invited in. I said, "Oh, okay." Well, I knew there was something up right away. I sat there and waited and waited and waited.

One hour, then an hour and a half, I sat there in the car, waiting. Finally, Bob Gordon came out and said, "Well, bud, I got some news for you." And he said, "My dad is back in as president and you're off the board. They're going to replace you with my sister. We'll pay you for coming down here and that's it." I said, "Okay," and I left.

During that month, Bass threatened all the family with cutting them out of the estate, and he had the power to do something with the trust and other monies that they had, and they weren't going to get anything unless he got back on the board. So, ultimately, I was pretty expendable. I think I did the right thing, I'm not sure I did the smart thing in making that move, but I know I did the right thing ethically.

31.

During my tenure on the board of directors in Glendora, California, I was also teaching. The association had created schooling for cemeterians years before, and I was the first one to attend the first class which was held at Bromwoods, a small college in St. Louis. A number of the leading proponents of the association at the time went to it, and we were instructed by various professors, who were not in the industry, about administration, accounting, maintenance, marketing, sales, and so on. It was a good school. It lasted for a week and it was almost a dormitory experience, and the closest experience I ever had to being in college. It was the first successful administrative school that the association ever had.

It only lasted for about three years, so we decided that we needed to have a real college with people in the industry doing the teaching as opposed to bringing in outsiders.

Arrangements were made to contract with the University of Memphis in Tennessee, and instead of the spartan accommodations we had they were now 'uptown' staying in dormitories. It's still held there in the summertime to this day.

For the first few years it was in existence I was a "professor" and taught the marketing class and they titled me, "Professor of Sales." People enrolled in the association's sponsored university, and had a choice of three or four curriculums and people who knew their business were teaching those curriculums. It was a lot of fun.

People from all over the country came there for classes, and if they completed them, they got a certificate called C.C.E.,

Certified Cemetery Executive. I'd gone through the classes at Bromwoods for a couple of years and at the time I qualified, but they'd never gone into the formality handing out those certificates. They finally did later at one of the annual conventions, and then I finally got mine. I was also doing other things at that time and I eventually stopped teaching there.

During all this time, Betty and I were not doing well.

In Glendora, I'd been working with the board of directors for a couple years as they had a big funeral home and did a lot of funerals. They also had two cemeteries there, one was very big, and the manager of the cemetery was a tall, good-looking blonde who always wore four-inch high heels, which made her that much taller. Her name was Sherry.

One time the board decided that it would be a good thing if the whole board attended the annual Christmas party, which was held in Glendora at the country club. We had our board meeting and then we went to the party. About one hundred fifty people were there that night, and this tall blonde, Sherry, was there in a really sharp looking red dress and she was master of ceremonies. I was very impressed with that, and so we got acquainted afterward.

Another woman, Penny, had befriended me two or three years before that, and she even came to Seattle and visited us. Betty would loan her a swimsuit and we would use the hot tub. Betty would never get in it but I loved it, it was just a great way to relax.

Jumping ahead a bit, Betty and I eventually parted ways, and then I was dating both of these women simultaneously. One was in Dallas, Texas and the other was in Los Angeles County. That got to be pretty hectic. I would see Sherry when I was in Glendora, and I would fly to Dallas to see Penny. Alternately, Penny or Sherry would come to me in Seattle.

I got pretty emotionally mixed up for over a year, as you might guess. Finally I decided to marry Sherry. (That didn't work either. We had a marriage for about three or four years, though were married for ten. California, where we lived when we got divorced, is a community property state, which gave her legal cause to divorce me.) Penny eventually married and still lives in the Dallas Ft. Worth area, in a little town called Granby.

Penny owned a company doing testing similar to McQuaig for large companies in the U.S. and was very successful at her career. She was a really neat lady, and I have lots and lots of fond memories.

Back at Yakima, Seattle, and Tacoma, we were enjoying good sales, things were going along really well. I had good sales managers at all three offices. Earlier, I had gone on that Colorado River float, and I really enjoyed river rafting.

There's lot of rivers in Washington to raft on so I got the bright idea that everybody who was interested would chip in for raft events. I got an old, used bus for our provisions, had it painted white, and had "Dan's River Rats" painted on the side of it. I'd provide the transportation, and I got T-shirts for everybody that wanted to participate in floating in the rivers. We had a lot of fun.

We would go on a Saturday, float during the day on the river, and at night, everybody had tents and we'd camp out, cook steaks, have sing-alongs and people playing guitars, and all that. It was just really fun. We did that for a year or two and floated in a lot of rivers - the Wenatchee River, the Snoqualmie River, and others.

In the meantime, I was going to baseball and football games in the old Kingdome Stadium in downtown Seattle. What a monstrosity that was, with terrible, terrible, terrible sound in it being all enclosed. The Seahawks played there and I got to see my Kansas City Chiefs when they played them.

And then Seattle started a baseball team, and I got season tickets to that. I had good seats on the front row just off the screen towards third base. I went with two other people through an ad in the paper and we bought good season tickets, they were pricey but we'd go to every third game. If one of us had somebody in town and wanted to go to a special game, we trade off.

At the first game Ken Griffey, Jr. ever played, I was sitting there watching him right behind the on-deck circle. He was swinging the bat, and then he looked over right at me and grinned. He was just a kid, about nineteen years old, but, boy, what a ball player he became. He followed his father's footsteps. He played in Cincinnati when he left Seattle. His dad, also a great player, also played for Cincinnati. They both were excellent ball players.

32.

I did a lot of consulting, speaking and conducting seminars throughout my career. When I went to Washington State, I included permission in my contracts to continue those efforts.

One time, I was contracted by Alan Creedy, the executive at O.G.R., Order of Golden Rule, a national funeral directors organization with headquarters in Springfield, Illinois. Alan asked me if I would put on a three-day seminar in St. Louis, and told me there would be about one hundred fifty sales people in attendance. I agreed.

They did a lot of advertising in many national publications. I put together a program and about nine or ten months later left Seattle for St. Louis. I flew to L.A. and discovered my flight to St. Louis was cancelled. All of us were put on a small bus and taken to Long Beach to catch a different flight than scheduled. I was to have dinner with the O.G.R. Board of Directors, so I called Alan to advise him of the delay. Long Beach airport was an all-outdoor facility. There was a restaurant on the second floor and about twenty of us were given dinner vouchers to use there.

When I started through the line, I noticed a passenger already eating that looked familiar. From across the room our glances met and he nodded and smiled back. I thought to myself, " Who is this guy? Where do I know him from?" I couldn't come up with the answer so I took a table by myself and proceeded with my meal. By this time, it was getting close to dusk and we were still awaiting a plane. After losing about four hours we finally departed.

There was lots of space on board so I took a middle seat and spread my materials out for review, and got a drink. About two hours later the flight attendant came by for about the fifth time to offer me a drink. I ordered another Scotch, and she said, "Do you know who is sitting up in first class?" She told me it was Stan Musial.

164

For those of you that don't know, Stan Musial was of the greatest baseball players ever. There is a statue of him at the main entrance to Busch Stadium in St. Louis. He had won about every award there was and was revered by baseball fans worldwide.

He had retired, but was very active in charities of all kinds. He lived in a very nice colonial style home in Forest Park, Missouri. In fact, I learned later he and Willie Mays, another fantastic ball player, had been to L.A. that day to sign baseball cards to raise funds for a children's charity. So, that's who was in the restaurant! I knew I had seen him before.

I had all kinds of materials for the seminar so I quickly gave the flight attendant a brochure with my picture on it and asked her if she would get his autograph for me. She agreed and about five minutes later she came back with my Scotch and his autograph, which I have to this day. And, now this story really gets interesting.

We landed in St. Louis about 1:00 A.M. Because I was in no rush, I was the last one to deplane. Who is standing at the cabin door? Stan Musial. What a surprise. He introduced himself to me since he knew my name from the brochure, and told me he was impressed with my credentials. Wow!

He asked if he could help me with a carry on and insisted on carrying my duffle bag loaded with materials. I had checked my suitcase and over my objections went with me to the luggage carousel. He wanted to know where I was staying. I believe it was the Marriott which had a shuttle, but Stan insisted he take me.

We got to his Cadillac convertible with a small turtle back trunk, and when he opened the trunk, his golf clubs were taking up most of the space. After apologizing, he put them in the back seat making room in the trunk for my bags. He then drove out of the airport across Interstate 70 to the hotel - it maybe took a whopping three or four minutes.

At the hotel, again, he took the majority of my bags. We entered and he was greeted as "Mr. Musial." At the desk I gave my name and Stan told the night clerk to upgrade me to a suite. Well, obviously, he owned the place! In fact there was a really nice restaurant that served food in carriages that were on an old-fashioned cobblestone street called "Stan and Biggies." I had taken a date there years prior. Stan asked me if there was anything else he could do for me, saying he would be back to the hotel for a meeting the next day. I said "sure, I'll be in a meeting somewhere with O.G.R." He said, "I'll stop by and say hi."

The next afternoon, sure enough, Stan stops at the doors and waved. I had over hundred people in attendance, so I stopped and waved Stan into the room. I told the audience a good friend of mine was here and asked him to come to the podium. When I introduced Stan, he received a standing ovation, made a few remarks, and then he left. (That was probably the best part of the program!) I never saw Stan again, but this story is too good not to share.

I have heard many stories about Stan Musial since. His generosity towards me was the same as everyone else he met. He didn't have to wait for me to get off that plane, he didn't need to take the time to carry my bags, drive me to the hotel, upgrade my room and take the time to speak to my audience. Simply put, that was "Stan the Man Musial." A true gentleman, sensitive to those around him, a tremendous athlete, and a great American.

33.

I had a houseboat while in Kansas City, and I'd sold it, but I liked boating so I decided to buy a boat in Seattle. And people said, are you nuts? Where are you going to put it? I said, "What do you mean? I want to buy a boat." They said, "Well, there's no place to put it."

I discovered that all the way up and down Puget Sound, there was no dockage available whatsoever. I hunted around and it took a while but I discovered that there was a place on Lake Washington, which came out to Puget Sound after going through the locks, and they were leasing stations on boats. I went down and investigated what they had and discovered they had a station available on a 31-foot Bayliner.

A "station" meant that you can lease that station for a year at a time and there were five stations on weekends. Different people rotated on weekends for Labor Day, Memorial Day, etc. It was rotated so that everybody got a shot at it and so you had your weekends all lined up in advance. When you were on board the boat and it was your weekend, there was a two-page checklist and you had to go around the whole boat and check everything off to make sure it was okay, because if you didn't check that off and things weren't okay and there was something wrong, guess what, you would have to pay for it.

The place where this boat was, Lord, it was very difficult to get in and out of. What made it even more difficult was that the boat was built in Alaska for racing and it had a very small draft on it, only 18 inches or so, and it was just like running a boat on ice, just practically skating. You really had to be on your Ps and Qs to pilot that boat.

I finally I got the hang of it, but it was hard, and the hardest thing was to dock it. The docks were located right below one of the most popular restaurants on the Sound. It was always crowded outside, and people would laugh at you getting the boat in and out. It was not easy, not a fun thing to do. Also, you had to have a pilot's license to take these boats on the ocean, so I had to go to school and study, and that was not easy to get. I've still got that pilot's book.

There were all kinds of submarines and navy ships over at Bremerton, and there were pipelines under the water, steel lines, cable lines, bridges, and just all kinds of stuff so you had to know what you're doing.

Once you got out in the Sound and you went on the inland passageway up past Mt. Baker, you were getting closer to the ocean, to the big water. There was a place called Deception Pass and it had a high, high, high bridge over it. When you went under that bridge and through that narrow pass, the currents were really dynamic and you had to know what you were doing.

Once you got past that and got out in the ocean it was clear sailing, and then you could go up to the San Juan Islands, to Canada, and on to Alaska if you wanted to. We would go up to the beautiful San Juan Islands. Sometimes we would tour around the islands and come back the same day, but lots of times, different couples would want to stay at the San Juans instead of going all the way up and back the same day. We all communicated what we wanted so if you were the couple that wanted to drive to San Juan, you'd take the ferry to get over there and we'd meet near there to unload all the provisions into the boat. Then the party leaving the boat would drive the other party's car to a designated parking spot and then get into their own car and go home. It was a smart system.

You could also sail to Victoria Island out of Vancouver. It's beautiful, with the Busch Gardens and all. We had that boat for a couple of years and it was lot of fun. I never really ran into any big problems with it thankfully. It was pretty pricey, but it was like leasing a car, and then the lease was over. It was worth it.

And then there's the story of Mike Cook, a really good sales manager whom I had brought from Kansas City with me. Once a month, he said he had to go into the veteran's hospital and get a blood cleansing for something he got during the war. Mike always smoked a lot of pot, though it didn't seem to affect his work as he was a tough sales manager. His good work, and that of a couple other managers, gave me the time to work with Forethought and do the other consulting deals I had around the country; they didn't need much watching over.

Mike called me one day and said he had come home and his wife was down in the basement in a corner crying. He couldn't figure what was wrong with her, and she said she just needed to get away from everything. He said, "Dan, I'm going to take her on a trip for a week, and I'm going to do this in the next couple of days, so you need to be here to run the show. I'm going to take her and the kids to California, and we're just going to have a good time." I had leased a newer BMW for Mike as part of his compensation for doing a good job instead of giving him a raise and commissions, which was pretty nice for him. I had three-year lease on it, and paid for it monthly out of my company.

So Mike took off in the BMW to go to California. And that was the last I ever heard from him.

I got concerned about it after a couple weeks. Mike had an Evergreen Washelli credit card with a $35.00 limit on it so he could buy office supplies and that type of thing, and they had to be approved by David Daly, the president; he always did approve them because whatever Mike got was necessary.

Jack Hackett was the general manager of the cemetery, and he said, "We need to call the police. He could be in the hospital." We called all the hospitals, we called the police, they put on an

A.P.B. on him, but they never found him. Then, the bills started coming in from the credit card a month later. We put a stop on that credit card so he couldn't use it. We tracked the bills as they came in, of course. He had bought gas $35.00 at a time, and the last one was in Kansas City, Missouri. I don't know if he ever went to California or not.

I checked his house and there was no furniture in it, it was all gone, the house was empty. Mike was making good money, and apparently had just decided to flee the scene. I do not understand that, I not understand it to this day. It seemed we got along pretty good, I didn't meddle with his management very much.

About a year and a half later, I got a call from the Kansas State Patrol that my BMW was sitting abandoned in a parking lot in Kansas City, Kansas, and I needed to do something about it. I had a wrecker get it, learned the car didn't work, so I paid the lease off.

So this was a lesson in human nature. Well, recall all those "blood cleansings" he'd been getting at the VA hospital? We checked into that, and he'd never been in that hospital in his life. We checked every VA in the area, in Tacoma, down by The Fort, and he'd never been in any of them. It was a strange story, but he disappeared. For fifteen years I never heard a word from or of him.

The end of the story is that years later, when I was in Philadelphia working for Loewen, twenty-five of us were at a dinner meeting, and who's there sitting in the meeting at the restaurant? Mike Cook. It turned out he was a sales manager in North Carolina for Loewen. I sat down beside him and said, "We need to talk."

He just looked at me and his face got red as can be, and I chewed him out. Of course, I had no recourse, I couldn't get him fired or anything. I learned his wife was working for him, and she was doing better at sales than he was. That story still makes me ill.

34.

After I had served a year as president of A.C.A., having gone through all the chairs, and after I had been vice president two or three times, and gone through numerous chairs, it seemed like the apex of my career professionally from a standpoint of association work. If you left as president, you stayed on the board for three years.

While I was president, the board and I had pushed and pushed and pushed to create a new association. It wouldn't be ours but it would be an association. It came about because I had chaired the board for two years with three past presidents, and shared a committee that met two or three times a year with the monument dealers at the Sheraton Airport Hotel in Chicago. The monument dealers and cemeterians were at each other's throats all over the U.S. and there were new lawsuits every year. They were justified on both sides of the fence, either the cemetery side or the monument dealer side because there was just cause for the lawsuits.

The ones making the money out of the whole thing were the attorneys. Every time we went to a convention, we'd have to raise funds from all the cemeterians and do a big bailout and phone follow up to raise money, and we were raising over a hundred thousand dollars a year for our legal fund to fight the monument dealers. We had a number of cases in Pennsylvania that were quite expensive.

While I was going out as president, I suggested that we meet with these people, come to some kind of conclusion and draw up rules and regulations that both sides, cemeterians and monument dealers, would have to live with or they'd be in violation of their own association. The board thought that was a good idea, so they appointed me to do that.

I got three past presidents to assist and we started meeting in Chicago. They were not pleasant meetings, they were riotous. There were four on our side and four on theirs. We all had justifiable causes, but with the exception of the executive vice president who was representing them, the two or three monument dealers were pretty doggone mature, they had their feet on the ground and wanted to resolve the conflicts, while their executive vice president wanted to continue them.

There were two vice presidents, Steven R. Morgan was ours, and theirs, and I finally got theirs not to come to the meeting so we could get something constructive done, and that took the better part of a year.

After two years of deliberation, we came up with a new set of rules and regulations between the monument dealers and the cemeterians, and that was passed by both boards, and it resolved it. Now we didn't have to raise all that money and do all that fighting anymore.

That was very educational, arbitrating and debating with people who are involved with lawsuits on the other side of the fence. We had some good times, we had some rough times, and the longer it went, the better and easier things got.

In my third year on the board, after being president, and after that whole thing, the board decided because we'd done so well that it would be wise if we were to get all the allied members of the death industry together and form a new association. We would have everybody meet and air their differences, discuss things, come to conclusions and air it all out without going to courts.

We began a new association called F.A.M.I.C., Funeral and Memorial Information Council, and we got all the executive vice presidents from all the associations to join it with the exception of the florists. The florists would never join us, but we had the cemeterians, the funeral directors, the monument dealers, the vault manufacturers, the casket manufacturers, the bronze manufacturers, we had them all. All executive vice presidents of the associations would meet in Chicago at the same hotel where we put together the America Cemetery Association and Monument Builders of North America.

The main reason I always wanted to meet there was because of an excellent, excellent restaurant right across the street called The Cave which featured really, really good Greek food. Everybody was on an expense account so we would all troop across the street to The Cave and have dinner. I remember it really was just like a cave as you walked in, and boy, it just reeked of garlic. You'd come out just smelling of garlic.

F.A.M.I.C. was formed and I became the first president. For a year, we debated and we met quarterly. We would make

171

agreements and go back to our respective associations and carry them out. Things would be approved or disapproved and we would correspond mostly by letter and we carried out lots of things. We had minutes, we had officers, I was the president, we had a secretary, a treasurer, and the whole nine yards, and we were doing pretty well. When we came up to the second year of F.A.M.I.C., however, nobody wanted to be president.

At a meeting, I got up out of the president's desk at the front, and walked to the back of the room, and I said, "Ladies and gentlemen, somebody is going to have to take over and become the president of this organization if we're going to keep it going" and I sat down in the back row. Nobody came forward. After sitting there for five minutes, I reluctantly got up and went back up front, and said, "Okay, one more year and that's it. I'm not going to do it a third time." And I didn't.

In my two years as president of F.A.M.I.C. we got written up in all the trade mags about the great things we were doing to bring people together in the industry. In the third year, I was coming off the A.C.A. board. I suggested to Bob Gordon, who I worked with while living in Seattle and Tacoma during all that time, that he take my place as president of F.A.M.I.C. and knew he'd want it in a New York heartbeat. Bob was a kind of a guy that liked a lot of notoriety, had a lot of ego, so he accepted the position, and he was president of F.A.M.I.C. for many years. F.A.M.I.C.is still in business serving the industry.

Around about this time, I got a call from Vancouver, B.C. from a gentleman I didn't know and who said his name was Ray Loewen. Ray said, "I hear all kinds of good things about you, about what you're doing with preneed funerals in Washington and I'm wondering if you do any consulting." I said, "I sure do." He said, "At my expense, would you come to Vancouver and talk to me about selling preneed funerals. I've got funeral homes but I don't have any cemeteries selling preneed funerals in Canada." I said, "Sure I will."

Ray Loewen was a Hutterite from Manitoba and owned some funeral homes there, and then he migrated to Vancouver and he owned funeral homes there. He had decided, with the growth of the conglomerates, that he might get into the business.

We met, and we got along well, he was a nice guy. Ray said, "Why don't you come up here?" He had five or six funeral homes in the Vancouver area. "We've got room at the crematory" which was in a little town near Vancouver. He said, "Go out there and teach our sales manager how to do it, train him and all the salespeople to sell preneed funerals." I agreed to this and did this for about a year, but it didn't go all that great. It was good, but it wasn't all that great. It was a tough sell in Canada.

Sometime a while later I was sitting in first class while going to a convention in Maui, and who's sitting in front of me? Ray Loewen. I reached out and tapped him on his shoulder and said, "Ray, how are you doing?" He turned around and said, "Well, Dan Reed, I'll be darned. Let me come back and join you." It wasn't very crowded on the flight. Across from me and one seat behind was Ray's executive V.P., Steve Childress. He was a man I knew from Texas, a lousy cemeterian who had gone broke and the funeral directors had run him out of town. Ray had hired him to run the Loewen Group. And Steve eavesdropped on everything we said… He was very paranoid.

Ray and I talked about what I'd done up in Vancouver, about things in general, and what was going on. Ray had just bought some funeral homes and cemeteries in California, his first foray into the U.S. as the Loewen Group. We had a good visit, and a good relationship. Steve Childress was concerned about me talking to Ray all the way over there. Although he was pleasant, I can read bodies and body language I knew that he was uptight about our conversation. I didn't see Ray in Hawaii, and I didn't hear anymore from him. I went back to the mainland, and I went on about my business.

35.

During my time in Seattle I got a phone call about one or two o'clock in the morning, and it was a fellow from Australia. He had been to a convention in Los Angeles and heard me speak. He owned seven funeral homes in Melbourne, the second largest city in Australia. At that time it was pushing three million, and was just a beautiful city. The Yarra River runs right through it, and it reminded me a lot of Philadelphia and the Schuylkill

River. The Yarra River and the Schuylkill River were equally as brown and dirty, but it made for a nice tourist city.

I said to the guy, "Do you know what time it is in Seattle, Washington?" He said, "Oh mate. I'm sorry, I'm sorry. I'll call you back tomorrow." He called me back the next day, which was the middle of the night for him, and he wanted me to come to Australia at his expense and talk to him about contracting and introducing how to sell preneed funerals in Melbourne. I was working at Evergreen Washelli at the time, so I had the freedom to go out and do other things I wanted to do on a consulting basis.

I got down to L.A., got on a plane to Sydney and then changed planes to go on down to Melbourne which is in southeastern Australia; Sydney is in the northeast. There's a big variance in their temperatures, climates, and their weather because it's quite a bit cooler in Melbourne than it is in Sydney.

I got there at one or two o'clock in the afternoon, and believe me, after an 18-hour flight you're groggy. You've just crossed the equator and a timeline so you gain a day, and your body is just out of whack. It's a long, long, long, long, long flight from California; there weren't very many flights, in fact I don't think there were any flights at that time from Seattle. I always flew business class because I had racked up so many miles, and that made it a lot more comfortable. I was on the fourth flight of the 747 that it made to Australia from Los Angeles.

I started going to Australia in 1987. A lot of things are different in Australia from the United States, just a tremendous amount. Tony said, "We are going to go to dinner tonight. Have you ever had Barramundi?" I said, "Barramundi, what's that?" He said, "That's the finest fish in the world. You, me and Richard, my general manager, are going to my favorite restaurant in the world, but my wife's not going to come because we're going to talk business."

He handed me the keys to the car he had for me, and said, "Your car is parked out in stall number so and so, and it's a black Rolls Royce." I said, "What?" He said, "Yeah mate, it's a Rolls Royce. We've got eight of them at the funeral homes, and it's not in use tonight so you take it and drive it." I said, "I'm not driving a Rolls Royce, the steering wheel is on the right side, and

I would be on the opposite side of the street to what I'm used to driving. No, I'm not going to do that."

He insisted but I resisted, and so he told Richard to give me the keys to his car, and he'd drive it. Most all the cars in Australia are imported and just as pricy as can be. They do have a Chevrolet plant in Southern Australia, and so I drove the company Chevy. So we had dinner, and Barramundi is indeed an outstanding fish. The next night, two barristers, their attorneys, ate dinner with us.

The cemeteries weren't in control of politics down there like in the U.S. but the monument builders were, and if you go into any cemetery in Australia you'll understand why. They sell monuments, all the cemeteries are full of them. I mean they truly got the lion's share of the dollars in the death industry.

One barrister explained to me that there were no laws written pertaining to selling preneed funerals, and no trust laws or anything in Australia. I made a couple of trips with the barristers to the capitol, and over time we got the laws put in place, they got passed.

Tony Generalli, who was from Sicily, owned seven funeral homes, and it became public that he was going to start selling preneed funerals. The funeral directors in Australia then kicked him out of their Australian National Association of Funeral directors. He was a maverick. Well, people in U.S who had started selling preneed funerals were also known as mavericks, and I was one of the biggest ones of all.

It took five or six months to get that done, and a few trips to Australia, and then we were ready to go. The third or fourth time I went to Australia, Tony and Richard met me at the airport and drove me to a nice two-bedroom flat on the second floor right on the Yarra River. There was parking underneath, and it was fairly close to the offices I had leased to house the sales people.

Tony lived in a suburb of Melbourne, down by the ocean and very, very swank. There were huge homes there, and Tony had a lot of money. He drove a Bentley, his wife drove a Mercedes, and he had all those Rolls Royces as family cars in the different funeral homes. He was very fastidious, extremely fastidious. If you went into his office and sat down, he would sit there and move the phone a quarter of an inch one way, pick up a pen, put it back down in a particular spot, push something else… the desk was clean, but he was moving stuff around all the time while he was talking, everything had to be in its perfect order.

One day he asked me if I was bus, and would I like to go for a ride. He said he had to see some people. I wasn't too busy so I agreed to go. We went around to drycleaners, to bakeries, barber shops, beauty shops. He stopped everywhere, and they all knew him. After a while, I got tired and just sat in the car and waited, because he wasn't in them very long.

A week or two later, I was telling Richard about that trip, and he smiled and asked, "Did you notice anything peculiar?" And I said, "No… not that I can think of." He said, "Well, if you don't know this by now, you are going to find out because many key employees know this: Tony heads the mafia in Australia. He is from Sicily and he is the head of the mafia." The funeral homes and all that was just a front.

Tony had six kids, all grown, and he was a good-looking guy with thick, curly black hair, and his wife was beautiful. He invited me for dinner one time on a Sunday with all the family there. If you have ever been to an Italian dinner, a Sicilian dinner, it isn't a sit down and eat for an hour or two affair, it's a sit down deal for the whole day affair. You eat and you drink wine and you talk, and then you eat some more and then you drink some more wine and it stretches out for hours. People get up, come and go, and come back and sit down. Tony was at the head of the table and his wife sat at the other end, and it was a big table, as you can imagine, with all those kids and their spouses and their grandkids. It was quite an afternoon, quite revealing, too, of the man's life.

For years he had a mistress, and had bought a home for her. She lived in a nice part of Melbourne, though not nearly as upscale as where he lived, and they had a daughter. The daughter was ten years old and on certain nights of the week, Tony would go over there, and spend the evening. And all the family knew it. The kids knew it, the wife knew it. Nobody talked about it. That's just how it was. So it was pretty enlightening for me to work with him. He was always very good to me, he treated me like a friend, and I was glad because I wouldn't want to cross him.

One time flying from Australia to Seattle I had to transfer through L.A. I belonged to the United Airlines Club, so I was sitting in the club at a table in the middle of the room on the phone with my good buddy, Dave Wharmby when a half dozen men came in and walked right up to me. A couple guys came around the table, tapped me on the shoulder, and said, "Sir we need to use your phone. Is it okay, can you please get off the phone?" I said, "Oh sure, sure." I ended my conversation, got up, and who was standing there in front of me but Henry Kissinger, Secretary of State. He and his aides had been somewhere in China or Asia and he had to make a phone call, so I gave up my phone so the Secretary of State could make his calls as he was quite a bit more important than I was. These occurrences sure happened to me regularly.

Another time I went to Australia all the airlines went on strike causing us to stop in Guam at three o'clock in the morning to refuel in as much as we would not be serviced in Sydney at that hour. Well, it's really hot in Guam. They turned off the air conditioning and opened the doors, but we couldn't leave the plane because we were in a different nation. After a while a one-ton truck of Shell gasoline came out, and a man started manually pumping gas into the wings of the plane. This took an hour and a half. By daylight we flew nonstop to Sydney.

In another time during my travels, I got in an elevator and there were two good looking women on it. I mean, they were just dressed to the nines, and flirtatious as all get out, and they'd been drinking. We got down to the ground floor and one of them looked at me said, "You are really a handsome man, I wish we had the time to get better acquainted," and the other one giggled and then they walked off. She looked back over her shoulder at me, still flirting. And who was it but Zsa Zsa Gabor! She was famous for hitting on men, so I know I wasn't the only one. It didn't bother my ego though.

Everything I was used to doing in business was totally different in Australia. When you hire a salesperson in Australia you have to provide a car if that's your full-time line of duty. Tony had to lease a bunch of cars, lease an office, and my agreement was that there had to be somebody from my company there continuously. It didn't have to be me, though it primarily was me, but that was in the contract. I could live with that because I was doing okay at E.W., and my contract was about to come to a close anyway.

The Australians love Americans and there weren't any problems hiring sales people because at age fifty-five they have to retire, and then they can work part-time. We hired a lot of part-time salespeople and they were pretty darn good. It was very pricy to start up from nothing, as there was nothing available to you in the whole country, and you had to create your own. Our printing bills and publishing bills were just astronomical. But Tony wanted to have a preneed funeral sales force in Melbourne, second largest market in Australia, and so we did.

I wish I could say that it was done with a great amount of success, but it really wasn't. We struggled, we hired people, we made some sales. I went to the field and taught people how to sell. I would stay three weeks at a time, and then I'd come back and I'd send somebody else. I had Dave Coates and another fellow I had hired go down for a week at a time, which they were excited to do, but I had to be there the majority of the time, though. So that was what was going on when I was winding things down at Evergreen Washelli and getting ready to start looking for something else to do in the U.S.

The Australian experience was a good one, and a lasting one. I didn't make a lot of money, and unfortunately I didn't do a really good job for him as hoped.

Years later, I was at a birthday party in northern Atlanta in Georgia with one of my best friends, Jack Frost, for his eightieth birthday. There were about three hundred people there, and sitting at his head table was an acquaintance I'd known from earlier years, J.D. Ingram, who was a mausoleum builder. There were six others at Jack's table: The Lieutenant Governor, Attorney General, and some of the moguls of the Georgia Assembly.

It was quite an evening. J.D. said to me, "I heard you worked in Australia." I said, "Yeah, that was years ago." He said, "Well, did you work for Tony?" I said, "Yes, I did, I worked for Tony Generalli Funerals," and he said, "well, I did too." I asked him what he did for Tony. He said, "I built a family mausoleum for him and his family. I built a twenty-crypt building with black marble on the front." So, Tony's going to go out in style, and he was a good guy, and I never hear anything about him nor heard from him again. As years went on, the conglomerates began to buy funeral homes and cemeteries in Australia, and they reaped the rewards of those laws being changed.

36

One of the few pictures of my dad and me later in life.

During this time, still in 1987, I got a call from one of my relatives apprising me that my dad had a major stroke, and was in the Veteran's Hospital in Chillicothe, Ohio. I made a few trips to see him.

One time Celine met me and we went to see him together. She gave him a big hug. He was non-conversant due to his stroke. He would just blink his eyes to show he understood what was being said. Celine told me to give my dad a hug, which was a very rare thing for me to do. I remember at reunions my Uncle Lindley would always hug his son, Lawrence, and I just never understood it because my father had never hugged me... ever. I hugged him, though, and it was awkward.

I never saw him alive again because while I was in Australia, Betty told me she'd gotten a call that he had died. There were only three flights a week from Melbourne to Sydney to the States, and I couldn't get on any of them, they were chock full. I finally landed a seat due to priority from a death, and asked Betty to call the funeral home and tell them I would not arrive until a week later. I was able to attend his funeral and see him buried with his ancestors in a little church cemetery called Boblitt.

An interesting piece to this story is that when I finally got out of Australia and Betty and I got to Columbus, we rented a car and drove to Chillicothe in a heavy thunderstorm. After viewing my dad, the funeral director told me a female attorney was waiting to see me privately in his office.

She showed me a hand-written letter and asked if I recognized the writing. Well, my dad, like me, did not have good penmanship, and his writing was immediately recognizable, so I confirmed to her it was indeed his. She informed me that it was his last will and testament, and that I had been left $5,000.

Well, that was a surprise to me because I had no idea how much money he had or that I would even get any. She then said that he also left $5,000 to each of my children, and that really surprised me, although he and my kids always got along really well. Then, she said to me, "If you want to contest his will you certainly can, but I will be representing him in court and because he has an administrator I don't think you would stand much of a chance."

Now my curiosity was really aroused, so I asked her what the estate was worth. She said that was privileged information and would not be divulged until the will was made public. The funeral was ready to take place so that ended our conversation.

Betty obviously was inquisitive about the meeting, so later I informed her of what I had been told. Some time later after I had returned to Seattle, the will was read and I got a phone call from a female cousin excitedly telling me about her inheritance. I still don't know how much was in the estate, but he had purchased a lot of timberland off the tax rolls, had harvested acres and acres and sold the lumber to the paper mills in Chillicothe. I had no idea he owned so much land. I still don't know how much he left, I think it was about six figures, but it was distributed equally to all of his nieces. Some of his nephews brought a lawsuit because they weren't treated fairly they said. Most, though not all of my female cousins really needed the money they got.

I was told, and this was not substantiated, that $250,000 was donated to the Shriners Children's Hospital. He was a 33-degree

Mason, a past master, and a Shriner so that went to a good cause. I am glad my children got some money because they all needed it. And so, my chapter of Dad came to an end.

My contracts were running out in Seattle and Tacoma, and they didn't need me as they were getting good results. I was making good money, and I had worked myself out of a job, really. I had good sales managers in all the operations. I had replaced Mike Cook with Mike Johnson who was doing a superlative job with a totally different style than Cook's. It was time for me to start thinking about some other things.

There I was with nothing to do. At this point, Betty and I weren't having real serious problems, but we just hadn't been content together, and so we decided it would be best for us to divorce. I loaded up our furniture and sent the majority back with her to, Belton, south of Kansas City, where she wanted to move. I got an apartment in Seattle, and so we split the proceeds and were divorced, which started yet another new chapter of my life.

HALL OF FAME

37.

My good buddy, Hugh Keatley, called me and said that he heard through the grapevine that my contract was up. I said, "Yeah," and he said, "I've got a really good opportunity down in Albuquerque, New Mexico," and I said, "Really?"

Chet Stewart and two brothers owned four funeral homes and two cemeteries there, family-owned, third generation, and they didn't have anybody who knew how to sell cemetery property or preneed funerals. So, I said okay, and he said he'd let them know and they'd get a hold of me.

I flew to Albuquerque and met with them, and I started what was to be a three-year contract. There was no sales force. They gave me a very nice office above their administrative office in the cemetery, but they would not let me sell preneed funerals as they wanted their brother's wife to head the preneed funeral organization, even though she didn't know squat about it.

As mentioned earlier, I had been dating and then finally married Sherry and decided to build a new home in Albuquerque. It was a really nice home at the foot of Sandia Mountain. I put a hot tub outside which she thoroughly enjoyed. We would hit the hot tub every night. Under the full moon, it was very romantic, and we could see the tram going back and forth on the mountain.

I bought a 35-foot Chris-Craft cruiser. It was the largest boat in New Mexico, which isn't saying much because there are no boats there. I kept it up in northwest New Mexico where a river dumped into a huge lake. We'd go up there on weekends, and spin up the river into Colorado. It was a good time, and always a beautiful drive.

The other great thing about living in Albuquerque was excellent, and I mean excellent, Mexican food. You just couldn't find any bad Mexican food and I fell in love with it, and learned about Hatch chilies. There's a big difference between chilies, if you didn't know.

Hatch chilies were grown exclusively at that time in New Mexico, and the powers that be of other types of pepper growers curtailed them so Hatch peppers couldn't be shipped fresh out of New Mexico to California, Arizona, Texas and so on. But, they could process them and sell them in cans, so, if you're ever looking for chilies, look for Hatch chilies because they're the best you can find.

On the streets in the fall when they picked chilies were vendors with great big gas fired ovens and they would put the big Hatch chilies in them and turn them over slowly. They were about eight or ten inches long, two or three inches in diameter, and when they were done, they'd put them in a plastic garbage sack. Everybody knew when you take them home you first had to put on rubber gloves, and then blanch them, cut them up and put them in your freezer, which we did every year. That was quite an experience.

I built a good sales force, and we were doing extremely well selling a lot of cremation, mausoleums crypts, and cemetery property. I sold out five buildings in the huge mausoleum complex. I couldn't sell preneed funerals there, and that brother's wife should have been selling do-wah-ditty, but wasn't,

183

but she was family so what were you going to do. I had eighteen salespeople and we were doing well, everything was Jake.

After a couple years, I came to the conclusion that I wasn't being paid the right amount of commission, and hadn't been from the beginning, but I was looking for a job then and wanted to work down there. But by now I had certainly proven my worth.

I decided to speak to the three brothers, one of whom I had hired and was selling cemetery property quite successfully for me. He and I got along famously and he extolled my virtues to the rest of the family, but he wasn't involved in administration, he wasn't a funeral director and didn't want to be.

I called for a meeting with them and he was there because it was family. I requested a raise in my commissions and overwrites, but they made the payroll, I didn't. They were paying me an overwrite and I was making pretty darn good money as usual, but this request was a negative to them, they didn't like it. I repeated that I thought I should make more money. They decided to consider the discussion and we would get back together in three months.

When we got back together they were stonewalling me, so, I gave them my notice and said I was going to work the rest of the year for them, and then I would be leaving. At the end of the year they had a big, nice going away party for me, with no rancor or anything.

In the meantime, I'd been contacted by one of my fellow Toppers, Dave Sullivan, who worked with Gibraltar Mausoleum in Indianapolis. They did contracting all over the U.S. and had a contract on a nice cemetery in the outskirts of Philadelphia. I went there on a year contract, and so we sold our house in Albuquerque and leased a really nice condominium in Philadelphia.

Sherry joined me to work as a family service counselor, and she hired her own crew. I had about twenty people, and we did a lot of phoning, a tremendous amount of phoning. The market there did not prove to be what I'd been shown because the majority of people who were buying property were black, which took the pretty much all white salespeople into the black areas of town, but they didn't want to go down there. This restricted what we could do with our marketing, so I hired a really sharp woman who had been in telemarketing. She ran a good telemarketing division for me, and so we eked out sales.

Gibraltar Mausoleum was going to build a mausoleum on the grounds of the cemetery, and so we sold over half of that mausoleum that year, which meant quite a few sales. Gibraltar would have meetings and they'd bring their managers in from other states, and of course I knew everybody and everybody knew me. Yet, when the year was up I opted not to renew because I had heard about an opportunity in Boise, Idaho through the grapevine.

Sherry and I flew out there and I interviewed with the owner, his father, and his brother, and we agreed on a three-year contract with the Cloverleaf Cemeteries and Funeral Homes. It was a good contract. They had been contracted before with Rich Sells, my good friend, before he joined the group at Hamilton in San Diego, and had done a pretty good job in Boise with about eight salespeople.

I was given a house there to live in for a short time, and then we rented a home, and then we started looking to a buy home. We found one in a nice area. Everything in it was great except the carpet. It was God-awful, some kind of a vivid green color; I never did like that carpeting.

I built a sales organization of about ten people, and we put in lawn crypts and started selling them for the first time in Idaho. We also started selling mausoleum crypts and built three mausoleums. We did really well in Boise.

While I was in Boise, my son Greg appeared on the scene and he came to live with us and stayed for about six months. He was great on roller skates, and Sherry and I went to his graduation from an old college, Chico State University, in Northern California. He was proud that he was the first one in the family that got a college education, and justifiably so. On a different occasion, while I was living in Seattle, Mark had come to visit us and it was just a short visit, but Greg stayed a while.

I got the sales force going and Sherry was the funeral home manager. I put together a marketing program, and we knocked doors as I didn't have a phone room yet. We would send one couple to Hawaii for a one-week paid vacation if they just

185

listened to our presentation, they didn't even have to buy anything. It was a great marketing program I put together, and we made it abundantly clear in all our advertising that it was limited to the first three thousand people around Boise: That's a lot of presentations.

It took us a few years to do that, but we got it done. The Chamber of Commerce was involved, and we had a dinner for the drawing, and it was all tied in with our advertising in the newspapers and on television. The head of the Chamber of Commerce did the drawing and I took the name and I went to the winner's house to award them the certificate. The newspaper tagged along and they took pictures of us.

It was the neatest thing because a young couple had enrolled in our program (we never 'sold' anything, people enrolled in the program) and had purchased lawn crypts. They were in their mid to late twenties, he worked in a factory, she worked in a store downtown, and they had one young daughter. On weekends he would take his old pickup truck and go out to one of the factories in Boise where he was allowed to have their scrap aluminum in exchange for him hauling it off. There were quite a few factories there, Hewlett-Packard being one of the major ones along with some other big computer manufacturing companies. He would work all day long, and take it to the junkyard and sell it, and that's how they paid for their monthly payment for the cemetery property. For that couple to win that contest, that was really neat and deserving. They went to Hawaii, and we got a lot of good publicity out of that. It was a very rewarding thing.

After that program was over, I decided to start telemarketing. So I hired a young gal named Stacy, and I had her knocking on doors. She told me that she thought she could do a better job with telephoning. We installed more telephones and she hired some people, including her sister-in-law, we started phoning, and boy, we did a good job telemarketing.

Living in Idaho with its great out country, I did some whitewater rafting. We drove all over Northern Idaho and discovered a little town by the name of Stanley, right at the foot of the Sawtooth Mountain range. The name is deserving because those mountain tops are just as jagged as can be. I fell in love with that quaint little town. We used to drive there on weekends.

There was a river with hot springs that ran through the town, and people built cabins on the river including the owner of the cemetery who had one for quite a long time. In the cabin there was a spot in the middle of the room where doors lifted up from the floor and you could go right down into the hot spring river, right beneath the house. You would get in there and float around, and there were fences so you wouldn't be swept downstream, although the currents weren't that strong. It was great. Stanley, Idaho is one of my favorite towns in the world.

One day I got a call from Hugh Keatley who was on the committee that headed up the Hall of Fame in the industry. He said, "Dan what are doing, you got time to talk?" and I said yes and he asked, "Are you going to Cincinnati?" (for an annual association meeting) and I said yes. He said, "Are you sure, you are going to be there?" and I said yes again, and then he said, "Well, since you are going, you might as well take the time to be inducted into our Hall of Fame."

I said, "What??" I was flabbergasted. To go into the Hall of Fame... I thought the apex of my career with the association was being the president, but that association was formed in the 1880s and up until that period of time there had been only eighteen people inducted into the Hall of Fame for outstanding contributions. I had seen people inducted into it, and was just glad to say I knew them and shake their hand. But, I was to go into the Hall of Fame... well that was a revelation to me, I was beside myself.

The owner of the cemetery at the time had a son who was never very happy about all the association work I did, because he was a funeral director through and through. About two hours after talking to Keatley, I got a call from Ron Robertson, whom I've known a long time and in fact had trained at one of my schools in Kansas City when he was just out of college, and he was working for Steve Childress, the Executive Vice President of the Loewen Group. Steve was also on the call and said, "Dan this is Steve and I've got Ron and Jeff Cashner, the president of the Western region, on the line, too. We are calling to see if you would be interested in taking a position with us as a Regional Vice President at Loewen to run the West Coast region." I said, "Well, sure I would. I have about three or four months to finish

187

my contract yet, however," and he said, "Not a problem, not a problem. Come to Philadelphia at our expense, I'll have Greg Strom call you to arrange it. We'll meet at the airport hotel and interview you to see if you have what we are looking for."

And then, Steve said to me, which was a coup de grace, "Now, Dan I want you to know, I am staking my reputation in this industry on interviewing you to take that job. It's a great opportunity." Well, that guy didn't have much of a reputation, the one he had wasn't good, anyway, and it didn't impress me that he was 'staking his reputation' to give me an opportunity to go to work for them, so I wasn't too excited about it. Greg Strom had been president of a bronze-level company, and I knew him from the industry. So I went, and there were six people sitting in the hall waiting to be interviewed and another was in being interviewed. I didn't know a one of them, so we introduced ourselves, and were talking, and since we're all there for the same reason that was kind of tense.

About three weeks after the interview, Ron Robertson called and said Dan, "We made our selection, and I want you to know that if you'll accept the position, you're going to be an officer of the Loewen Group, and you will be responsible for six states and a part of Canada in running sales and marketing. I want to know if you will accept it." I said," Yes, I sure do accept." That was a big day in my life in Boise, Idaho.

One of the stipulations for working for them was I had to move from Boise, because it was too far off the beaten track from the west coast. It had a good airport but you had to connect through Salt Lake City or Seattle to get anywhere, so he said I could move wherever I want to move on the West Coast. This was a no-brainer because Sherry, being from the Los Angeles area and her children being there, jumped on that in a New York second. So, we decided we'd move to California, starting a new chapter in my life… again!

38.

The mid 1990s saw tremendous growth of the Loewen Group. Many acquisitions were being made. Regional Vice Presidents (R.V.P.s) were installed in Hawaii and Canada, and they were really growing quickly. In 1995 when I joined the Loewen Group, it was the second largest organization in the world in the ownership of cemeteries and funeral homes, and the first largest in the ownership of funeral homes. The majority of their business was conducted in the United States, but they were actually a foreign corporation doing business in the U.S. They headquartered in Philadelphia for the U.S., and their home offices were in Vancouver, B.C. I was the newest member to join as they had reorganized during the summer when I got that first phone call.

The presidents of the five regions of the U.S., Ron Robertson, and Greg Strom were all on the move recruiting vice presidents for marketing. We had strict budgets, and every year they increased; we would go to Philadelphia yearly for three to four days based on how long it took us to come together on our budgets. The five regional presidents were responsible for operations and sales, and so they straddled the fence with cemeteries and funeral homes with operations. Ron was the national sales executive, and we also answered to the president of the region, so we had two bosses all the time.

When operations were purchased by Loewen in California, Washington, Oregon, Montana, Idaho and other western states, I would inherit some good sales managers and some lousy ones. There was a sales force in place making sales, and now I had total responsibility for all of the marketing, how we went about it, how we put presentations together, and how the managers read them. They responded to me, period. It was a highly, highly regulated system and I didn't take it lightly.

One of the first things I did was make a trip to visit all of my operations; that was just elementary. I noticed right away that what people were doing was just a mishmash, a salad, if you will. Everybody was doing things their way, some of them were good, most of them were pretty bad, and none of them had the marketing prowess that I had gained over the years.

The first thing I did was create a standardized presentation. I told all the managers in my travels that there was a presentation that they were going to learn, that they were to follow it, and that they were going report to me on every salesperson on a weekly basis. Some of the managers didn't believe in reports, and were more shoot from the hip managers, and 'well, he did a good job, he got a sale, pat him on the back,' "attaboys" and that kind of thing. That went out the window with me right away. I was there to run an organization.

By this time, Sherry and I had moved from Boise to Orange County. We contracted to build a new home in a subdivision called Palmia, which was an upscale subdivision of about five hundred homes built by a huge developer. It took a while to get our home built because it was built in blocks at a time. After we selected our home style and determined what street we would live on, we had to wait for six months from start to end for them to complete our home.

It was a really, really nice area. They had a state-of-the-art putting course, tennis courts, swimming pools, and a clubhouse. There were five different styles of homes in the subdivision, and "Number Five" was the largest and then they got smaller going down so on to "Number One." Where we lived there were no Ones or Twos, only Threes, Fours, and Fives, and there were only so many of each on each street. We got a "Five" and that was a beautiful home.

During this time, my son, Mark met a lady from Ensenada, Mexico. I didn't know very much about their courtship, and just two days before their wedding, Sherry and I got a phone call with that announcement, so we did not attend. While traveling in central California I visited them in Los Banos, and I met his wife, Griselda. They had a nice home and she was an excellent homemaker. They had a small acreage and Mark had a few head of cattle. I didn't see them again until they had moved to Shelton, Washington where my grandson, Marcel, was born.

Eventually, Mark came to work for me and traveled to Idaho, Washington, and Montana on his assignments. By this time, they had a daughter, Damaris. Some time later, Mark and his family moved to Ensenada, Mexico, where he did a lot of day trading on the computer. Years later, when I'd moved to Missouri, he came to work for me at Daniel E. Reed and Associates and moved his family nearby in Monett. Since that move, I've been able to see them regularly, and really enjoy our time together.

Greg, my youngest son, has always been a challenge to his siblings and me. It is not a pleasant subject, and we have not spoken for a number of years for many reasons. There were many strained times, and some good times, too. He and his wife, Gail, live on a farm in North Carolina.

1995 was also the year that I went to Cincinnati to be inducted into the Hall of Fame. The event was held in a great big reception area at a primo place, the Netherland Hotel. The Loewen group had, unbeknownst to me, commissioned a local company to put a huge banner up that said "Congratulations to Daniel Reed, inducted to Hall of Fame, a faithful Loewen employee." That was great because Loewen was really going head to head with S.C.I. and Stewart Enterprises, but mostly S.C.I. at that time. Everybody in Loewen knew I hated S.C.I. as bad as they did, so we were on a mission. And of course, S.C.I. was there.

Fred Newman and me

During the cocktail party that night Ray Loewen and Larry Miller were there, and some attorneys came in and they came over to congratulate me, when Larry and I noticed Ray had a long face. I said, "What's going on, guys? You don't look too happy." They said they just came from Mississippi, and we were in a lawsuit and it wasn't looking good.

They told me right there in hushed tones that there was a five hundred million dollar judgment brought against the Loewen Group, and that put chills up my spine. Here I was in a zenith and getting things going, and here's a massive lawsuit against us. It was the second largest lawsuit ever brought against a United States corporation at that time, the only larger one was with Texaco. We went on with the party and I was inducted into the Hall of Fame, I got a standing ovation, and the next day I went right back to work.

I was standardizing presentations and the marketing for the sales managers which was easy for some but not for others. My key operation was in Modesto, California and it was run by a really neat guy, Tom Holman. He had six kids, had moved from New York City to California years ago and got a job selling cemetery lots and eventually he became manager before Loewen bought them out. It had a large funeral home, large cemetery, and it was the biggest sales force I had.

When I met Tom, I had invited him and his wife to dinner at the Red Lion Hotel. Tom was nervous and he said, "Well, Dan, I guess there are a lot of changes coming." I said, "Well, whatever changes are coming, it always happens in any organization." He said, " I know, I worked for S.C.I. and left like you, I couldn't stand it." I said, "Well, there's really not too much to worry about because you are doing a good job here, and whatever you are doing you keep on doing it, if you need help, you ask me. I will come here once a month and visit with you. You will send me your reports once a week. We'll talk about the reports on a weekly basis, as I will with everybody, on a conference call, and other than that, do your thing." His wife reached across the table put her both hands on mine, and said, "Thank you for that, thank you. He's been worried to death, and I told him it will be all right." I reassured her it was going be okay. But that's the thing these corporations put people through, this fear and stress, and it reaches all the way down the line.

Tom had a fellow that was running his family service program named Johnny who had worked in Arizona for a good buddy of mine, Bill Hawkins. Johnny had four family service people.

After about nearly a year on the job I had gotten things consolidated, we were all using the same presentation, everybody was trained the same way, and I was beginning to make sense out of the reports that I got on every salesperson every week. I'd take them with me on the plane, I'd go through two hundred plus individual reports, everyone in the group, and then it got to be a lot more than two hundred and I couldn't handle it alone any longer, and I had to get an assistant regional vice president. We went through that rapid growth into 1998.

One time on my monthly visit I said, "Tom, you are not getting out of the family service department what you should be getting." He said, "Well they are doing a good job, Danny." He said they were making hellishly good money. I said, again, "You are not getting what you could get" so he said, "what should I be getting?" I said, "Well, first of all you've got four people. You need twelve." "Oh, no, Danny," he said, "Listen, I'll lose some people if you put twelve people in family services." I said, "I told you a couple years ago just to run things the way they were, but I am asking you to let me come in, work with Johnny, build a family service program and increase the sales dynamically, increase your income, increase his income and increase the production of the cemetery and funeral home." He listened to me, and said, "Well, you are the doctor, you call the shots. I am willing to do it." I said, "Tell Johnny that I am coming up and spending a couple of days with him."

I returned to Modesto shortly after that and I asked Johnny if he had ever had Japanese food, and he had not. I said, "Well, tonight you are going to get a chance to eat it. We will explore Japanese food, and you can pick and choose what you want. If you don't like it leave it on the plate. And, we're going to talk business." He agreed so we went out, and I introduced family services to him.

He said he'd heard about family services, but he had never been involved in it; Bill Hawkins had told him about it when he was running sales for Bill in Scottsdale. I said, "Johnny, we are going to start a family service program and you are going run it, so you need to learn it. I will spend time with you, teaching you what to do and how to do it."

He was hesitant because he was just like Tom. I don't know if they colluded or not, but he said, "You know, we've got two women in there making extremely good money. They are making a hundred thousand dollars a year each." I said, "I know that, but I am not concerned about how much money they are making, I am concerned about how many sales you are getting and how much you are making." He said, "Okay. I will do whatever you say."

So that began the family services program in Modesto and we went from four to twelve people. We lost the two top producers who went to the competitors, so we replaced them, and then we almost doubled the production at Modesto. Johnny and Tom were happy as all get out, and I was happy because of productivity. They were happy because of the increase in income they did for themselves on their own merits.

Modesto was my test market. I put family services in all over my region in the way that it was being used there, and I had something to showcase.

Loewen decided to buy operations in Palm Springs and Costa Mesa, and I was in on the acquisition because I had to do all the prognostication and sales figures and everything for them, which was not an easy thing to do. I inherited a female sales manager at Costa Mesa and two or three of her top salesmen, one of whom came to work for me in Toledo, Ohio when I was with the Hamilton Group, which we'll get to later. Incidentally, as of this writing, she is still in the business, working for S.C.I. and hates every minute of it.

There was a couple, the Flanagans, who had a funeral home for years in Costa Mesa, but they had moved to Palm Springs and built a beautiful funeral home and a cemetery across the street from my offices. It was just top of the line.

Where I sat in my offices in Costa Mesa adjacent to those offices were four crematories and they practically ran around the clock. Cremation is very prevalent on the whole West Coast.

Honorine Flanagan was a tyrant. She ran that operation, and people were scared to death of her. She intimidated and managed through fear, which is the worst way to manage. Her husband, John, was in jail for reasons that will become apparent.

I learned about a lawsuit that had been brought against the Flanagan funeral home for a cremation in which they didn't get the proper cremains returned: They got somebody else's. During the lawsuit, it was discovered that the Flanagans had been commingling bodies - for years: They would stack two or three bodies at a time in the crematories and, they were even cremating dogs and cats, so you didn't know if you were getting your neighbor from down the street, Fido or Felix the cat or your mother when you got the cremated remains back. They all came uncovered and Flanagan just mixed them together. Most people think of "ashes" after cremation, but there is no such thing. They are fragmented bone reduced to about the size of the end of your little finger, and they usually go into an urn.

I hired a salesperson who had been in the business before in Palm Springs. I hired this great gal, Karen Montez, a redhead, to be my secretary as we started our Palm Springs operation. I didn't have much to do with Honorine, who stayed on as a general manager, because, frankly, I had no use for her or her assistant, who she intimidated all the time; how she could treat a man like that is beyond me. I didn't like her, she didn't like me, so we agreed to disagree without saying it. Karen Montez and I started hiring salespeople, and I hired a great guy from St. Louis who later became my assistant regional vice president.

I was so impressed with Karen. This was the kind of a gal that could answer the phone, keep on typing, be addressing envelopes and doing five other things - she multi-tasked magnificently and could do anything. If you told her to do something, she didn't say, "Where should I go?" or "how am I going to get it?" She'd say, "Okay," and she'd go do it. She was extremely resourceful. Good grief, if there were more men and women like that in business! You give them a job to do and they go do it. They don't ask, "Do I have to cross a river?" or "is there a bridge to cross?" or "do I have to climb a mountain?" They just go do it. That was Karen. I fell in love with that woman. She was the most effective and successful executive administrative assistant I'd ever had.

Stacy Edwards had done a really, really good job running my phone room in Boise, Idaho. When we were apprised that we were going to open up telemarketing groups across the U.S., I was to have two, one in Portland, Oregon and one in Las Vegas. I opened up the one in Portland first, and who did I call to do this? I called Stacy Edwards. She did a great job for about a year, and then my son, Mark, hired her to manage an operation in Montana.

So then who did I call? I called Karen Montez. I moved her and her family there in about 1997, and she loved it, and still lives there as of this printing. We started a program, and I made audiovisual tapes for the people to be trained on so when they were hired they would go into a room and watch and learn until they had the presentation down. Then they'd get an assignment in the phone room. We did a good job running a lot of appointments. Then we opened the second group in Las Vegas, and I sent Stacy's sister-in-law to Vegas as she wanted to run the phone room there.

We now had seven phone rooms across the country, and I had the best hold ratio of any of the phone rooms: When we made appointments, they stuck, and we were running at just a little over 40% close month in and month out: When you get a 40% hold ratio with a bunch of salespeople, that's pretty darn good. We were calling for offices all over the states I had then, and the salespeople would take the leads and run with them.

Tom Holman did not want to run those phone room leads, so I wrote him up. Most of the salesmen managers weren't worth their salt, were lazy. Well, now that the rooms were doing so well they jumped on it like a monkey on a banana, and we were very successful running telephone rooms.

I went into the phone room one time in Las Vegas. I walked through, and I listened for a while; there were about twenty people working the phones then. After a while, I called the sister-in-law to come into the room, and said, "We're going to shut this room down." She asked, "Why?" and I said, "Because. Just listen."

I was a very pragmatic manager and believed in going by the book. You had systems, the systems worked, and you followed them. I learned that when I was with Gibraltar Mausoleum Corporation in Philadelphia: They had a system and they did great, great, great sales because everybody followed the system. One of the things they did was have sales meetings six days a week, meaning Monday through Friday and every Saturday. I wasn't able to hire some good salespeople because they refused to work Saturdays, but the whole system worked, particularly with presentations.

Dave Sullivan was a stickler about presentations being learned verbatim, word-by-word, page-by-page. He'd come in, go to any salesperson, open up a presentation book to any page and say, "Give me that page." If they couldn't give it verbatim, he'd look at the manager and you knew the manager was going to get chewed out. That's just the way it ran, and it was good. I ran it that way in Boise, and it was just the right way to do it. It worked, and it worked with the large sales group I had with Loewen.

So, there in that room, I turned the lights off, and I said, "Okay, everybody stand up. This phone room is shut down, we're done." I said to them, "I've walked through here and listened, and some of you saw me and some of you didn't because you were working, which is good, but you're working the wrong way, you're working the hard way. There are a lot of you in this room that are not following the script that you were trained on. You will do the script that you were trained on or you will leave our employ. It's your choice. You can make up your mind. You can tell your manager what you want to do. You're either going to do the script the way we want it done, or you're going to leave. Period. That's it." And I walked out.

39.

By this time in the Loewen group, with the phone rooms going, with the all salespeople being hired, with all the sales managers, I couldn't keep up with it all, so I was given the authority to hire two assistant regional vice presidents. I put one in the north and one in the south, and assigned a lot of the work that I was doing to them. We were continuing to make acquisitions. Mark came to work for us as a sales director.

The hierarchy in my region was as follows: I was the regional vice president, I had two assistant regional vice presidents, I had four directors of sales, and the directors of sales had so many sales managers each, based on their territory. Well, Mark became a sales director and he travelled to Idaho and Montana. He knew the system, he knew how strict I was on the system, and he did a good job.

On a conference call that took place every Monday, chaired by Ron Robertson, who was referred to as "R-2," Ron announced a yearlong contest involving all levels of salespeople selling funerals and cemetery property. It would be publicized heavily to create competition and would be held at the M.G.M. in Las Vegas. This was good-spirited competition put forth by R-2.

Then, about halfway through the contest, R-2 announced a talent contest just between the R.V.P.s that would be held opening night. Each R.V.P. had the responsibility for securing talent from their region. Who did I have pursue this? Karen Montez, as usual, and she got busy to carry out my assignment. Each R.V.P. had fifteen minutes to showcase their talent. She found a husband and wife team with guitars and great voices to sing a medley of songs, my son, Mark, did a knockout version of the famous comedian Rodney Dangerfield and his routine of "I get no respect," and there was a great drummer.

The night of the contest, three judges sat in the front row: The C.E.O., the President, and the Comptroller. We had about five hundred attendees in the room from all over the country.

Incidentally, everyone receiving an award had all their expenses paid and it all started off before dinner with a riotous crowd.

A R.V.P. from Florida who was very popular in the company and always wrote the highest volume month in month out was an avid biker. He rented six motorcycles and had bikers from his region outfitted in black leather caps, slacks, shirts and jackets, and the show opened with the bikers coming on stage with a roar. The crowd went nuts! They did figure-8s, circles, and other tricks for fifteen minutes.

My group was next, and Karen was my M.C. Then, when the fourth group was doing their set, a streaker come prancing across the floor, zipped in and out of the performers, and brought the house down including the judges. The guy actually had skin-colored shorts and socks on, but really looked naked.

Well, guess what: The streaker was me! I had concocted the idea weeks before, enlisted Karen to help me, and without anyone's knowledge, I went backstage after my group's bit, got undressed, put on a really curly wig, put on the skin-colored outfit, and did my streak. It was crazy! Well, the judges and the people sitting in the front rows recognized me (I have a beard, remember) and before the evening was over everyone knew the Loewen Group's streaker. My region won the talent contest though it had nothing to do with my actions; I always thought the bikers should have won. Pictures were put in the newsletter and it was quite an experience, a whole lot of fun.

Ron held meetings the next day, and we rehearsed the awards presentation. It was a lovely night and everyone was dressed formally. The ladies were beautiful in their gowns. At the head table were the top officers of the company and all of the R.V.P.s. All of the winners of the different categories were introduced individually and congratulated by the head table. It really was a great year for all of us and we felt very secure about the coming years.

We would go to Philadelphia once a year for meetings, and to Vancouver, B.C. twice a year to meet with all the brass and discuss marketing. It was a good company, and we were really on the go. We had seventeen thousand employees in the U.S. On the administrative side of the company, which I was included in, there were eighty officers. Eighty. They had responsibilities of accounting, financing, banking, acquisitions, all kinds of things. The Regional Vice Presidents were in the top eighty officers and as such we had an option, if we wanted, to take stock with the company.

When you're making good money, and I was, I was making a substantial six-figure income, you know you can only buy so many steaks and so many suits, and spend so much money. They had a very generous offer on stock. If you would transform your earnings into stock, they also gave stock to you, so I became a pretty good stockholder.

As we grew and kept adding on cemeteries and funeral homes, an interesting addition came up with the acquisition of funeral homes and cemeteries in Palm Springs, California. When I went to Orange County, as mentioned I had an office in a funeral home in Costa Mesa, My offices were nice, but most importantly I was close to John Wayne Airport. I did a lot of flying, just a tremendous amount of flying, every week. Every week I was in the air somewhere. And you talk about miles, I had racked them up going to Australia.

We were just do-wah-ditty, making all kinds of sales, and then all of a sudden I started getting some calls from some vendors whom I knew personally from years in the business. They were a bit embarrassed and said, "Dan, we're not getting paid for the bronze markers, we're not getting paid for the vaults," whatever the situation was, "and we need to have our money. It's in arrears and when we call Vancouver, all we get is a stall. What's going on?" I told them I'd get back to them with an answer very shortly, and I immediately called Vancouver.

Well, they had been pulling names to see who was going to get paid this month and who wasn't. I insisted and did get most of their money paid up. I went to Vancouver for a meeting, and by this time it was apparent to everybody that cash flow was a real problem because with the ongoing lawsuit, we had been shut off by the banks, and had been borrowing money in New York. On Wall Street we had been shut down and were living on cash flow, and that won't do it when you are a growth company. A growth company has to have capital.

For that meeting in Vancouver, I'll never forget it. I took a Kansas City Chiefs tie. The Chiefs had had a good season that year, and it happened to be Ray Loewen's birthday. I went in, knocked on his door, and he said, "Yeah, Dan, what's going on?" We were getting ready to go to a meeting in about fifteen minutes," so I said, "I might as well just come in here and suck up. Happy Birthday. I brought you a Chiefs tie, if you want to wear it, fine, if you don't, give it to somebody." Ray looked at it, and said, "I appreciate that. How's things going?" I said, "Well, I think things are going good from my point of view, but I don't think things are going good from your point of view."

He said, with a frown on his face, "How so?" I'm standing in front of his desk, and I said, "We're not paying our bills. It's known in the industry all across the U.S that Loewen is in trouble financially." He said, "You know, Dan, you just don't understand how I finance."

I said, "No, I admit to you Ray, I don't understand how you finance, but I do understand cash flow, because I've been short on it a lot in my life. And we're short on cash flow." Ray said, "Well, it will all work out, don't worry about it. Let's go to the meeting."

There were about eight of us who met, and later we had dinner that night. At dinner, Ray asked us all to unload on anything we had going. I don't know if I put some idea in his mind with that two-minute standoff meeting between us or not, but we went around the room, and I expressed my views again about the cash flow. There was kind of a silence in the room with my contemporaries because they didn't comment, but I did.

We finished our dinner and we all went to have drinks. I asked Ron if I could talk to him, and he said, "Yes, I'd be glad to talk to you. I've got to meet with a couple others first, but we'll get together."

Around 10:30, Ron came to me at the hotel bar. Everybody from the company was in there drinking. We got our drinks, sat down in a corner, and I said, "Ron, I'm giving you my notice. I'm not going to leave you in a lurch but I'm going to leave here in three months." He said, "Dan, it's been a good ride, hasn't it?"

I'll never forget that. He didn't ask me why, he didn't ask me what I was going to do, he didn't ask me if there was something wrong. He said, "It's been a good ride, hasn't it?" He knew what I was doing. So, I gracefully "retired" from the Loewen Group.

They put out a big notice in their company newsletter about me retiring as Regional Vice President. And that was that.

During the time before I left, I got a sixteen-page registered letter from the Loewen Group, as did the other seventy-nine officers of the company, and it said our stock was frozen. We could not sell it; that would be illegal because of insider trader laws. Sherry read the letter with me and we looked at each in stunned silence.

Over the ensuing months, I watched my stock go down, down, down. It was at $42 a share when S.C.I. offered to buy us out. Here was the company that I hated the most offering to buy us out, and we tendered that offer. We staved them off and didn't sell the stock, it wasn't consolidated.

About a month after I had given my resignation and retired, Loewen Group went bankrupt. Upside down. Totally. I don't know if it was just common sense or not. I had a lot of things in my life I was pretty dumb about, particularly in some of the decisions I've made, but I do have foresight, and it was accurate that time.

40.

Well, what to do? I'm in Orange County, and I don't have anything going on. I was living my life, we were going with the wind. We had partial season tickets to the California Angels there in Anaheim so I was going to see the games. On quite a few Sundays I went down to San Diego with Sherry or with my barber, who was an avid football fan, to see the Chargers play.

And eventually, I thought to myself, "Well, here I am all by myself, what am I going to do?" I decided to talk to some funeral homes locally about selling preneed funerals for them. I lined up two or three funeral homes in Orange County, and went to San Diego County, which was about seventy miles away, and lined up a big funeral home in the northern area of the county, and started hiring and training salespeople.

I didn't do anything spectacular. I was doing quite a bit of selling myself, and we were doing well selling prearranged funerals for Forethought. They had been sold out and redone two or three times and they didn't know me and I didn't know them.

I was using Forethought for my life insurance, and I didn't get along with them too well for a number of reasons which I thought were justified, so I got lined up with a company in Utah called Great Western Life Insurance Company.

Now, that's a strange thing to talk about, the Great Western Life Insurance Company, because it was owned by a funeral director who owned seven funeral homes in Utah, and had started an insurance company to take care of his own needs.

Back when I was in Boise, a man named John Lindquist from Ogden, Utah came to see me and said, "I've heard all the things about you from the past, what you've done, and what you're doing here in Boise. I'm starting an insurance company and I'd like to have you come in and head up my sales for me." I was on a contract, and it was slightly ahead of the time that I was called by Loewen, and I couldn't break it. Sherry and I had a home there, so I deferred on going to work for Great Western Life Insurance Company. But, here I am years later and I remembered John, called him, and they were doing pretty well.

So, I started selling for Great Western while I had my new company in California called Pre-Arranged Professional Associates, "P.A.P.A." I incorporated that in California and I was making my own payroll, doing my own thing going back to what I had done with M.C.C.I. on a much smaller basis.

Sherry initially was not happy with my resignation from Loewen, but when it went bankrupt she understood. She was unhappy that we lost all the stock, and she never got over that which became the beginning of the crevasse of our marriage.

I had done pretty well in Orange County and had a good, good funeral home there. I also had done pretty well in San Diego County and did a lot of sales myself. I met a guy named Rick Sadler. He was a tempestuous kind of guy, very overbearing, a funeral director who was managing a prestigious funeral home for a guy that was an alcoholic, and he had a pretty good size staff, mostly women. Rick had a family working for him. He hired the father and his three daughters, and he was having an affair with one of the daughters. The father was an ex-professional boxer, and he and I got on okay; he drove the van all over to deliver bodies to the cemeteries and those types of things.

An interesting side story to that, years later, when I was in Detroit working for the Hamilton Group, I went to a Greek restaurant I had heard about that was very good. Somehow or other I knew the owner from previous restaurants I had been to, so I asked for him when I went there, and he came over and sat down.

We shook hands and talked about when we met and so on, and he said, "What are you doing now?" I told him about my work in southern California, and that I had met a guy that knew him. He asked his name, and I told him about the ex-boxer. He said, "You work with him?" and I said yes, and he said, "That guy saved my life! Not once but two or three times. When I was a kid going to school here in Detroit, there was a gang after me and they always chased me. He would come out and protect me, and would just beat the hell out of those people. He's got a standing invite anytime he's in town, dinner is on me. He's a heck of a guy and you tell him I said hello when you go back."

It really, really, really is a small world when you're as active as I have been at all the different points and places in my lifetime. It's amazing how what goes around comes around, just amazing. The old saw "You better treat everybody nice on your way up because you might meet them on the way down," well, there's a lot of truth to that. I've always treated everybody nicely, I've been fair, and tough, yes, but I always treat everyone fairly. I treat people well, as if they are all equals. I wasn't always treated that way but thankfully most of the time I was.

Rick Sadler and I would get into it a few times. We got into a big argument once and I walked out of his office, got in the car and drove back to Orange County, had a scotch and dinner with Sherry. The next time I went down there, Rick said, "Dan, can we talk?" and I said, "Sure" and we went into his office and closed the door.

Rick stood there, and he put out his hand then he said, "I owe you an apology. I was way off base. I lost my temper. I said some things I shouldn't have said, and I want to beg you for your forgiveness."

So, here it was happening again to me. That happened with Patty, that happened with Dave Coates, and here it was with Rick, and to this moment, Rick and I are very, very close friends and have been ever since. We've never had another cross word between us.

I had stood my ground with Rick, and the next time I was in his office he told me about a new TV program that was coming out called "Six Feet Under." The producers have looked at funeral homes all over the U.S. and they picked his funeral home to do the program! The show was full of stars, and he wanted to know if I'd participate. I said, "No, I've been on television and radio, no, I don't have the time to do it, Rick, because it's going to be demanding and you have to be there all the time." I deferred, but that program became very, very popular, and ran for several seasons. It was a funny show.

I got Pre-Arranged Professional Associates growing, and one day I got a call from a guy I had met on a couple of occasions at conventions. He said he'd been asked by Ron Kruger to set up a lunch appointment saying he wanted to talk to me. I asked what it was about, and he said, "I'm with the Hamilton Group here in San Diego." Well again, what goes around comes around.

Paul Hamilton had come to me back in Cedar Rapids when he owned three funeral homes, and he wanted me to move to San Diego with him and be his sales executive. He had sold that company to S.C.I., and started a new company and went back in the business of buying funeral homes. Paul Hamilton was pretty aged by that time and wasn't active in the business, but he had built a good team and had nice offices in San Diego.

I agreed to meet for lunch, and we met in Dana Point, California, a really upscale area with some marvelous, top of the line hotel accommodations. Before the waiter could even get the water glasses set down, the president of the Hamilton Group turned to me and said, "Dan, we want you to come work for us." I said, "Well, that's a surprise." He said, "Well, we think you can help us and we can help you. I brought a contract with me and you can take it home and read it if you want to, you don't have to give me an answer today, but if you do come to work for us, you would take the responsibility of being our National Sales Director. I can't give you a title of Executive Vice President, I've already got that, and we've got two Vice Presidents sitting here so I can't give you that, but we'll give you the title of National Sales Director and we'll pay you handsomely on an overwrite for all the business. We've got business coming in which would give you a pretty good income to begin with, and you can build it from there." I listened and said, "Well, that sounds interesting."

I went home to broach the subject with Sherry. We lived in Palmia, in Mission Viejo, California in a beautiful home. Out back of the house, outside the dining room and living room on our lovely patio we had built a waterfall about four feet high. We had a picnic table and chairs out there year round, and spent a lot of time out there by that waterfall. It was very soothing, and ran all day and night. It was all lit up at night and it was just beautiful.

Sherry and I both drank scotch. She always drank JB, but that was too mild for me. One of the things about my time in Australia was that you could come back with six liters of alcohol duty free, and in Australia they sold a lot of Glenlivet and Glenfiddich Single Malt Scotch Whisky, the top of the line. When I was living in Seattle, I'd come home with six bottles every time, so I had a closet full of scotch! After Betty and I were divorced, I lugged all that scotch around and I still had plenty of it left, and most of it was Glenlivet.

So, Sherry and I sat down and had a scotch, I reviewed the contract, and asked her what she thought. She asked "Would you be working in San Diego?" I said, "No, I'll be working all over the U.S." She didn't like that. I said, "Well, look, it's a good opportunity." I was making a good living with P.A.P.A. then. I said, "This really is going to work into something good." She again said, "I don't like it" and she just walked off.

SURPRISE

41.

Well, I was sorry Sherry didn't like it, and that had no influence on me. None whatsoever. I went down to San Diego, signed the contract, got everything set up, they gave me a schedule for going to see all the operations, and I took off for a few weeks flying around the country.

In California, I drove to some of the operations as there weren't that many, but they had a number of operations in Washington, Ohio, Wisconsin, Louisiana, Michigan, and Idaho. I visited them all and in the meantime they had all the regional vice presidents welcome me and make me familiar with everything.

The Hamilton Group decided to have their annual national meeting at the Batesville Casket Company's place, The Farm, because in Hamilton's funeral homes the majority of the caskets they were selling were Batesville caskets, and so Batesville loaned it to us.

Years before I had been there with Forethought, so it was interesting to see it again. At the national meeting, I again was introduced to everybody and some people I hadn't yet met. They were all advised that I would be responsible for all the marketing and all the sales, and that they would work with me. Well, some of them did, and most of them didn't because they were funeral directors, and they just don't get it.

I was in Toledo at one of our funeral homes early in the morning; I was always one of the first ones there. I was going to Detroit that day, and then planned to grab a flight the next day back to Orange County; I generally went into John Wayne airport. Well, that morning, the news was on the television. The date was 9/11, 2001, and there was the horrendous tragedy with the airplanes in New York City. I stood there in the funeral home watching, just stupefied. I remember very distinctly being in Toledo when those planes crashed into the towers. I saw the replay of the first one and then, the second...

I got to Detroit, got my hotel room that night, got up the next morning, got over to the airport, and everything was closed down. I didn't know that before I left the hotel. The airports were jammed and there were no planes flying anywhere in the U.S. as you recall.

I looked at that mess and turned right around, went back out, got into the hotel limousine, and went right back to the hotel, asked if they had a room and they said yes so I checked back in. It's a good thing I did that immediately because all those people were stranded and began looking for rooms.

I stayed in that hotel three days before airports started opening up again. I went over to the airport a couple of times to check on things, and there were just long, long lines everywhere.

I stood in the line for a long time and finally got to the Southwest Airlines counter as I wanted to get back to John Wayne Airport. A woman worked with me, and it took forever, but she finally got me a flight out that afternoon to Phoenix as she just couldn't get me into L.A. I flew to Phoenix, rented a car, and drove back to Orange County.

I was back to travel, travel, travel and it was an interesting part of my life, an interesting part of my career. One of the nice byproducts of it was that I had a sales manager in the northwest area of Washington State, which is great fishing country. There were two funeral homes and a cemetery in Port Angeles, and he was doing a reasonably good job, nothing exciting, but he loved to fish. As I was heading up there one time, he told me he'd take me fishing. He had a nice boat, a 30-foot Tollycraft, and he knew right where to go to get halibut as he loved halibut fishing.

Now, halibut fishing is a lot different than most sport fishing in that you put your anchor down in the ocean. We were out where we could almost see Victoria, B.C. We were still in American waters, just south of Canadian waters; Vancouver was to our northeast, and Victoria Island was almost straight north from where we were, you could just see it, and he knew right where we were going. We had to get up early so we slept in the boat on the dock overnight, and got up at five o'clock. I had to get a fishing license, and then away we went on the boat. We went out there and we put the lines down.

Halibut live really deep, about three to four hundred feet deep or deeper based on where you are. You put your bait on great big hooks and you generally have two or three hooks, maybe four on a line spaced about a foot to a foot and a half apart. I had never done this before. You have big weights, you let the line out, and when that weight hits the bottom where halibut lie as they're bottom feeders, then you raise that up about three or four inches so it's just off the sea floor. Then you sit and wait, you sit and you wait.

We waited for about an hour and a half, and bam, a fish hit my line, and I said, "I got one," and he said, "Well, just start reeling in. It's going to take you a while." I think it was down not quite four hundred feet.

It's not that the fish are fighting you, it's that between the weight and the fish on this big heavy-duty line, it was just doggone heavy. I reeled, and I reeled, and I reeled, and I sat down and I rested, and then I reeled, and I reeled, and I reeled... It seemed like it went on for half a day.

I finally got that fish up right by the boat. We had a big net ready. Some people, depending on the size of fish, would take a gun and just shoot it, just kill it right in the water. But this fish wasn't all that big, it was about thirty-six inches. Halibut can get huge, they call them "barn doors," they can get up to six and a half feet long, but this was a young halibut.

We got the fish on board with us and the doggone fish was slapping all over the bottom of the boat. My sales manager was trying to get it, and he slipped and hit his breastbone on the gunwhale and that really hurt him. We finally got the fish into the locker, and he said, "That's a nice fish, but do you want to keep it?" I said, "Hell, I caught it, why wouldn't I want to keep it?" He said "Well, it's not very big. It's a young fish. Why don't you return it back and we'll get some bigger ones." I said, "Okay, that sounds like a winner."

He put the fish overboard and away it went and it was the one and only halibut I ever caught in my life. We didn't catch another fish that whole dang day, and I gave the halibut away! We got back to his house, and he had halibut in the freezer so he gave me a whole bunch and put it in a cooler, which I checked on the plane when I left. That was one of my favorite trips with the Hamilton Group.

I traveled and traveled and traveled. I'd be gone a week to ten days at a time. Things were getting more excruciating at home from the standpoint of having a "family." I always tell the story that Sherry and I were married for ten years, but for most of them we did not have a marriage; ten years we lived together, and that's about the way it was.

I was going to San Diego to have our corporate meetings, and then I'd be right back out traveling again. I enjoyed going to my business in Louisiana. One time people took me out to dinner and I had alligator, which was the first time I ever had it, and the last. After one trip, I came home, went upstairs to my office, and as usual the mail was piled up a foot high on my desk. I started going through it, and I came across a letter from an attorney's office. I opened it, and inside were divorce papers. That shocked me to be honest, it really shocked me, despite the state of our marriage. A letter from an attorney.

I went downstairs and said to Sherry, "What is this all about?" and she said, "Well, I'm just tired of the way we're living. I want out of here. You're never home. I told you I didn't want you to take that job, and you know we're not getting along, so I just filed for divorce."

Well, that was one hairy divorce. Evidently she'd been wanting to do it for a while and had been running around with a couple of doctors. I didn't know about it at that time, and I really didn't care, it didn't affect me.

I went down to her attorney's office for a meeting. In California, if you're married ten years there's no contesting for divorce, it's 50/50, split all the way through, and there was no alimony. We had to sell the house and split the proceeds. We had invested money in the stock market, so that would be split.

There was one thing that really got to me about that divorce, and that was that meeting in her attorney's office. They wanted my Social Security, and ten years of marriage in California qualifies you for that. Sherry knew that - and she waited to file for divorce until the ten years was in. I went berserk. I said, "I've worked all my life for Social Security, you're not getting any of it." I had a life insurance policy at that time worth $400,000, and she took 25% of that leaving me the other 75% to be split between my three kids, because that had been my intention.

We had gotten buyers right away for our house. They were living in a large, expensive home in the next subdivision in Rancho Santa Margarita and they wanted to downsize. We all met in our home, them with their realtor, and I negotiated an additional $10,000 in that sale, closing it myself; the realtor didn't do it, Sherry didn't do it. I said to them, "If you want this house, and it's everything you're wanting, it's worth $10,000 more than you're offering." So, my counter came up in a reduction to the sales price, but with $10,000 more than what they had offered. Sitting there, they capitulated, and I did what I call a silent close. I sat, and waited for them. They finally agreed to it and we shook hands, and the realtor said he would adjust the figures. I made $5,000 for Sherry sitting right there at that table.

As time went on, I was paying more in premiums on that damn life insurance policy than what the policy was worth. It was in the divorce decree, but I cancelled that policy. When Sherry heard about that she was all over me on the phone about getting her money. As of this writing it's still up in the air, but that $400,000 is down the toilet, long since gone.

The demise of the marriage started with losing all that stock money with Loewen, and then when I took the job on the road. After we sold the house, I'll never forget, I went back in after all her stuff was out and my furniture was all packed. I was painting everything, all the halls, all the walls, all the rooms of an empty house. Well, in comes Sherry and she wants to know what I was doing. I said, "What does it look like I'm doing? I'm cleaning this place up. It's got to be done." She said, "Oh, okay. Well, I just stopped by to see if you're doing okay and if everything is all right. What are you going to do?" Well, I knew what I was going to do, but it was none of her damn business what I was going to do. I was really upset with her over the divorce. It was mean, mean spirited, and just a mean damn thing. She was trying to get everything she could possibly get from me and I didn't want her to know anything about what I was doing.

42.

While the divorce was pending and I was traveling for Hamilton, I had been up in Milwaukee and was on the way back to Los Angeles. I called my good buddy, Fred Newman, and told him I had gone down to the Lake of the Ozarks in Missouri a couple weeks ago. I'd always liked the Lake of the Ozarks because I had kept my houseboat there when I lived in Missouri. There were nice homes on the lake, and I thought I could go there and get myself a boat and a house on the lake and enjoy it.

On my trip there, I had rented a boat for half a day and went around the lake to look at homes. There were a lot for sale, but they were out of my price range. The longer I was on that lake the more these big boats were coming around. It wasn't like it used to be, I mean, my goodness, these huge boats were just all over the place. That little boat I was in didn't stand a prayer out there with all those wakes and everything so I took the boat back in. The guy was concerned and asked, "What's wrong? Is there something wrong with the boat?" I said, "No. I just don't need it any longer."

I told Fred all this, and he suggested, "Why don't you go to Table Rock Lake? Real estate is a lot cheaper there and you can be on the lake, have a boat and do what you want to do." I asked, "Where's Table Rock?" and he said, "It's down by Branson and Springfield."

I got a flight into Springfield, rented a car, drove to Branson, checked into a hotel, got the Yellow Pages and looked up realtors. I found a guy and I told him what I wanted, and he asked my price range. I said, "Well, somewhere between $150,000 and $200,000." He said, "Okay, I'll get them all lined up and we'll meet in the morning and we'll start our tour."

We met and toured a few homes, and my lord, they were huge homes! Boat houses, garages outside, three and four bedroom homes, and I asked, "Are all these homes that you got lined up this big?" He said, "Oh, yeah, this is it. These are good buys." I said, "Look, I don't need a house that big." He said, "Well, you told me 150, 175, 200 caps," and I said, "Well, these homes are not what I'm after, they're not what I want." He asked, "Well, what do you want?" I told him, and he said, "Well, I don't know. Let's go back to the office."

The lady that owned the company was there and he introduced me to her and told her the features of the house I was looking for. She said, "I have just the house for him." He asked, "Where's that? It's not on the list." She said," We just listed it this week. You weren't here when we went on the tour, but I was. It's a brand new model home, never been lived in, three bedroom, all brick, and it looks right down on Table Rock Lake. It's not on the lake, not a lake front, but it looks down on the lake." I asked the price, and she said, "$165,000." I said, "Well, let's go look at it."

It was almost dark by the time he and I got down there, and I swear to you what sold me on that house... it was just dusk, I went through the whole house, and came outside, and whip-poor-wills were singing. When I was a kid and lived in the hills of Ohio, I loved whip-poor-wills. Years later when I'd had a contract down in Franklin, Tennessee, I had an apartment and I heard whip-poor-wills at night in the woods. I just love them. So here's this whip-poor-will singing, and I said, "How much did you say you want for this house?" He said, "165." And I said, "Offer 145" and he said, "She won't take that," and I said, "Offer it to her."

He dropped me off at the hotel, and said he'd put in the offer tomorrow. This was a Sunday evening, and I told him I had to leave town, and would call the next day. I called him, and he said, "Well, I told you she wouldn't take that offer, in fact she got pretty angry about it." I said, "No way. Well, what would you counter with? I like that house." He said, "Well, she's asking 165, you countered 145. Why don't you come back with 150." I said, "Just 5,000 more?" He said, "Well, you never know, you can always come up from there." I said, "Give her the offer, 150," and she accepted it. So I bought myself a home on the lake in a little town called Cape Fair, Missouri.

My good buddy, Bill Hawkins, and his family owned a really nice summer home in Pinetop in Arizona. I called him while he was there, and he wanted me to come and stay with them for a couple of days, so, I went on that beautiful drive through Arizona to Pinetop. We were out picking up pinecones, and there was a terrible lightning storm going on, just terrible, but we survived it, and I've still got those pinecones to this day. After that visit, I drove on to Missouri and to Cape Fair. This was about 2003, and so ends and so starts another chapter in my life.

THE RETURN TO MISSOURI

43.

I had six or seven totally different lives, totally different environments, and totally different geography.

My furniture and belongings arrived in Cape Fair from Orange County, I got settled in, and I really liked my new environment. I got to hear those whip-poor-wills every night. I started flying in and out of Springfield, which was about a forty-five-minute drive, and I would always fly into Chicago to then connect to some area in the country.

There were a lot of stairs to climb going in and out of O'Hare airport, and all the hotels I stayed in, and my knees had begun to really bother me. I had given a three-month notice to Hamilton, and it took me about five months to get everything squared away and part from them on very good terms.

And so, here I was in little Cape Fair. My daughter, Celine, and her family were closest to me, about two hundred miles away in Kansas City. I knew no one in southwest Missouri except the guy that had sold me the house. I had absolutely no contacts. I was alone and I sure as hell didn't want any women around as I was sick and tired after that divorce. So, I was in a good area to be by myself, and just relax, and again, these knees were really bothering me.

I had played racquetball for over twenty years. Back before it was racquetball, it was handball, and then they came along with rackets and then they improved the rackets, and it was a lot easier. You didn't have to soak your hands in salt water with your gloves every day that you played. It was just a much faster game, the skillsets were different, and I really enjoyed playing racquetball.

I played in Kansas City with a fellow that was a good friend of mine, Don Bybee, who was president of KNBR/KMBC, the two top radio stations in the area. We became good racquetball buddies. He spoke at a couple of my annual Christmas banquets, and was just a heck of a nice guy with a nice family, and was very, very strong in the Mormon religion. With the church, every fall he and his kids would go out and pick potatoes, carloads of them, to help people without food.

Don and I played racquetball downtown at the Kansas City Athletic Club early in the morning. One time, there was a guy in the locker room sitting there talking to us, although at first we didn't realize it. He was on the end of the bench in front of some lockers, and Don and I were having a conversation, and he kept talking, and all of a sudden we realized that he was talking to us, so we paid attention to him.

He introduced himself. He was in charge of the public relations for the Kansas City Royals and he work directly for Ewing Kauffman, and was a really nice guy. Well, he talked up a storm. He didn't play racquetball, he was a little chubby, but man, could he hold a conversation on anything you wanted to talk about. Well, the guy's name - and he's been making a great living for a while now- is Rush Limbaugh. Rush was quite a guy, quite a character, and we got to be good locker room buddies. It's funny how I always meet people!

When I was in Seattle, I had joined the YMCA downtown. There were a couple women that worked for me that were darn good racquetball players, and I played with them occasionally. One time I was getting showered and this little fat guy, not very tall, not very old, probably in his early forties came over next to me and he said, "Excuse me, my name is so and so" and he was a doctor who did arthroscopic surgeries and colonoscopies. He said, "I've been watching you play racquetball and you are pretty darn good. I have never played racquetball but I would like to learn. Would you teach me?" I said, "Sure, I'd be glad to."

The thing I liked about playing racquetball is that it didn't take up your whole day. You'd go in and get on the court for an hour, take a shower and be back out on the streets ready to go to work. You didn't spend all day like on a golf course. I never became a golfer, I only played golf once or twice in my life.

I started teaching this guy, and at first he didn't move around too well on the court, and it took about three or four months of me teaching him the various rudiments of the game, and then he started getting pretty good. He expressed his sincere appreciation for my time.

The Y had the names of all the racquetball players listed in the different ladders, A, B, and C. I was never an A, but I was always a strong B, I could beat As occasionally, and I beat Bs and Cs regularly. It was a very competitive game. I noticed his name in the C ladders, and I'd watch him occasionally, and then, he moved up to the B ladders. Then, over about a year, as he moved up in the B ladders, he was losing weight and got in a very good shape.

After some time we played a couple of games, and he was vastly improved, just vastly. We went in to shower and he said,

"Dan, have you ever had a colonoscopy?" And, I said, "What's that?" I was in my forties then, and he explained what it was and more about his work. He said, "I really appreciate what you've done for me in my life, so here's my card and if you want to make arrangements with my office, I'll give you a colonoscopy, on me. I'm glad to pay the hospital bill. Everybody should have one."

He convinced me to have one, and so that was my first colonoscopy. Well, in a big surprise to me, he took nine polyps out of my colon, and fortunately they were all benign. But just think, what if I hadn't gotten that done? You never know if there's a problem as there's no pain or anything with colon cancer, so he did me a big favor. He suggested that I get a colonoscopy every two years for a while, which I did.

As you can imagine, all those years of racquetball had really worn my knees out. In my last days of playing I would stop and take a time-out, I'd get down and take my knee and stretch it and wrench it so that it would get back in place. But it was bone on bone.

I went to a convention in Las Vegas, and a guy came up to me named Buck Weaver. He had heard about me and asked, "You want to come over to my court and play racquetball?" and I said, "Sure, but I didn't bring my stuff with me." He said he had plenty of equipment. We went over to a really nice racquetball court, in fact, it was where they held all the national championships for years. Well, he moved around slowly on the court, not really hitting the ball hard, just lobbing the ball here and there, but he just beat the daylights out of me. I could not win with him.

Afterward, we sat down, and he didn't drink so we had coffee, and he told me he was in the advertising business. He had had a television show in Las Vegas for years called "Buck and His Buckaroos." It was a kid's program that came on Saturday mornings for an hour. He had ponies and the kids would get on and ride them, and it was a great show and it was televised nationally. Buck was a big ham.

He had put together a booklet that was brand new in the advertising world, and after we visited, he adapted it for the cemetery and funeral industry's prearranged sales. A few years later, when I had gone to work with Loewen, I had started buying this book as it was really good, and I had the drag and pull with the right people to get them to utilize it. We had 1200 sales people at our zenith with Loewen, and eventually I had them all using it, and Buck paid me a royalty of a nickel a book. That was some 'extracurricular' money that I made, so who says you've got to be on a golf course to do business? A doctor maybe saved my life, and another guy got me into a lucrative side-money deal, so, racquetball turned out to be okay, except for the knees.

In Cape Fair I bought a boat to use on Table Rock Lake, a 36-foot Bayliner. They have a small gunwhale on them, and when you walk around it's only about six to eight inches in width. It doesn't give you much room for navigation. I was having a hard time navigating that with my knees.

When I lived in Orange County I had orthoscopic surgery on both knees, and it had helped immensely. But, continuing to play racquetball continued to wear the joints. So I did some research about injections of hormones that cause growth of the membrane that's in between our bones, and it supposedly really helped people with either bad hips or bad knees.

I went to a doctor in Springfield to see about getting the injections. He looked at my X-rays, and he looked at me and said, "Dan, I'm not going to take your money. It will do you no good to get these injections because you've got to have something for it to adhere to so that the growth hormone works. And you have absolutely nothing but bone to bone."

He asked me to move across the room for him, so I did, and of course, I was walking like most people do with knee problems, waddling from side to side. He said, "Man, I don't see how you can even walk. How in the world do you do manage?" And I said, "Well, I walk with a great deal of pain." He laughed and said, "Well, I guess you do." He continued, "If you want me to, I've operated on thousands of knees and I will schedule you if you're ready. I think we should get your left one done first because it's worst, and then, a few months later we'll do the right one."

I looked at him and I said, "I've seen guys with knee problems on the racquetball court, and on the golf course, and on the tennis court, and if they get one knee done, they never go back to get the other one done." He said, "There's a lot of truth in that." So, I said, "So, we're going to do them both at the same time," and he said, "Well, I don't do that," and I said, "Well, if you don't do that I'll find somebody that does."

He looked at me and he said, "You're a tough old coot, aren't you?" I said, "Well, I'm pretty strong minded, yeah." And he grabbed my knee and said, "Well, you know what, you'll be the fifth person I've ever done this for in thirty years of practice. But if that's what you want we'll do it. And I'm going to tell you in advance, you're not going to have a leg to stand on and I mean that. You will not, and you're going to have to do a lot of physical therapy, and it's going to be very, very painful." I looked at him and said, "Let's do it."

I got scheduled for my knee operations, and in the meantime my five months was running out with Hamilton. Soon I would be "retired" again, now with a boat that I could hardly get around on. I had two bad knees, and again, had no acquaintances or friends of any kind in southwest Missouri, so I decided to sell that boat.

I called the Springfield News Leader even though I'm forty miles away in Cape Fair. I asked them if they delivered to my area, and they said only on Sundays. I said I wanted a subscription, and I wanted to place an ad. With my marketing background I wrote and placed a nice big ad for this boat, and they started delivering papers to me.

I was still traveling for work and would come home every other weekend. I'd go through the paper to see how my ad looked, what my competition was for selling that boat. Then I noticed there was a separate piece of orange and brown paper inside the classifieds, and it was for people seeking people, men seeking women, women seeking men, men seeking men, and women seeking women.

So I tore that one page out and I left it on the table, and it laid there for a couple of weeks. I left and came back, and had two more papers, and there it is again. So, I put it aside again, but this was the beginning of a whole new chapter.

44

I generally worked out in the field about ten days, and came home for three or four days. The newspapers piled up on the kitchen table, and I'd gotten a few calls about my boat but none were very promising.

But I kept reading those ads about people seeking people, and most were horribly written. I thought, well I can do a lot better than that, so I wrote an ad for those personals.

The way the process worked then was you'd put an ad in the paper, they gave you a personal code number for a voice mail account, and interested people responded with their own code number to keep things perfectly private and safe. It was quite an elaborate program at the time.

For the title of my ad I put in all caps "NEWBIE" and then "new to Southern Missouri, have a new home on the lake, have a new boat, have a new car, have lots of OLD friends across United States, but I am looking to acquire NEW friends locally for relaxation, conversation" and so on and so on. I put the ad in, and the next week I when I got home, a hundred and twenty-six women had responded to my ad!

With the message system, you could save or delete messages. You'd press 1 to save it, 2 to listen again, and 3 to delete it. So I listened, and there were things like, "I really like square dancing." 3. "I really like to go to flea markets and look things over, that's really entertaining." 3. And it kept going like that. 3. 3. 3. Out of a hundred and twenty-six calls there were seven, only seven that I saved.

I played them over again, and they all sounded very good, so I responded to them all in the order they came in. When you responded to them then you would give your home phone number and they would call you.

I ended up taking five women to lunch at a restaurant of their choice. It was funny, four of them chose the same restaurant. One of them chose a really nice place, the Touch Restaurant, which is an upscale restaurant in Springfield, and I was impressed with her. I dated about three of these women.

Then I got a message from a gal who told me she had just returned from Switzerland. She said her name was Margaret. She said, "I am interested in your ad. I would like to know more about you, please call me," and left the number. I called her and she sounded really charming and educated and upscale and all that, so I said, "Well, let's think on this and I'll call you back." She said okay.

I called another woman who had responded to the ad, and took her to lunch, and then about a week later I called Margaret back and said, "I am calling you back as I said I would. I enjoyed our conversation last weekend, and would love to know if you feel we should pursue this." She said, "Yes, I do," but she said, "I have to tell you the truth. My name isn't Margaret, it's Carol Jones." I said, "Oh okay, Carol." There was a long pause on the other end of the phone.

I said, "Where should we meet," and all that. Then she spoke rather calmly and slowly, and said, "Well we can meet at my house." She lived in a country club-type place with golf course, restaurant and all that. She asked, "Do you have suits?" Well, I had a lot of suits hanging in the closet, and I said, "Yeah, I got a couple…" I thought that was funny but it went over her head. She said, "Please wear a suit when you come because we are going to dinner at my club and it is rather dressy. It's a gated community and there is a phone at the gate and you'll need a code to get in. When you get there, call me and I'll give you the code." I said okay and so we made a date.

I drove up there in my Lincoln, got the code, the gate swung open, and I drove around that big place and got to her home. The garage door was open, there were three cars inside, all really nice cars, and she was there by the door. We introduced ourselves, went in, and she asked if I would like a drink. I said sure, and she asked, "What's your flavor?" I said, "Well, if you've got mixings for Martinis, I prefer gin." She said, "I make a good Martini." And so she did.

She was a good looking, a tall, statuesque gal, a bit younger than me but not by a lot. I looked around the room, and she had more money in her furniture than I had in my whole house. So, this was top of the line. We had a couple of drinks and talked about a lot of things.

She said, "Instead of going over to the club, why don't we go out to one of my favorite restaurants in Springfield." I said,

"Sure, whatever you like. I'll drive." So we got in the car and she asked, "What kind of car is this?" And, going back to that day with Henry Ford in Michigan, I said, "Oh, it's just a damn Ford." She said, "Okay." Well, she apparently didn't know a Ford from a Lincoln.

I didn't know it at the time, but the reason that she had hesitated so long on the phone when she told me her real name was that she was the largest realtor in southwest Missouri. She had over a hundred salespeople, about fifty offices spread out in different towns all over and in Springfield, and she was the go-getter for real estate in the residential market. So, when she gave me her name it didn't impress me because I was unaware of her, and I guess I didn't impress her that her name didn't impress me.

We drove down to this nice restaurant and pub, which is still there to this day, the Metropolitan Grill. She couldn't get past two booths without people stopping to talk to her, and she made a nice point of introducing me to everybody. They all knew her. And that started my relationship with Carol.

Carol was a nice lady. Her sales manager had been her boyfriend and they had broken up about two months prior to that, and so she was on the rebound. We dated and we went here and there and we had a good time. She always had lunches to attend, Chamber of Commerce, Rotary, she was invited to all of them, and I went with her because I didn't have anything else to do, but then I got tired of it. I had been there, done that on a much larger scale, and it just wasn't my cup of tea anymore, I just didn't need it. So we both came to the conclusion that we got along well, we were good friends, good companions, but we weren't destined for a long-term thing, and that was all right.

In the meantime I was still getting messages occasionally even though I had stopped the ad. One day there was a message, and the woman said, "Oh and besides that, I forgot to tell you, I do like to go dancing and I do like to travel," and that was it. I thought 'what the hell was that?' and went on to listen to the rest of the messages. Then, in front of that message was her original message in which she talked about liking good restaurants and good entertainment and different kinds of shows, and so on.

And, that… that was my Pat.

As usual she did everything a little bit backwards, but she got it done. So I thought, 'this is something,' and I called her. We got along well over the phone, and I made a date with her. She really sounded good on the phone, and I had gotten such a big kick out of her message, the end before the beginning. She gave me directions to her home in Springfield.

I got to her house, and she opened the door, and boy, here was a "ten" standing there, a really good looking broad, and well dressed and well mannered.

She invited me in, and then said she was going to take me on a tour of Springfield, which I didn't know much about other than the airport. We went to a nice restaurant called Trolleys. The 18th day of October we had our first date. I remember it well, maybe better than she does. She sat there and watched me eat. I didn't know what fascinated her about the way I ate, but later she told me she was very conscious of people's table manners, as most were terrible, and mine were excellent. So, I guess I passed a rough test there.

We started dating and really hit it off. I took her down to see my boat, and she even helped me when it was time for winterizing it. Shortly after that time, I sold the boat to an orthodontist and I got out of it about what I put into it.

That fall we dated quite a few times, and my knee operations were coming up, which I set specifically for November because there was lots of sports to watch on TV. The doctor had cautioned me in advance, because I lived alone, to find a rehabilitation place where people could take care of me and I could get my rehab, and so on. I reviewed a list he gave me, and I picked out a really nice place. Coincidentally, it was just three blocks from where Pat lived.

I had the operations, and the very next day they had me get up and do some walking, which I did, gingerly, and then they had me doing some stretching exercises, which I did, gingerly. After about three days in the hospital the doctor came in and said, "The nurse is telling me you are doing really well getting started on this. We are going to move you to the rehab floor and see how you do there. If you do well, in about a week we'll get you out of here."

I was up there for five days, and one morning he said, "You are just doing extremely well. All your rehab, your emotions, everything, so we are going to send you home, and we are going to have a physical therapist come help you with your rehab, and there will also be a nurse coming in twice a week to check on you, and help you out."

I was able to cancel the place where I was supposed to go, and went home instead. A neighbor, Bill McHargue, who lived pretty close to me and I had gotten pretty well acquainted with and who later came to work for me, came to the hospital to take me home. I had to take two steps to get in the house, and those two steps were the tallest steps I ever climbed in my life, I think. I had a devil of a time getting in there.

The physical therapist would come over and do rehab with me every other day, and that went on for two or three weeks. It was not fun, I tell you. I stood there with tears in my eyes, and whatever they told me to do, I did half again as much when they weren't there. I wanted to have my legs back where I could walk again without pain. And it worked, but the rehab was very, very painful just as the doctor said.

It was six weeks before I could drive, which took us to the first of the year. After I did the rehab work and was driving again, I was back to dating Pat, and we were getting along really, really well. I told her one day, "You know, I just think the world of you." Well, she had told me early on, "There are two words that we don't use in our relationship: One starts with "L" and the other one starts with "M," and they are forbidden in our relationship." I said okay, as it wasn't hard to figure out what those are.

But by this time, we had gotten past the "L" word, and I was using it more frequently than she was, although she used it on occasion, and when she did I would smile and tell her, "Be careful, no "L" words."

Pat was working full time at Dillard's clothing store selling high fashion women's clothes. She had gotten that job after twenty-plus years of selling paper wholesale on the road for Nationwide Papers, the wholesale merchant for Champion Papers. When the company decided to sell out, they took their key personnel and put them on a retirement plan, but they had to go find a job, and so she went to Dillard's.

After a while at Pat's suggestion, we decided that in our best interest we should get away from just a date on a Friday or Saturday or Sunday night and see if we were really compatible, for real. She said, "Let's go somewhere for two or three days," and I said, "Okay, where you would like to go?" Pat said she didn't know, because she really hadn't traveled all that much. She had traveled around Kansas and Missouri but not very extensively. So I said, "Let's go to Seattle, it's a neat city, with good food, a totally different environment," and she said okay. We went to Seattle for three days and just got along great. I took her all over, and took her to the home Betty and I had built, and she was very impressed.

That trip kind of settled it. I wasn't dating anybody else, and she decided that I was the one she was going to date, and from there on, our romance just grew dramatically. Her sister and her brother-in-law, who lived in Lawrence, Kansas at the time, came to visit her and she wanted them to meet me. She was very tight with both of them, had been for years, so I guess I had to pass a test.

They came down to my house, and it was while I was still doing rehab and could hardly do a damn thing. I had wanted to change my furniture around because I was tired of it being the way it was, so all of a sudden we're moving furniture here and there and somewhere else, and then someone said, no, this has to go there…

Well, they spent about three hours moving the furniture in my living room all around, and I really appreciated it, I thought it was great of them. Years later Pat told me that they weren't too thrilled about my asking them to move the furniture right on meeting me, so I guess I didn't make much a of positive impression, although I have since. They vacationed with us, they came here to our house and we would go to their house in Summerlin near Las Vegas every year. In the winter, I took them all to my timeshare in Mexico, and we had a great time. It's a great place to be, Ixtapa and Zhiatenjuo. We've all always gotten along very well.

45.

While I was recuperating, I was bored as Pat was working all day, so I thought, 'what the heck I am doing sitting here and watching the paint dry.' I went out and called on a couple funeral homes to see about selling preneed funerals for them.

The first one I went into, to this day they are just ruthless, ruthless people and they treated me like crap when I was in their office, and I've never forgotten it. I went to the Wal-Mart in the town of Ozark, and I asked them how many funeral homes were in town as I had just gone to the one that I saw in the obituaries in the Sunday paper. They said there was another, a very nice funeral home about two miles east of there. I went to it, and introduced myself to a fellow named Randy Barnes. I gave him my card and asked him if he would have an interest in me selling prearranged funerals for his business, and he said, "Yes, come and sit down, talk to me."

Randy was very, very gracious and his daughter was there and she was just a knock out, just beautiful, as was his lovely wife. We visited for about an hour and we decided that I would start selling prearranged funerals. Well, I had to get everything together as there was nothing to start with. I had some leftover materials from P.A.P.A., but there really wasn't all that much, so I got some things together, created a direct mail piece, and I started selling prearranged funerals for him. I hired two people for him and they did really well, and I went out to start selling for more funeral homes. I formed a corporation called Daniel E. Reed and Associates, D.E.R.A., a Missouri corporation.

By that time, Pat and I had agreed to form a legal partnership because that "M" word did not fit into what we wanted. We went to an attorney that was highly recommended in Kimberling City, near Cape Fair and Table Rock. He drew up the legal partnership papers for us, and we came out as legal partners registered with the state of Missouri to this day.

The way legal partnership works is this: Everything that I brought to the party is mine, everything she brought to the party is hers, and everything that we get together after that is ours. If there is a "divorce" amongst the two parties, they have to sell everything that they've acquired together and it has to be split evenly, 50-50. We've been together since 2004, and we have never had a word over money, which most couples disagree on. We put money into a joint account and we spend it. If there were any major purchases to be made other than just normal things, we discussed it, and it's just worked out great.

That attorney recommended me to an accountant in Kimberling City, so I went and introduced myself asking if he would give me the ins and outs about doing business with him, and he agreed and advised me on some things. I still had my attorney in Topeka, Kansas who had been my attorney when I purchased the cemetery back then and when I set up all my contracts. Ed Carpenter was my lead attorney, and so I advised him of what I was doing, and he set up and kept everything on scale for D.E.R.A.

I called Homesteaders Life Insurance Company up in Des Moines, and talked to Jack Stepanek, whom I had met over the years at conventions. I said, "Jack, I would like to start a general agency and I am wondering if one is available in this part of the world." Jack said, "Let me ask you a question: Have you ever been bankrupt?" I said, "Nope." He asked, "Have you got an insurance license?" I said, "Yep." He said, "I'll send you the papers. You'll be a general agent for us in Southwest Missouri. We'll give you some help in setting up funeral homes," to which I said, "I don't need it, thanks. I don't need any help other than getting the paperwork set so I can teach all my people how to do it right."

So that was the beginning of D.E.R.A. before I even hired anybody. I had a general agency with Homesteaders Life in West Des Moines, Iowa. That's a good old company, over a hundred years old.

I went out and started calling on funeral homes, which, of course, I was very adept at doing, and southwestern Missouri was just a fertile, untouched market, almost totally. There were a lot of smaller towns with just one or two funeral homes, and I picked the ones that I thought would be best suited, and generally got them, and if I didn't I'd go to the other. I built D.E.R.A. from that first funeral home in Ozark, and I grew it up to just a little over forty funeral homes in Missouri and Kansas, and in the zenith, I had around forty salespeople.

I did really well. I did what I knew how to do successfully from previous times, so it didn't take long to get to forty salespeople. I had sales meetings once a week either in Kansas or in Missouri; the people in Western Missouri would go to Kansas and the ones near Springfield would come here. I did all my recruitment ads. I did all my hiring. I did all my teaching, and I did all my field training.

I want to make something very clear. One of the biggest fallacies about sales management is not knowing the difference between teaching and training: Teaching takes place in the classroom and most sales managers are very good at that. Training takes place in the field and most sales managers are very inept at that because they are too lazy, they just don't want to do it. Or, they have gotten the title bestowed on them for some reason and they are the "sales manager," but they are not sales managers until they can take their people to the field and train them by showing them what ropes they've learned and the way it works.

And so I did that, with every person I hired, including Pat. She decided after a short period of time that maybe she could sell prearranged funerals because of her sales experience, and she hated standing on her feet on concrete floors eight-plus hours a day. And so I said to her, to come ride with me.

I took a few leads and she went with me to a God-forsaken rundown trailer home park out of Rogersville, Missouri. We went in there and it was a sorry, sorry family with two young kids who were as dirty as could be, they had cats all over the place, we sat on a couch that had the springs looking out at me from the upholstery. And, I wrote two contracts in an hour and a half, made myself about six hundred dollars.

We walked out and she said, "I can do that." And I said, "Well, if you can, and you want to come to work for me, give your notice or do the training first at home while you are still working." She said she'd rather do that, so I got the materials together and gave her homework to do, and I went on about my business while she was learning how to give a presentation. She did ultimately come to work for me, and she did very well. She made a lot more money than she was making working at Dillard's, and she was part of my group.

As years went by and the organization got larger and larger and larger, Pat also helped me a tremendous amount at home with paperwork. I also trained people here in our home, and that was a lot of work, bringing in four to six at a time. She'd set up lunch, coffee, rolls, Cokes in the afternoon, and she cleaned up the mess after they left. She was instrumental to me in getting the organization going. And ditto with all the sales meetings. She was there to help with a lot of things, and everybody knew that we were a twosome and nobody questioned it, and they shouldn't anyway because they all liked her. With her help, I did really well in growing that company.

Before that time, we decided we were going to build our own home, and so I sold my home at the lake and did pretty well on it, and she sold her home, which she had lived in for years and years.

We got a builder and we built our home together in a subdivision and we are in it to this day. It's not an opulent home, but it's an upscale, nice home, very open floor plan, and just appealing to everybody who walks into our home. We put a big deck on the back, and I kept the hot tub that I had down at the lake and put it out there. I had to get a big, high crane to get it off my deck down there and move it here. We moved it before we screened in the deck, so it was a built-in hot tub, no doubt about that. It's a big one, and can easily accommodate eight people. I love that hot tub. Her boys helped us with the move, which was very helpful. We moved into our new home in August 2005.

By this time my company was really expanding. Mark and his wife and two kids were still in Mexico. We communicated regularly, and he knew that I had started this company, and he said, "I need to get out of here and make some money. Can I come to work for you?" I said sure. So he moved in with us and he was here about a couple months, learning what I wanted done and how I wanted it done. He did a really good job because Mark is just an excellent salesman.

I suggested to Pat that she go into family services, which are a bit different because the leads are a lot different than with direct mail or telemarketing. I was doing no telemarketing and was doing a lot of direct mail. I had an outfit in Ohio that I worked with for years doing all the direct mail promotions for me. The guy that owned the company was a good friend of mine and we had been in the Loewen Group together.

At the end of the second year of me being in business I decided to throw a Christmas party. Remember I mentioned back when I started dating about the lady that took me to that really nice French restaurant called Touch? I went to Touch and rented a private dining room upstairs and I invited the funeral directors to come to my banquet. I invited them and their wives, and one key employee, and there were about forty people there. It's interesting to reflect that two years before that I didn't know a soul in southwest Missouri.

We had a nice Christmas banquet and I thanked them for the opportunity of doing business with them. I was doing nothing but making money for them and for me. The next year, I had another huge banquet at Bass Pro, and we had about seventy people attend. We had entertainment, a big, nice buffet, and the C.E.O. of Homesteaders flew down in a private jet with his regional manager and his assistant who worked with me in Missouri. They gave me a big trophy for "outstanding accomplishments," and I still have it sitting on my desk. They wrote me up in their national newsletter that extolled the virtues of the production I had done.

We were running a little over a half million dollars a year in business, approaching $600,000 in a pretty small market. By small I mean people don't spend a lot of money for the funerals in most of the funeral homes. Some of them did, but not most of them, so I was making pretty darn good money, and had the tiger by the tail. I made a couple of people sales managers including my son, one in Kansas, two in Missouri, and then made them responsible for recruiting. I did all the hiring, I did all the teaching, and they did the training. I assigned that, but eventually I was meeting myself coming and going, and the work was just too darn much.

Now, experience teaches lot of things, but experience had taught me over the years by either an observation or in actuality that a good manager is the core and makes the wheels go around, and if you don't have a strong leader, somebody that's respected and follows the dictates, you're going to have an organization fall apart.

The key example of that was when I left Albuquerque and went to Philadelphia. Within three months of my leaving, that eighteen-person sales force went down to three, and they turned the lights off in those nice offices because nobody could manage it, lead it and run it appropriately. I knew the same thing was going to happen to me, that if I was to turn over the management to somebody, it would just gradually run down hill, and I didn't want to do that. I'd worked hard building this organization up to what it was making me a goodly six figures sum annually. So, I contrived an idea.

46.

I shared my concept with my C.P.A. who said, "Damn, where do you get these ideas? I have never heard of such of thing." I said, "I don't know, I just came up with it." He said, "Well it is great, you can do that."

So, then I ran it by my attorney, and he said, "Well, here's Reed again, with another die-breaker," and I said, "Yeah…" and he said, "it will work if you want to do it," and I said, "Okay, you draw up the papers I need to have, and I am going to present them to everybody at the annual banquet that I have at Christmas."

I had a breakfast meeting for all of my salespeople in Clinton, Iowa, and that was when I put my whole offer into existence. My attorney had driven over for it from Topeka, Kansas.

To set this up, during the years of growth at D.E.R.A., I had weekly contests, I had monthly contests, I had team contests, I had all kinds of contests, and it motivated and excited people, and the contests were a lot of fun. With this plan, I really had to think about what to do because I didn't have a market to sell this company, because there was nobody that could run it, and none of my peers were going to move to southwest Missouri to buy my company.

So, I concocted this: What I was going to do for the full year was not have any contest at all. During that year productivity would be based on rewards, and the rewards were stock in my company. And the stock in my company would be given out in lieu of cash. My two top salespeople didn't want the stock and they weren't long with me and I knew that, and I gave them cash awards, but everybody else had to sign legal papers that morning that they were involved in the purchase of Daniel E. Reed and Associates.

The way it worked was every month in a sales meeting I would show the productivity, the balance sheet, and the income statement of my company for the prior month. And the first month that these people saw that they were shocked. They knew I was making good money but they didn't realize it was that much. A lot of them just didn't believe it.

I ended up having the biggest year in sales with this corporation because people just went nuts. They wanted to have that stock, and every month I would issue stock certificates at the sales meeting, and they were really excited about it, except for those two guys who just took the cash and looked down their nose at it, and that was all right, that was their business.

The contingencies of this stock certificate were as follows: First, if you became an owner in the company by the issuance of one share of stock, you could not sell that stock unless you sold it to a stockholder. That curtailed people from trying to sell this stock to one of my competitors. I didn't have many but they were there.

The second thing was that stock was increasing in value every month they owned it due to their shares increasing in value because of the sales. This went really well, and about halfway through the year some of the more enterprising ones began to buy stock in cash, and then sell it for whatever they wanted to sell for. They had a one dollar par value, and the stock value was worth a lot more than that, so if they got that stock by good productivity and somebody else acquired it for the same reason, one person could go to another person because they were a stockholder and offer to buy or sell.

So there was quite a bit of buying and selling that went on in between people in the company as the year progressed, and two or three of the more aggressive ones were after all the stock they could get.

The productivity increase still remained constantly high and people got their stock every month. I had written into the contract that they signed that the company was going to go up for sale, but only a stockholder could buy it, and they would buy it at the par value worth of the company. It was a fair deal for everybody.

I made this announcement around the country to some of the moguls, and they were flabbergasted, they couldn't believe it. I'd come up with that idea and it worked. It worked to the degree that at the end of the year we had some people who owned quite a bit of stock, and some people who made some money in lieu of cash and sold their stock for more than the dollar par value was based on what their terms of negotiation were between the buyer and the seller. I was not involved in it at all. All I did was issue new stock, take in the old stock, and issue new stock to the purchaser. I had no idea what they paid for it, and didn't care. At the end of the year we had written almost $600,000, and as a general agent that had made me a considerable sum of money.

Three people approached me to buy the company. I turned one down because he did not have the skills that I thought were necessary to run my company. The other two, a father and son, had skills but they were limited in that they were pretty pragmatic, dogmatic, and there's nothing wrong with being pragmatic but they were really overbearingly dogmatic. But, I sold the company to them for $400,000. They put no money down, I had a five percent interest load, and I gave him five years to pay it off, which gave me monthly payments at around $6,000. They had the company, I retired again, and that was a case of taking nothing and building it into something that had a value to it and then in selling it at the value.

So, I was retired again!

Well, as has always been my bent, my real enjoyment in life is travel. I like good food but I like travel better, and I had done a lot of travelling in my career. On my honeymoon with Sherry, we had gone to New Zealand, and I worked a bit while I was down there, but we really had a good time. We went to Rotorua and saw the natives and their rituals, we went to Auckland which is a nice city, we went out to the sheep ranches, and it was totally enjoyable. Years later I took Sherry on cruises with the

Renaissance Lines and we cruised to Turkey, Greece, and Italy. I took her on a trip to China for ten days, which was a magnificent journey, and we did all the things that people do, saw the terracotta figures and Chonquing and so on. Travel was my forte.

Pat had never done a lot of travel, so I wanted to get her exposed to traveling. The first thing we did was a land tour of Italy which was just fabulous. We went to the Vatican, we went from Venice all the way down to Naples, south of Rome, and it was really an exciting, enjoyable trip.

I took her on two river cruises a year apart. We sailed the Main, the Rhine, one cruise was from Amsterdam to Budapest. We'd get off at small and large towns for a while, we saw Vienna, Austria, went to Nuremburg, and did all the things that tourists do. They were all just very enlightening. We did a lot of traveling and I wouldn't trade the world for the times we had.

After about a year and a half, things were beginning to go haywire for the father and son, Ron George Senior and Ron George Junior, and they were losing a lot of salespeople. They were doing a lot of recruiting, a lot of teaching, very little training, and things that aren't built solidly aren't going to last too long. They came to me and asked for a stay of making payments for sixty days. I agreed and they didn't make any payments for two months, and then they started paying again, but then they came and asked for a reduction in payments, and I agreed to that.

Long story short, they got about half of the company paid for before they went bankrupt, and they took the D.E.R.A. name and made it pretty bad with the funeral homes, with the salespeople they hired and lost, and the salespeople I had that they lost. My son was one of the first ones to leave, and it went down the toilet.

47.

In 2008, I was approached by a long-time acquaintance from New Jersey, Larry Nikola, who told me he was going to build a new funeral home in Savannah, Georgia, called Bonaventure Funeral Home, as well as purchase a cemetery in Savannah. I agreed to a two-year contract, and started recruiting and training at the cemetery while the funeral home was being built. Every program I tried did not work successfully, sales were very limited, and the sales force had high turnover.

I had an apartment in Savannah and would fly home every other weekend. When the funeral home was completed, I moved my offices to the second floor, and continued recruiting and training. Although I went to the field personally numerous times, the funeral home was just not being accepted in Savannah by the masses. It was beautiful, but that didn't seem to matter.

When my contract completed in two years, I returned home with a pretty darn good failure. Possibly one of the reasons was that the deep South had a mistrust of northerners, and were very steeped in their traditions with old funeral homes. I'm not making excuses, but we were looked upon as modern day "carpetbaggers."

So there I was again, so what the heck, why not? Let's do it again except on a lot smaller scale, something I can handle. I picked off the three best funeral homes that were nearby, that have consistently been good markets for productivity, one in Ozark, one in Rogersville, one in Ash Grove and Walnut Grove, Missouri. They were small with one funeral director, and I got along fine with all of them.

They were anxious to have me come back, and so I started a new sales organization and I formed a company called Advanced Planning Consultants, Inc., and here we go again. I didn't want a lot of salespeople, so I hired some people in West Plains, trained them and put them in business down there, and they did a reasonably good job, nothing outstanding, and I didn't hire anybody at all for the two funeral homes that I was selling for. I wanted that for myself.

I did a direct-mail program. I'd drop mail once a year at each funeral home, and I could live off the fruits of my direct-mail program, and worked for myself. When I had sold D.E.R.A., Pat had retired, and she had a retirement stipend from the company she'd worked for, and so she didn't need work. I went back to selling preneed funerals by myself and I loved it, I enjoyed it, I really thoroughly enjoyed it.

234

Everybody asked me when I was going to retire, and I said well, I guess I retired a number of times, but the vaccination has never taken. It kept me busy, it kept me active, it kept my mind going, and I liked the challenge of going out and convincing people to do what they ought to do to help themselves.

I was never as good a salesman as my son, but I was better than most of the people I hired and trained. I had a closing average of 78 to 82 percent. I had a persistency factor that would run between 92 and 95 percent which is unheard of. If they were sold, they were sold, and they didn't cancel. Every year I thought I'd quit, and every year I did a mail out for all three funeral homes and that would keep me going for another year.

I finally decided in 2014 it would be my last year of selling. I really, really, really was going to stop working. I told Pat and she laughed, she didn't think that would happen, but it did. I didn't do any additional mailings, and when the leads ran out in November or December, I did away with my corporation, my bank account, and closed it all down at the end of 2014.

So now what? People had suggested to me over the years that I write a book about my life but I never seriously considered it. Then we had this marvelous niece of mine who came to visit us, listened to my stories, and as a result, now you have a book in your hands!

EPILOGUE

ℬ

I've got to tell you it's been a really good ride. I was able to make long-term friends all over the United States, and true, good friendships last.

I have a few friends and acquaintances in Springfield, and I work out two days a week at the health club, and I do water aerobics. We've got a treadmill here at home so I push myself, I get on, and I walk.

I still do all our gardening; we've been gardening for years and raise a tremendous amount of vegetables. It's an organic garden, no dirt in it, all organic and it takes some taking care of, but that's fun, that's a good outlet.

I watch my St. Louis Cardinals, I watch my Kansas City Chiefs, we enjoy our families, and just enjoy life. It's been a good ride, I've enjoyed most of it, it's been lot of fun, with a lot of challenges, a lot of hard work, and it's all paid off pretty well for me.

ℬ

The great baseball player, Yogi Berra, had many comical philosophies, one of which I never forgot. He said, "When you come to a fork in the road - take it." Well, I did that, many times! Most of the choices were good but some sure were bad. However, at the end of a dead end, I never looked back.

ℬ

I would urge you to review my Sheriff Jim story about the sheep (in chapter 19.) Great logic taught me to really get different points of view before making a decision.

ℬ

After the move to the big city part of my life, I began maturity in a very rural area in the hills of southern Ohio. To this day I remember well that when you come to a door or gate that is open, pass on by, don't shut it. On the other hand, if you come to a door or gate that is closed, be sure to close it after you pass through. Do you ever notice how many people violate this common sense of courtesy?

℘

Other than inheritance, there are three ways to make money legally:
1.   Through your efforts.
2.   Through the efforts of others.
3.   With money.
Number two was the best method for me.

℘

Selling and Marketing

I hope you have enjoyed traveling with me on the many different journeys of my life. My last story has to do with the vast differences in the title. As you have gathered by now, my opinions are pretty definite. Not always correct, but mostly! Indulge me please while I pontificate.

There is a wide gulf between a good marketer and a good salesperson. Surprised? They interrelate and are co-dependent to accomplish their goals.

The old idiom, "Well, he or she was just a born salesperson" is rarely accurate. You see, all of us have natural born characteristics, namely dominance, sociability, resistance and compliance, D, S, R, C. Where our dominant strengths and weaknesses are play a huge part in personalities. McQuaig and Penny (president of Personality Insights) taught me this (see Chapter.24).

A person with a high sociability factor is outgoing, talkative, and in general likes people. While this is favorable it does not necessarily make a good sales person. Another example, "Oh, he or she has a great gift of gab." I learned that these traits are not the key rudiments to be a successful salesperson. Equally important is to have a high dominance trait coupled with a low compliance trait. It makes it easier if we know our own traits to

237

evaluate our strengths and weaknesses. So, if we look at a person who has a high D, a strong S, a low R, and a very low C, we have a much better chance with proper teaching, counseling, and training for a person to be successful in sales.

D
   high
S

R
  low
C

I have seen in my career a lot of high Ss that talked themselves out of sales because they either don't have a low R or a high D. My illustration may help you understand better a perfect profile. Our top producers and manager prospects fit pretty close to this model.

The fallacy to all of this is a poor management team to develop these traits, or a lack of a good marketing plan! Good managers are not necessarily good marketers. Unfortunately for a person wanting to become adept at selling, there is not a school or college out there trenching salesmanship. There are many books and audiovisual files available on the art of selling, but unless a person is fortunate enough to have a good sales manager and management team, the chances are slim to none of sustained success.

There are numerous college courses available to learn the art of marketing. However, most marketers in our country and worldwide are not salespeople! The first premise of marketing is to understand all of us are motivated to buy a product or service by one or more of the five motivations, namely: Need, love, pride, profit, and fear. If there is a product or service that appeals to more than one factor it makes it much easier to sell.

Marketers, generally speaking, achieve their sales through good advertising and/or promotions. While helpful, good salespeople need neither of these. In today's world the vast majority of sales are made through good professionally accepted marketing.

The days of direct, creative selling by a well-trained salesperson are gone. That's sad! Well, things change. Try entering a home today without an appointment, it won't happen. Voila, telemarketing. Then, when the public tired of phone calls, viola, the internet. There will be further advances in marketing. It bound to happen.

So--my stories of success will not be repeated. We need creative thinking in order to replace our outdated methods. Someone will contribute to new philosophies. Maybe it is you or yours.

May I repeat, "It's been a good ride".

&

Tact: The ability to tell a person to go to hell and have them happy to be on their way. (Something that served me well.)

&

One of my favorite quotes comes from John Wooden, former U.C.L.A. basketball head coach who wrote:

> Talent is God given - be humble
> Fame is man-made - be grateful
> Conceit is self given - be careful

This quote has always reminded me to reduce the use of the word "I."

HERITAGE

Looking at my heritage, I know very little about my mother's side and quite a bit about on my father's side.

My grandfather's name was either Heenan Moses or Moses Heenan Reed, though I think it was the former, and he married a lady by the name of Elizabeth Robinette, who went by Lizzy. I never knew my grandfather because he died pretty young, but they had thirteen children. One died at birth, a stillbirth, and another one died of pneumonia at about one year of age, one was named Minnie, not sure about the other one. There were six girls that lived a long life, and there were five boys, one of whom died young.

The oldest was Ethel and she married Clarence Parks. They had three children, Esther, Orland and Robert.

Next was Uncle Marion and Aunt Gladys who had two girls, Edith and Elaine. He was a farmer in Iowa.

After that was Aunt Elma, and she was married to Howard Downs, and while she never divorced him, they were separated most of their lives, and they had one child, Geneva, who always claimed me as her brother, because when I was just a kid I lived with them for four years, right when I started grade school. She always called me her kid brother. Aunt Elma built her own log home and then her own house.

Next in line was my dad, James, and he married Lucille Nejdl, who was older than him. She had been married previously and had a daughter from that marriage. I came along and was about eight years younger than my half-sister, Evelyn Werner.

After my dad was my Aunt Tina, but her real name was Mary. She was married to Edward Robillard, and lived in Niagara Falls. They had four boys, Edward, Floyd, Ralph, and Earl. I had four boy cousins I hardly ever knew.

Then came John, and very sadly he was killed at about 20 working at a box factory in Rittman, Ohio. He was crushed to death, and never married.

Next was my Aunt Rose, and she was married to Roma Larch. They had six children, five girls and a boy who came along late. The eldest was Donna, then Delores, Daisy, Davillah, who later renamed herself Darlene, Delphia, and then was Darrell.

The next was my Aunt Flossy, her given name was Florence, and she married Knox Chamberlain, and they also raised six kids, five of their own and a boy they adopted. His name was Gene Retzler, and he was just a super kid. The eldest was Ruth, then Carl, Betty, Knox Junior, Ralph, and then Gene.

After that was my Uncle Harold and Aunt Helen. She had terrible teeth and so did her father. She was a nice aunt and I lived with them for a year when I moved back to Ohio from Montana. I was in about sixth grade then. My uncle was a heavyweight boxer and he did pretty well, he fought some of the biggies. They had two children, Doris and Billy.

Next was Uncle Lindley and his wife. I never lived with them. They also had two children, Lucille, who was named after my mother, and Lawrence. They lived north of Cedar Rapids, Iowa all their married lives.

Lastly was Aunt Lucy, and she married Gene Smith. She raised me a little bit when I was a kid. She and Uncle Lindley rented a farm together and I lived with them for about a year. She taught me how to tie my shoes and how to whistle. They had two kids, Helen and Gerald.

I had twenty-three first cousins. I was the best-known cousin of the bunch because I traipsed around with all of them. I stayed one summer with my Aunt Flossy and Uncle Knox on their farm. I lived for a year with my Uncle Harold and his wife. I lived with my Aunt Elma, and cousin Geneva. I lived with Aunt Lucy and Uncle Lindley for a year.

I'm glad I've got this great photo of them (next page):
Back row, left to right: Marion, Flossy, Tina, Lucy, Rose, and Lindley. Front row, left to right: Harold, Elma, Grandma Lizzie, Ethel, and James, my dad.

242

On my mother's side, as mentioned earlier, I had my Czech grandparents, babi and děda, pronounced "bubby" and "gedda," On one of the three or four trips my dad and I did cross country between Ohio and Montana, we stopped in Cedar Rapids to see them.

I remember going into this old, old, old grocery store with wooden floors. It was a musty smelling grocery store and they had a place out back they lived in, somehow they eked out a living selling groceries. I remember Evelyn and me riding on a tricycle up and down the long aisles on those old wooden floors, and when I got ready to leave, my grandfather gave me a box of Cracker Jacks.

I was so excited about those Cracker Jacks because I never had them before. When my dad and I got in the car and he started driving, pretty quick I opened those Cracker Jacks, and tasted them, and they were pretty doggone good. There was little toy somewhere inside the box, and as I was eating along I looked at my hand, and I noticed a whole bunch of dried worms! I don't know how long that box had sat on the shelf, but I was eating dried worms and Cracker Jacks, so that was the end of Cracker Jacks for me.

Evelyn and me in Montana

I never did much visit anyone until years later when I moved to Cedar Rapids, Iowa, and connected with my sister, Evelyn. I had only been with her in that grocery store and then one other time when my dad brought her on a train to Montana, and I just barely remember that.

When we connected in Cedar Rapids years later we became very fond of one another, and became very, very close. Unfortunately I lost her, I lost her from that damn cancer.

I stayed in touch with her husband, Al Oujiri, and in fact went to a reunion with them in Cedar Rapids a number of years ago about two years before he passed away. He was a great guy. I don't know if they had a very happy marriage or not, I hope so, but in his later years he seemed to be very nice man. I know when he was younger he had terrible, terrible headaches, and he'd go to the basement, and stay down there for hours and hours in the cool and dark to try to feel better.

Luckily for him, a few years after losing Evelyn, he met and married a marvelous lady, Elaine Schulte, who literally saved his life one time when he had a heart attack while on vacation near the Ozarks in Missouri. They had a good long life together.

The four daughters, my nieces, each have their own personalities and have spread like the four winds. One lives on the west coast in Oregon, Lauren (Laurie), the youngest, a writer and life coach.

The next youngest is Karen, now living in Texas, happily married and also a writer. She has a marvelous son who has a great personality, and a precocious granddaughter.

The second oldest is JoAnn, now living in New York though lived in Maryland a long time, and lost her dearest husband to leukemia; I helped her with estate questions after he passed. She has two kids and two grandkids.

The oldest is Susan, who was quite an actress and dancer in community theatre in Cedar Rapids, and she has two marvelous kids, thanks to her raising them, a grandson and another grandchild on the way. She lived most of her life in the Cedar Rapids area and now lives in Minnesota.

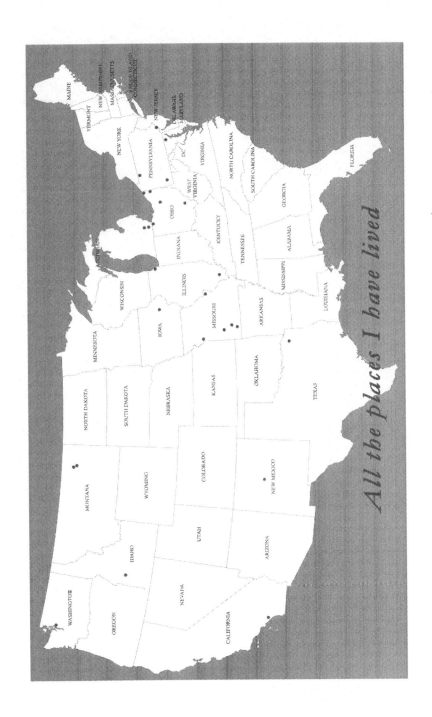

All the places I have lived